HOUDINI

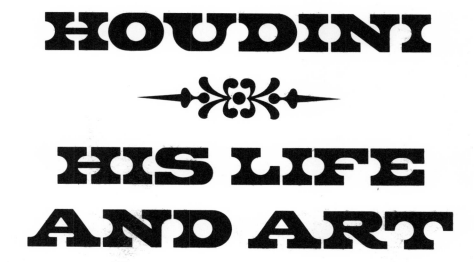

HIS LIFE
AND ART

HARRY HOUDINI THE JAIL BREAKER

INTRODUCING HIS LATEST & GREATEST

PRISON CELL & BARREL MYSTERY

HOUDINI is strapped & locked in a barrel placed in a police cell which is also locked and in less than 2 seconds changes places.

£100. WILL BE PAID TO ANYONE FINDING TRAPS, PANELS OR FALSE DOORS IN THE CELL

NEW ORLEANS ITEM
CHALLENGES
HOUDINI

"Sporting Chat"
of THE NEW ORLEANS ITEM
Dares Houdini

of the Orpheum Theatre to allow himself to be manacled by a member of the Police Department, selected by the Item, and then

to DIVE INTO the MISSISSIPPI RIVER

releasing himself under the water, which is a test Houdini claims to be able to do under all conditions.

Having accepted this defie, the test will take place at the

FOOT OF CANAL STREET,

Houdini allowing himself to be heavily manacled, and will leap into the Mississippi River from the gang plank of the

"J. S."

Steam...

moored at the foot of Ca...

The Leap can be...

SUNDAY, NOV...
REMEMBER...

CHALL...

SEAMEN
CHALLENGE
HOUDINI.

...DINI,
...nsbury Park Empire, London, N.

...he undersigned Able-bodied Seamen, hereby

Challenge you to
...pe from a Sea-Bag

...mp Steamers to secure MAD WITH GROG SAILORS.

...restraint, made from heavy sail cloth, encases ... from the neck down to the foot, arms crossed ... heavy belting straps encircling the body, every... behind the back. A strong rope lashed ..., said rope to be nailed firmly to the floor ...oving about.

...make the Attempt to Escape
VIEW OF THE AUDIENCE,
...have no concealed confederates.

...r your reply, we remain,
...JOSH COLLYER. H. S. PATTERSON.
...J. E. WAITTE. MICHAEL CALLAHAN.

...epts the above Challenge
...tion that there must be no danger
...tion from any fastening placed
...Test takes place at the Second
FRIDAY NIGHT, FEB. 28th, 1913,
...the FINSBURY PARK EMPIRE.

Norfolk, Va., ...
(Aboard U.S. ...
...Houdini,
...onial Theatre, City.

...are respectfully reques... ...ng test, on behalf of th... ...now at the navy yard. ...e undersigned hereby ...g powers to the utmost ...o defeat us, you will hav... ...task of your career. ...h to challenge you to ...Theatre a U.S. Govern... ...ng suit, which is at p... ...S Severn, tender to S...

...llow us to place you in thi... ...ists of high pressure wate... ...which encases the entir... ...to and including the fe... ...he breast and neck plate ... ...ck fastening it to the lowe... ...then placing the brass and ...er your head, and securing ...the suit with the usual b... ...uts in the usual manner. ...h up by handcuffing your ha... ...and locking your feet toget... ...the ajustable kind. ...this challenge, kindly let u... ...so that we can obtain the re... ...to take the Diving suit from ...u must know that it is gov...

Respectfully,
C. E. WEICKHARDT
R. V. PETRITZ
J. BERLINBACK
C. I. PERRY.

...oudini has accepted the above challenge, ...this remarkable test will take place on ...the Colonial Theatre stage

...D-NIGHT

Donaldson-Ackiss Print

COOPERS
Challenge
HOUDINI

HOUDINI—Sir,
We, the undersigned Coopers
HEREBY CHALLENGE YOU
to escape from a large
RUM PUNCH HICKORY BARREL
after we have headed you in it in the regulation manner

We issue this Challenge, as we should like to know if it is in the power of any human being to ESCAPE FROM A BARREL AFTER IT HAS BEEN "COOPERED" AND "HEADED IN" BY COMPETENT COOPERS.

If you accept, we will bring a barrel in which you can be seated comfortably, and we will give you plenty of holes for ventilation, SO YOU WILL NOT SUFFOCATE.

We remain, Sir, faithfully yours,
ROBERT REDFORD
Cooper of the Albion Brewery, Shepherd's Bush
EDWARD JAMES CLARKSON, 2, Herschell Rd., Forest Hill, S.E

HOUDINI
Accepts the Challenge
and invites the Coopers to bring the barrel to the SHEPHERD'S BUSH EMPIRE, on Wednesday Evening, June 7, 1911, when he will attempt to perform this unheard of feat in the 2nd House

---

...ALLEN...

...Houdini, .
...ra House, City:

...ndersigned having wit... ...ome to the conclusion t... ...ur performances, and ... ...o allow us to make an... ...t coated nails. If you... ...YOU UP in this ... ...T ESCAPE without... ...not care to try it ...

...ouis Laflam... ...ouis Landry,

...LLEN & SON, BOX MANUFACTURERS

Accepts
...challenge for
...t, Feb. 14
...HOUSE

...orderung!

Bremen, den 6. November 1912.

Houdini
Bremen. (Circus Corty Althoff)

...haben von Ihren Befreiungs- und Entfesselungs- ...hört und stellen Ihnen hiermit die Bedingung, sich ...von uns angefertigten Holzkiste, in der Sie von uns ..., vernagelt und verschnürt werden, zu befreien. ...e Kiste wird vorsichtshalber nochmals von uns, bevor ...nutzung genommen wird, geprüft, vernagelt und darf ...er Befreiung nichts an der Kiste beschädigt sein.

Hochachtungsvoll

Eduard Bachmann, W. Jnwick u. K. Plaggenmeier,
Tischlermeister der Firma Heymann & Neumann, Bremen.
Th. Honnerjahn, Heinr. Stubbenbruck,
Heinr. Richers u. Gustav Sennholz,
Packer der Firma Heymann & Neumann.

Herr Harry Houdini hat diese Herausforderung ...angenommen und sich bereit erklärt, heute Freitag ...den 8. Nov. im Circus Corty Althoff das vom ihm verlang... ...Experiment zu versuchen, unter der Bedingung, da... ...die Kiste nicht luftdicht verschlossen wird.

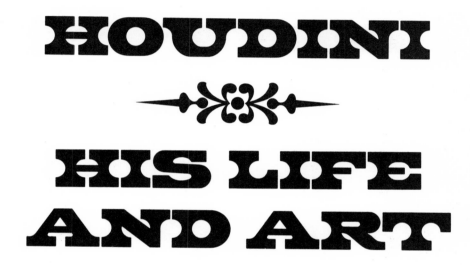

HOUDINI

HIS LIFE AND ART

By The Amazing Randi and Bert Randolph Sugar

GROSSET & DUNLAP
A Filmways Company
Publishers New York

 This book is dedicated to the many aspirants who defy
their parents, their peers, logic, common sense, and the
odds to pursue the Muse of Magic. Among them may be
a successor to the Great Houdini.

Library of Congress catalog card number: 76-15709
ISBN 0-448-12546-3 (hardcover)
ISBN 0-448-12552-8 (paperback)
First printing
Printed in the United States of America

CONTENTS

FOREWORD BY SUGAR

Harry Houdini. The very name brings back memories to the dwindling number of theatergoers and to those who stood outside theaters to watch him hang like a ham upside down. To the average adult, he is a storied figure in theatrical history, a man who gave color to his age, somewhat in the fashion that John L. Sullivan gave color to his or P. T. Barnum to his. To the younger generation, he is merely a name fictionalized in the current best seller *Ragtime*.

At a time when national heroes have passed from the American landscape, it is difficult to fathom Houdini's full impact. People who couldn't care less about magic know his name. George Bernard Shaw once said that as one of the three most famous people in the history of the world, real or imagined, Houdini took his place beside Jesus Christ and Sherlock Holmes.

Harry Houdini was many things to many people. His list of tricks reads like the contents of a yellowed version of Ripley's *Believe It or Not*—handcuff escapes, rope escapes, disappearing elephants, walking through brick walls, escapes from milk cans, Chinese water torture cells, trunks thrown into rivers, and so on. A colossal egoist, a genius who brooked no contradiction, a bold adventurer, a writer, a collector, a supreme showman, a man with boundless and self-renewing energy, a complex human being, a performer with a burning ambition for personal glory, a devoted family man, a lecturer, and a man who responded to any and all challenges, Houdini and his reputation extended far beyond the bounds of the stage; but it was as an entertainer that he held center stage for a quarter of a century as the "Maker of Miracles."

In this context, he was as versatile as he was ingenious. He was a technician, although as a technician he had his equals in Kellar and Thurston. He was an escape artist, an art form he created and then excelled in. But most of all, he was a showman, creating his real magic through publicity. His repeated assaults on the psyche of America made him a legend, dominated the nation's papers and attention in a way unknown before or since, and still continue today, fifty years after his death.

One popular story of the day had Harry Houdini in Detroit presenting a dramatic, extracurricular performance in accordance with his usual custom of giving the public a free exhibition to stimulate interest in his show. He arranged to be hurled, handcuffed, into the Detroit River from the Belle Isle Bridge. When the morning of his outdoor performance dawned, the manager of the theater awakened Houdini to inform him that the river

was frozen solid and that the performance would have to be cancelled. Never one to let anything stand in his way, Houdini shot back, "What's the matter with the river stunt? Can't you get someone to saw a hole in the ice under the bridge?"

According to the legend a hole was cut in the ice, and at the appointed time, Houdini made his way through thousands of spectators who had gathered on the bridge and on the adjoining shore. Mrs. Houdini, bedridden with a fever, was not with him, as she usually was for his performances, but awaited his return in their nearby hotel room. Houdini stripped down to his trunks and was carefully manacled by the Detroit constabulary. He exchanged some banter with newspapermen, and then, on his instructions, he was pushed off the parapet of the bridge and vanished into the icy waters with a splash.

On such occasions, Houdini always had planted in the crowd a skilled underwater assistant as a "saver," for emergency purposes. The man kept a rope with him, and according to his instructions from the ever-careful Houdini, who planned every one of his escapes with exacting attention to detail, if Houdini did not appear by the end of the third minute, he was to make the rope fast, toss over the free end, and go down after him.

Usually Houdini would reappear on the surface in a little over a minute. But this time, two minutes passed without any sign of him, and then three. The emergency man had difficulty manipulating his numb fingers to tie the rope in the cold.

By the end of four minutes, longer than Houdini had ever stayed underwater, police surgeons and other physicians who had been invited to watch the performance expressed their unanimous opinion that something had gone wrong and that Houdini had performed his last stunt. Or so the story goes. The newspapermen began sending their messengers off with hastily written notes proclaiming the end of the "Master of Mystery," the "man who could get out of anything."

Finally, after what seemed like an eternity but was, in reality, only eight minutes, the emergency man threw the rope down into the water and began to climb down it. But before the frightened assistant could get into the freezing river, Houdini's head and arm flashed out of the water, and the next instant he was supporting himself by the rope on the surface.

Back at the hotel, Mrs. Houdini was resting uneasily when she heard newsboys out on the street screaming, "Extree! Extree! Read all about it! Houdini dead!" She ran from her room to get the paper, but just as she returned with it clutched tightly to her breast, Houdini himself burst into the room, still dripping and blue with cold—but alive.

He supposedly told his wife, "I reached the bottom and freed myself of the manacles as I usually do, but there must have been more of a current than I had calculated, and when I came up there was solid ice above me, and I couldn't locate the hole. So I went down again and looked, and looked, and swam about in the water a little, but that confounded hole had vanished as if it had suddenly froze over. After a few minutes I needed air. I got an idea. I let myself come up gently, and sure enough, just as I had thought, there was air space between the water and the surface—about half an inch wide. By lying on my back and poking my nose into this area gently, I could fill my lungs. I then swam around a bit looking for the hole, but still couldn't find it. Then I'd take another breath. I couldn't see much and it wasn't too warm down there, but at least I had oxygen. After what seemed like an eternity, I saw the rope drop down into the water, not very far away from where I was, and you bet I made right for it! And that's why I'm here."

No matter that on the day of the jump from the Belle Isle Bridge, November 27, 1906, the Detroit River was not frozen over according to the accounts in the local papers, the story fed the legend of Houdini. And like Pinocchio's nose, the legend grew and grew with every telling and retelling, growing in dimension as Houdini's fame grew, but never growing stale.

Mighty as he was to the myth-makers, in person he was short of stature, so much so that his vanity demanded he wear elevator shoes. He stood five feet eight, with an enormous head, short legs, and small feet. On stage he resembled a well-developed pugilist. Close up he was impressive for his military bearing, which caused one observer to view him as being like "those enlarged and idolized busts of Roman counsels and generals." His face was not so handsome as intense, wide-browed with a well-defined nose. His penetrating eyes seemed to pierce through you and follow you wherever you went. His hair was bushy, almost springy, with the consistency of a tightly-wound Brillo pad, which gave him a Paul Newmanesque quality. His stage voice was practiced, with strong enunciation given to almost every syllable; he reminded some listeners of a barker and sounded to others like a man with a slight German accent. His manner was straightforward, even quaint, with none of the suavity of other magicians, and often he signaled the end of a trick

with a conventional "Will wonders never cease?"

Houdini imparted romance to the audiences of America and Europe for a quarter of a century, standing them collectively on their heads with his feats. This man-legend provided them with an identification for their own desire to escape the regimen of their lives. For man has always dreamed of "escaping" from the shackles—real or imagined—of everyday life, and has made his heroes those who could escape: the Jean Valjeans and Huck Finns of fiction and the Papillons of real life. Here, standing before them, was the embodiment of their fantasy—Harry Houdini, the death-defying "Self-Liberator." The audience empathized with his dilemma. They identified with his problem. And his escape provided them with a melodramatic happy ending, a catharsis after the emotionally exhausting buildup.

But, even more than in his escapes, Houdini's greatest unstated appeal was to be found in the limitless human yearning for a taste of tragedy, that is, that this indeed "might be the day" when he didn't escape from his bonds, as man himself couldn't.

Harry Houdini worked harder, longer, and with more dedication to attain his goal of performing miracles than anyone ever thought possible. It is this complex man that we attempt to capture here, as difficult to do on paper as he ever was to capture in chains. For if his life reads like the clichés of a cheap novel, it is because, in part, Houdini wanted it to read that way, and only he himself could distinguish what was real and what was fiction. Now he is gone, as are those most closely associated with him, and we are left with fictionalized truths and promotional or self-serving stories. In an attempt to distill and synthesize all of these stories down into one true story of Houdini the man, rather than Houdini the legend, we have determined, where possible, to reflect on what was, not what could have been or even "what best serves the story line." The possibilities of viewing and reviewing Houdini are limitless. There are, after all, the sociology of the times as well as the psychology of the man to consider. But it is the biographical approach that best serves the purposes of both this book and Houdini; therein we can more clearly define both Houdini the man and Houdini the legend by reemphasizing the truth of the facts as we know them.

Bert Randolph Sugar
Chappaqua, New York
April 6, 1976

FOREWORD BY RANDI

Not too long ago, during one of my after-show question periods before a large college audience, I was asked a question that really set me back a bit. It was asked in all candor and innocence, though at first I thought it to be facetious. "Was Houdini a *real* person?" Never before had the legendary character of Harry Handcuff Houdini been brought to me as it was at that moment.

Yes, Houdini was a real person. He was so real, so alive, so important a man in my chosen field of prestidigitation, that a college sophomore could come up with a demand to know whether such a fabulous man ever really walked the earth, or whether he was the product of someone's fertile imagination. His actual deeds and the stories that have been fabricated about him are almost indistinguishable this half-century since his death, and I am sure that no one could enjoy that situation more than Houdini himself. Perhaps he sits, even now, upon some celestial throne designated by Heaven for the royalty of conjuring, flanked by Dunninger, Blackstone, Thurston, Cagliostro, and the many others who deserve their places in that firmament, and chuckles as we lesser personages strive to tell his story—as it *really* happened.

It is certain that his name is brought to mind every so often by the myriads of periodical editors who call writers to their desks and assign them the task of writing "something new" about Houdini. And it is equally certain that each writer so burdened scratches about in his literary catch-all to come up with a "new" Houdini angle that will get him off the hook. The authors of this book have avoided invention and pursued, rather, the human being behind the showman the world knew as "the elusive American." And that human being is a huge and very appealing one, indeed.

Authorities who have written many books and articles about Houdini, have in some cases treated him as some sort of holy personage who had no weaknesses and never made a mistake. Obviously, such a picture is a monochromatic one. Then, too, many events in the stories about him have been perpetuated in order to glamorize a life that hardly needs such enhancement. The authors of this book are determined to set the record somewhat straighter than it has been in the past, while not detracting from the fascination that accompanies the subject. One does not diminish the sun by describing sunspots.

Obviously, a prominent character in the drama is the little lady who stood for thirty-two years at the side of Harry Houdini as his wife. That her life was anything but dull goes without proof; that it was often less than happy, and at times even approached boredom, is less well documented heretofore. Bess Houdini lived with a whirlwind, and her story needs telling too.

Houdini's brother Theodore, the only one in the family who followed the entertainment profession along with him, lived on to taste the strange flavor of that situation wherein he could never be as far up the ladder as Harry, but was doomed to live in that half-limelight which lingered on after death claimed the man for whom it originally was lit and shone so brightly. Hardeen, as he was known professionally, had never attained the position Houdini had, and even when he was left behind to claim the throne, failed to do so. Houdini took the throne, the crown, and the kingdom with him when he went.

When the publishers of this book approached me, they did so in the middle of the greatest "magic boom" of this century. A generation left disillusioned by all that it should believe in from politics to science, has reacted by pursuing the chimera of the supernatural, a beast that Houdini himself sought to slay during his lifetime. Ironically enough, his feats have now served as fuel for the silly claims of self-styled miracle-workers, and, as might be expected, the half-century since his death has blown up those accomplishments out of all proportion. Perhaps this book will settle some of the myths and place the credit where it should be—at the feet of the greatest prestidigitator and illusionist of the age.

This interest in nonsense and nonscience has happily also brought about a revived interest in the legitimate frauds—among whom I gladly number myself. We who perform apparent wonders for purposes of entertainment, as did Harry Houdini, rejoice in this lucrative and satisfying interest shown by young and old currently. And I personally take this opportunity of calling upon my fellow conjurors to make sure their efforts are not looked upon as genuine, but that they make very clear the real purpose of these deceptions—entertainment, nothing more, but certainly nothing less.

I find the present arrangement—two authors—an interesting one. Bert Randolph Sugar has approached the subject from a factual, biographical point of view; I am prepared to look behind the facts of the story to discover the ways that Harry Houdini shaped his own destiny, and to postulate the reasons for his actions. My experience in the conjuring field should equip me to perform this investigation while Bert Sugar keeps the facts of the narrative sharply in focus.

We have relied heavily upon photographs and historical material from press files and from many collectors

and museums to tell part of the story. Frequently, documents seen here are reproduced for the first time, and photographs have been traced back to the earliest prints, and in some cases to the original negatives, to retain every nuance of reality possible. We are very grateful to those who have given us permission to use these materials, and hope that our story will do them justice.

I am personally very satisfied to have been called in to coauthor this book, for I have for many years wanted to be able to tell a modern audience what I feel Houdini went through in the moments when the chips were down and the wheel was spinning. Unless you have been dangling above a city street wrapped in a straitjacket or manacled and slammed into a barred cell to test your abilities at beating the big odds, you cannot imagine just what it is like.

The shadow of Harry Houdini hangs over me constantly, like a strange, burdensome cloud. Every time I perform a feat of escape, I have "done a Houdini" to the press. And though it may be taken as a compliment to be compared to the greatest of all magicians, it is nonetheless a secondhand compliment. In vain, I ask audiences to refrain from comparing me with the man, but to little avail. And I know all too well that I can only come out of such a comparison as runner-up.

For it is more obvious now than ever before that Harry Houdini is the Master Magician of all time. No one has ever so captured the imagination and love of the public as he did. No other magician has been so perennially present to generations who never saw him at work. And no magician so richly deserves these distinctions.

In this business, if you are not an egotist, you are a failure. Houdini was the egotist *par excellence*, never missing a chance to put his name up before the world, whether he was leaping shackled off a high bridge or testing the dungeons of an ancient European castle. In the Houdini Museum Hall of Fame, in Niagara Falls, Canada, there is a little-noted document among the hundreds displayed that sums it all up. It is a Keith Circuit vaudeville program in the center of which is an elegant portrait of Harry Houdini and a personal autograph from the great man himself. The signature reads, "Houdini. That's enough." And it was.

He took the world that he found himself in as a poor boy, and inside of his brief fifty-two years of life, he wrested from it all the fame and adulation that one man can expect to get—and then a bit more. He was a magician, an historian, a champion of causes, a flaming star, a legend, and an enigma. He was Harry Houdini, and this is his story.

The Amazing Randi
Rumson, New Jersey
April 10, 1976

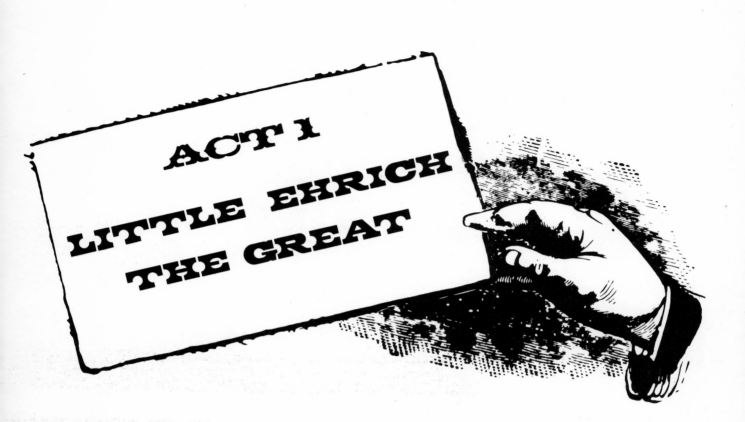

ACT 1

LITTLE EHRICH THE GREAT

Winston Churchill, Chaim Weizmann, Herbert Hoover, Somerset Maugham, Robert Frost, Guglielmo Marconi, Ernest Shackleton, and Gustav Holst were all born in 1874. So was another unusual man—Harry Houdini. Of that much we're certain. And that's *all!* For Harry Houdini's birth, as well as the rest of his life and even his death, is shrouded in uncertainty and mystery, as befits the man described as "the greatest necromancer of the age—perhaps of all time."

Houdini always said "my birth occurred April 6, 1874, in the small town of Appleton, Wisconsin," and he was proud of the fact that the "United States Government recognized the significance of this date, in 1917, by waiting until it arrived before declaring war on Germany." As far as his family and fans were concerned, the date and place of his birth made him as American as George M. Cohan, who was actually born on July 3, but believed he was "a Yankee Doodle Dandy/born on the fourth of July."

Tracing Houdini's actual origins is almost as difficult as following his tricks, for history, in part, seems to have been rewritten, or at least, in the language of the magician, much of it has been "misdirected."

His father was Samuel Mayer Weisz, the son of a rabbi in the western provinces of the Austro-Hungarian empire. At the age of twenty-three, Samuel emigrated to the Pest portion of the city now known as Budapest to pursue his one ambition—the study of the law. Finding the law closed to Jews in Hungary in 1853, he turned to the familiar profession of his father and forefathers—the study of the Talmud.

Widowed and with a one-year-old son, the young rabbi wooed and won the hand of twenty-three-year-old Cecilia Steiner in 1864, and fathered three more sons in the next six years. The fifth son of Samuel Mayer Weisz—although later he would be referred to as "the seventh son"—recorded in the registry of the Pest Jewish Congregation, the Pesti Izrealita Hitkozseg, as having been born in Pest on March 24, 1874, was called Erik and would become known to the world as Harry Houdini.

Houdini's birthplace and birthdate had always been accepted as those he claimed—Appleton, Wisconsin, April 6, 1874—until just a few years ago, when the Society of American Magicians investigated the mystery of the Master Magician, his two birthplaces and two birthdates, and discovered the entry in the registrar's office of the Jewish Congregation of Pest. This alone did

Rabbi Samuel Mayer Weisz.

not end the controversy, for although he was born in Budapest, the miniature time warp is, according to the former director of Harvard College Observatory, "definitely the difference between the Gregorian and the Julian calendars." In other words, when the designers of the Gregorian calendar attempted to reconcile the error in the Julian calendar, they dropped several days. March 24, 1874, became April 6, 1874, according to the new Gregorian calendar. Like George Washington, Houdini had two birthdates—March 24 and April 6, 1874—a fitting beginning to the life of an illusionist.

The arrival of another baby and another mouth to feed did not alleviate the gloom that pervaded the Weisz home that year. Samuel Mayer Weisz, like so many other learned men who had become rabbis in Hungary and other heavily populated Jewish settlements in Europe without an ordination, had no congregation or job to support his burgeoning family. Driven by the desire to have both a pulpit and a salary, he read every paper, looking for advertisements for a rabbi either in Europe or the new country, America.

Just a month before Erik's birth, Samuel answered an ad in *Doctor Bloch's Wochenschrift*, a German periodical filled with items of Jewish interest from America. One of the items that caught Weisz's attention was a little ad from a newly formed congregation in Appleton, Wisconsin, called Temple Zion. They wanted a rabbi. No matter that it was over six thousand miles away in a place he had never heard of; this was his big chance, a pulpit of his own.

Weisz answered the ad in German, and within a few weeks he was rewarded for his ambition. The president of the congregation offered him not only the position, but for an unheard-of sum of $750 a year! Weisz sent his acceptance the same week his son was born, and spent the next three weeks collecting the few possessions they had in the Old World for their trip to the new. Late in the spring of 1874, Samuel Mayer Weisz left Budapest bound for Appleton, Wisconsin, to become Rabbi Samuel Mayer Weiss. Temple Zion added the "Rabbi" to his name, and the immigration authorities who met his ship from Bremen took care of his last name, anglicizing Weisz into Weiss to conform to the German spelling of the word *white*. And so, the Reverend Dr. Weiss arrived in Appleton, Wisconsin, in the early summer of 1874 to become the first rabbi of a new Reform congregation of just ten German-Jewish families.

The town of Appleton in 1874 had a population of only 8,000. Located on the Fox River in Outagamie County, the village lay in the heart of the dairy farming belt, with some vestiges of the fur, cattle, and horse trading of olden days still prevalent. The home of Lawrence College, Appleton, like most Wisconsin cities of that time, was heavily populated with Germans. The small Jewish settlement in Appleton had all come from the little Bavarian town of Gemunden, and the Hammells, Marshalls, Loebs, Fishers, Strassers, Lyons, and Hynamens were primarily horse and cattle dealers and merchants.

Rabbi Weiss assumed his duties immediately, conducting the Friday and Saturday services in German upstairs over Heckert's Saloon on College Avenue. The rest of the week, he taught Hebrew and German at Lawrence

College. When Cecilia Weiss was not helping her husband in his new capacity by overseeing the Zion Ladies' Aid Society doing *mitzvahs* for poor families that needed help, she was home raising her family—the traditional matriarchal "place" for the wife of a learned man who devoted himself to his studies. For according to the Talmud, "A learned woman is a monstrosity. She is neither male nor female; run from her like the plague."

Little Ehrich—the spelling was changed in the New World, his first step towards Americanization—was a strong and happy baby. The romantic legend of Houdini written by one biographer, through the eyes of his wife Bess, described Ehrich as a baby who never cried. Only one characteristic gave his mother a little uneasiness—he slept barely half as much as her other babies had. At times when an average, well-ordered infant would have been deep in slumber, young Ehrich would lie in his crib, awake and content, for long periods, his bright steely eyes roving curiously from one object to another. This self-sufficiency and constant curiosity have been construed as superhuman qualities possessed by Houdini from birth. Although there is some basis in fact that he never slept more than five hours a night during his adult life, there is nothing on which to establish the accuracy of this description of his infant wakefulness; it is probably just ex-post facto myth making.

According to another biographer, Mrs. Weiss claimed little Ehrich hardly ever cried, and when he did, she would comfort him by picking him up and holding him close to her breast until the sound of her heartbeat stopped his tears.

Apparently everyone who ever knew little Ehrich Weiss agreed on one thing: his early fascination with locks. Cecilia Weiss made many of the old world "goodies" her mother and grandmother had made, including *apfelkun*. This freshly baked apple confection proved to be the siren's call that first brought together the infant Houdini and locks. One day, according to Houdini, when his mother had left the kitchen for a few minutes, he caught the smell of one of her specialties emanating from a closed cupboard. Taking advantage of her absence and the unlocked state of the cupboard, he found and finished up the freshly baked dessert. Mrs. Weiss, taking note of the innocent theft, sought to remedy the situation by having a lock put on the cupboard. But the next baking day, little Ehrich sniffed the aroma of the pie again and opened the cupboard door despite the lock.

Mrs. Weiss, now facing a situation not unlike that of Old Mother Hubbard, put a padlock on the door to reinforce the cupboard's own lock. Once again, little Ehrich conquered all the obstacles and triumphed over matter with his agile mind.

One person who remembered little Ehrich was Lewis Marshall, who died in 1975 at the age of 103. Raised in Appleton, he remembered "Harry" Weiss as "a nice, likable little fellow who used to monkey around with locks and do sleight-of-hand and tricks for us." "Harry" was also remembered, not quite so fondly, by his townfolk as a "high-spirited" and troublesome little boy who one night unlocked the front-door locks of all the merchants on College Avenue.

One thing that kept little Harry out of trouble was the trapeze and bar set that the Weisses set up behind their home on Appleton Street. This was the outdoor staple for children of the 1880s much as swings were to become the vogue for children in the 1920s. While most kids played on their trapeze and bar sets, little Harry worked at his until he was proficient enough to gain the envy of the neighborhood kids and skilled enough to give shows and charge admission.

Throughout his career, Houdini gave out false clues and false dates in interviews and press releases to confuse every biographer. He led them down a primrose path as to the true facts of his life. In 1918 he told a writer that "at the age of seven he observed a traveling showman walk a tight rope in the main street of town, varying this feat by hanging by his teeth from the cable. Not knowing that a special mouth-fitting contrivance was required for this trick, Houdini tried it in the backyard the same afternoon—and lost five teeth."

From that time on, little Harry was always seen down at the vacant lot next to the railroad tracks watching the traveling circuses. Sometimes he slipped in by crawling under the canvas tent, other times he went in as the crowd was exiting. Somehow he was always able to get in and seat himself in front of the sideshow. It was not the fat lady or the living skeleton or the ossified man advertised as his own tombstone that held Harry's attention, but the magician or conjuror who produced rabbits, flowers, flags, long streamers, and almost anything imaginable from his seemingly inexhaustible silk hat. According to Houdini, one hot summer day the magician momentarily dropped his hat in front of little Harry, and an entire world opened up to him. The boy saw that there was nothing supernatural behind the tricks, no occult power to bring them to fruition. He could do it! Just as he could do his acrobatic tricks on the bars and trapeze.

The interview—and legend—has it that two years later, when Ehrich was nine, Jack Hoefler's Five Cent Circus came to Appleton, and Ehrich applied to the manager for a job as an acrobat, wire walker, and sleight-of-hand performer. "October 28, 1883, was the date of my first appearance before an audience," he later wrote. "I appeared as a contortionist and trapeze performer, being advertised as 'Ehrich, the Prince of the Air.' My contract called for thirty-five cents a week." Bedecked in red woollies to give the appearance of a trapeze artist, he performed "the Dead Man's Drop" and, as he later claimed, a variant of the contortionist's trick of bending over backwards and picking up articles with his mouth: the young Houdini, true to the legend, went the competition several times better by picking up pins with his eyelids, or eyes, or eyebrows, depending on what story you read.

This one small taste of "sawdust" stayed with little Harry, or "Ehrich, the Prince of the Air," for his entire life. Thereafter, whenever the summer's divertissement of a traveling circus came to Appleton, he could be seen making his way towards the lot near the railroad tracks that housed the troupe, looking for new wonderment and new thrills that only a boy interested in magic and circuses can understand. Harry Weiss was going through his I-am-a-kid-and-I-want-to-be-a-magician period, a period that really never ended, leaving Houdini with a little boy inside him throughout the rest of his life.

As the infant Erik grew into little Ehrich and then into little Harry, his father was experiencing difficulties with his congregation. Although the new Temple Zion had been built on Durkey Street, the prevailing sentiment of the parishioners was that the fifty-year-old rabbi never really "fit in," was not "well liked," and that they should look for a new and younger rabbi. The elders of the congregation sought out a landsman from their old hometown of Gemunden, a Hebraic scholar named F. J. Solomon, and persuaded him to come over and act as their rabbi, although he, like Weiss, had no rabbinical training.

And so, on a cold morning late in the year 1883, Rabbi Samuel Mayer Weiss, according to Houdini's own personal reminiscences, "awoke to find himself thrown upon the world, his long locks of hair having silvered in service, with seven children to feed, without a position and without any visible means of support."

"We thereupon moved to Milwaukee, where such hardships and hunger became our lot that the less said on the subject, the better," Houdini added cryptically in his own hand. What is known about that period in Milwaukee is that after Weiss had moved to the larger city, he tried to support his family in the traditional manner of out-of-work rabbis. He became a *shocket* and a *moyel*, a kosher butcher and a rabbi who performed *brisses*, or circumcisions. The small amount of money this brought in was woefully inadequate, even when supplemented by little Harry's contribution made by shining shoes and selling papers. The family had to move time and again to stay ahead of the rent collectors.

In his "adopted" country, little Harry believed, it was possible to start with nothing and still be successful. He had the first qualification: he had nothing. During his fourth year in grammar school, he left to help his father. According to one of the stories Houdini liked to tell, where the apocryphal is not always distinguishable from the factual, he took a job as an apprentice with a local locksmith to learn more about his first love—locks. Within a few weeks he was able to pick every lock in the shop. He even learned how to make a picklock out of a small piece of wire that could master any fastening.

One day the sheriff came into the shop, dragging a prisoner, a man of sizable proportions. The man had been arrested and then discharged. When it had come time to free him of his handcuffs, however, no key could be found to fit the lock, and so now the prisoner stood bound in front of the locksmith and little Harry, waiting for his iron bracelets to be taken off by whatever means could be devised. Try as the locksmith might, he could not break the obstinate steel. According to Houdini, "While the master locksmith was trying to open the handcuffs, the whistle blew the dinner hour. Having a sharpened appetite, he called me to his side and said, 'Harry, get a hack-saw and cut off his handcuffs' and then went out with the police officer to dine."

Left alone with the handcuffed stranger, Harry set to work. As the minutes ticked by, it became painfully obvious that the irons had given little to Harry's inexperienced efforts. The imprisoned man grew more and more restless. "Wait a minute," Harry said, and with that he fished out a tangled mass from his little boy's pocket. Somehow, in that mishmash he found his picklock and set to work. A minute or two later one cuff fell off, and the second quickly followed. Harry stepped back hastily and shoved the picklock back into his pocket while the man rubbed his wrists and eyed him thoughtfully. At that moment, according to the story, the sheriff and the locksmith returned from the beer break and told the newly freed man to "clear out," putting an end to any thoughts he may have had of trying to use either picklock or Harry. Houdini would have you believe— in telling of it later—that this was the only man who ever got close enough to him to watch him open a pair of handcuffs.

The rest of the time in Milwaukee, when, as Houdini himself later admitted, "I rarely had the bare necessities of life," he continued to fantasize that he was really "Ehrich the Great" ("Anyone can tie me with ropes and I can still get free!") or "Cardo the Great" ("I ain't got nothing up my sleeves"). But his fantasies were merely his escape from the cruelty of his lot.

Finally, little Harry's fantasies got the best of him and he ran away from home, escaping from the oppressive misery that only those who have experienced deprivation and poverty can know. He wanted to pursue his dream of somehow, someway, somewhere earning enough money to send back home and fulfill his promise to his father to look after his beloved mother and never have her "want." The best way to do that would be to find work. By 1886 Ringling Brothers had started their first circus in Baraboo, Wisconsin, a mere sixty miles from Appleton. But whether this was the attraction that drew Harry or whether he merely needed the chance to escape and be on his own is not known, for there are few details concerning his runaway year. What is known is that he made it to Delavan, Wisconsin, and from there to Rockford, Illinois, where he sneaked aboard a freight train south—heading, he thought, for Galveston, Texas. Instead, by the classic misdirection that Houdini was known for throughout his life, his freight went to Kansas City.

The only concrete evidence of Harry's one-year odyssey throughout the midwest was a postcard sent home postmarked "Hannibal & St. Joseph R.R. 1886," which is in the magnificent MacManus-Young Magic Collection in the Library of Congress. In a young boy's penciled handwriting, the card reads: "Dear Ma I am going to Galveston Texas and will be home in about a year. My best regard to all. Did you get my picture if you didnt write to Mead Bros. Wood Stock Ill. Your truant son Ehrich Weiss."

With a burning desire to make something of himself and also to make some money to send home, he went through the towns of Hannibal, Missouri, and Coffeyville, Kansas, latching onto traveling circuses where he could. One night, according to Houdini some thirty years later, he challenged some local townspeople to tie him up. It occurred to the sheriff who was actually doing the tying to put a pair of handcuffs on him. "If I put these on you, you couldn't get loose," Houdini remembers the sheriff as saying in one of the little booklets he sold in the front lobby before his act. Houdini says he told the sheriff to "go ahead and put them on," and then Houdini freed himself from his first pair of handcuffs in the very area where legend of another sort had been made just a few years before by the James boys.

Tiring of his purposeless wandering, Harry set out for New York, the fabled city where opportunity and gold were available on every street corner. By the time he arrived in 1887, he had not only become "a man" of thirteen, but he also was able to rejoin his father, who had

Young Ehrich's letter home to his mother, dated 1896 (left), and a page picked up from one of Houdini's magazines, published later in his life, showing him at various ages (right).

20

1877

3½ YEARS OF AGE

8 YEARS OF AGE

AGE 15

13 YEARS OF AGE

19 YEARS OF AGE

HOUDINI AT DIFFERENT AGES OF HIS CAREER

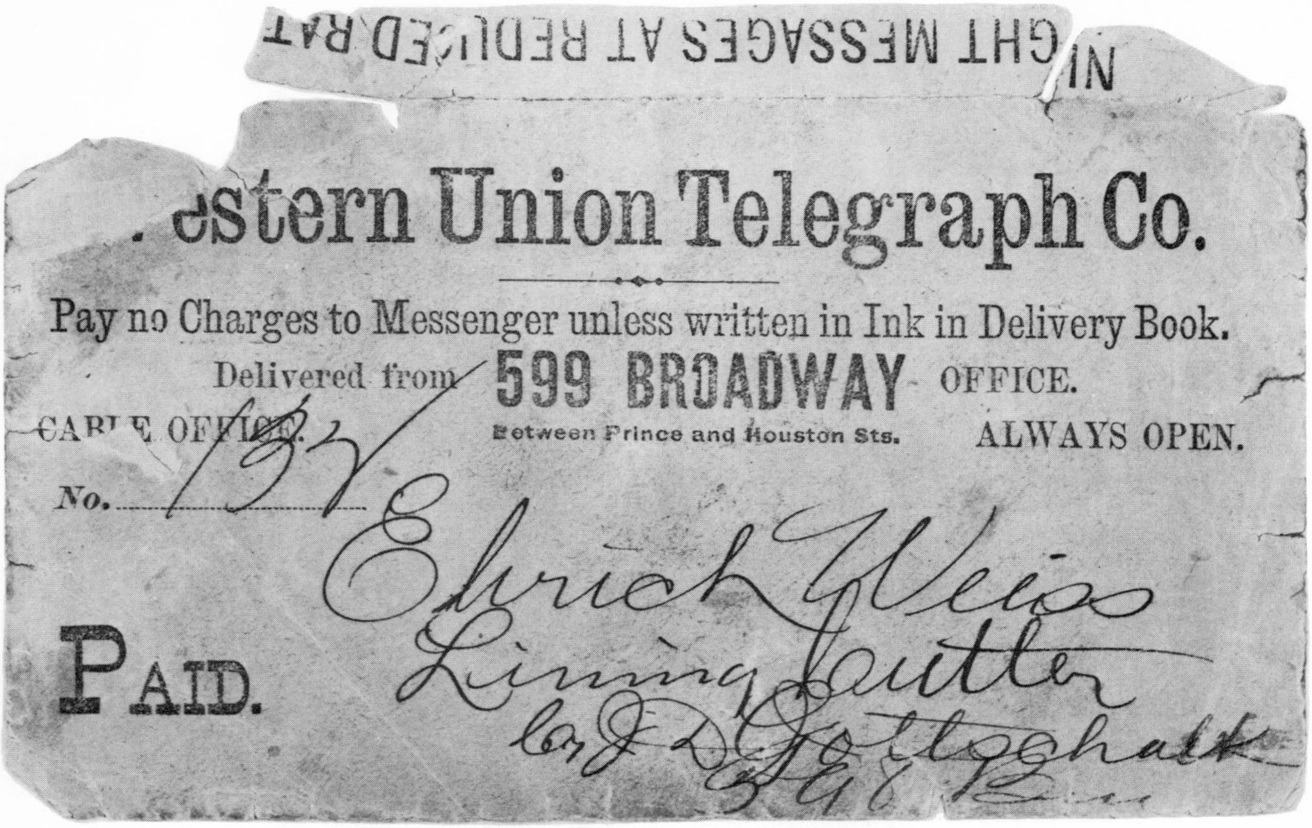

NIGHT MESSAGES AT REDUCED RAT

estern Union Telegraph Co.

Pay no Charges to Messenger unless written in Ink in Delivery Book.

Delivered from **599 BROADWAY** OFFICE.

CABLE OFFICE.   Between Prince and Houston Sts.   ALWAYS OPEN.

No.

PAID.

*Ehrich Weiss
Lining Cutter
Co J D Gottschalk*

left the family in Milwaukee to seek greener pastures where an out-of-work rabbi had more opportunities.

Harry had received a letter from his mother telling him that his father had gone to New York to found a small religious school, convinced that a city with a Jewish population of more than half a million would support his efforts more than Appleton or Milwaukee had. Determined to find him, help him out, and bring the rest of the family east, young Harry sought to locate the erstwhile rabbi. After weeks of combing the streets of the city, Harry found his father in a small rooming house on East 79th Street. The son soon found a job as a messenger and quickly earned enough to bring all the Weisses together again in a small ground-floor apartment on East 69th Street. "We lived there, I mean starved there, for several years," Houdini was to inscribe in his diary. Cecilia Weiss once again set up the household with the remaining six children—Nathan, William, Harry, Theo, Leopold, and Gladys—all crammed into the three-room apartment. Harry, true to the promise made to his father to look after the family in case of any adversity, assumed the mantle of the protector of the family, leaving his father to his studies and his small Hebrew school. At the age of thirteen he was truly a *mensch*.

While his younger brother Theo took a job with a photographer, Harry finagled himself a job in New York's growing garment industry as an assistant to a necktie-lin-

ing cutter. He got the job by removing a Help Wanted sign from the door and telling all of those waiting in line that the job was filled.

While Theo's boss was teaching him sleight-of-hand tricks with coins, Harry was learning magic from a boy who worked next to him, Jack Hayman, at H. Richter's necktie factory on lower Broadway. This was, as nearly as can be traced, the actual beginning of the Houdini legend.

Forecasting Harry Weiss's future at this stage was like looking through a kaleidoscope and finding many different patterns. But the one that shone brightest was magic! What little boy who has ever witnessed—or performed—a magic trick hasn't vicariously invested himself with that exciting, adventurous, and mysterious world? Little Harry Weiss was no different. Because his childhood had been stunted by deprivation and hardship, he yearned to continue it, to cherish that little spark of a kid that was still in him. To transport him back to a childhood he never really knew, he sought out the one area that has fascinated kids and kids-at-heart since time immemorial: magic. He studied everything he could get his hand on—books, tricks, biographies. He visited magic shops, traded small talk, bought sets of "tricked" cards, and became "sold" on becoming a magician.

But perhaps the greatest stimulant to achieving his ambition was a little secondhand book he came upon in one of the outdoor bookstalls that lined Fourth Avenue one Saturday afternoon in his sixteenth year. It was the life story of France's greatest magician and entertainer, *Memoirs of Robert-Houdin, Ambassador, Author, and Conjuror,* the man who developed many of the greatest illusions in the world. Harry scraped together the few pennies he had in his pocket and haggled for the book, as precious to him as any treasure would ever be to any prospector. Racing home with the battered volume under his arm, he went right to his room and immersed himself in the life of the famous magician. As legend would have it, the next morning his mother found him, still clothed, sitting on the edge of his bed poring over every page. If Harry Weiss had not previously determined to become a magician, his mind and goals were now set. He, too, would become a "Maker of Miracles." The old volume had not only given him the key to unlock the miracles of magic, but it had also given him a new hero and changed his life, much as the man named Robert-Houdin had had *his* life changed by receiving—by mistake—a book on magic instead of one he had requested on clockmaking. If there was a moment when the insubstantial dreaming took form, this was it. But if the book gave him a new hero, it also gave him a new name, for Harry Weiss decided to emulate his new hero not just in deed, but also in name. By adding an *i* to the name Houdin, he could become "like Houdin," much as Houdin himself had taken his wife's maiden name, Robert, and added it to his own last name. And so the infant born

Erik Weisz, who had become Harry Weiss to his friends, now became Harry Houdini.

From that day Harry and his friend Jack Hayman became the Brothers Houdini, performing wherever and whenever they could for their family or anyone else who would watch.

Their first show was held in the cellar of the Weiss apartment house, with a dry goods box for a stage, a lantern for footlights, and a gunnysack for a curtain. The headline attraction was the Houdini Brothers, Weiss and Hayman, who had laboriously and—according to their parents—perilously rehearsed some acrobatic and magic tricks, mostly "silks" and "cards." Admission to the combined show was five cents, although one member of the audience *schnorred* in for the four cents he had in hand, making the total box office receipts eighty-nine cents for the eighteen kids, parents, and relatives on hand. After a long, arduous performance, given—according to one observer—"to gratifying applause," the perspiring performers decided to "divvy up" the proceeds, which they felt was little enough reward for their efforts. They told their stage manager, a little boy named Mark Nelson whom they had hired for a dime, that he wasn't going to receive his money. Young Nelson, after protesting to no avail, "got even" by calling together as many of the neighborhood kids as he could round up and revealing all of the secrets of the two welshing performers. The next day Harry and Hayman found themselves the object of jeers instead of the awestruck admiration they had ex-

One of Harry's paycheck stubs during his necktie-cutting days, circa 1890 (upper left), and the bust of Robert Houdin (right).

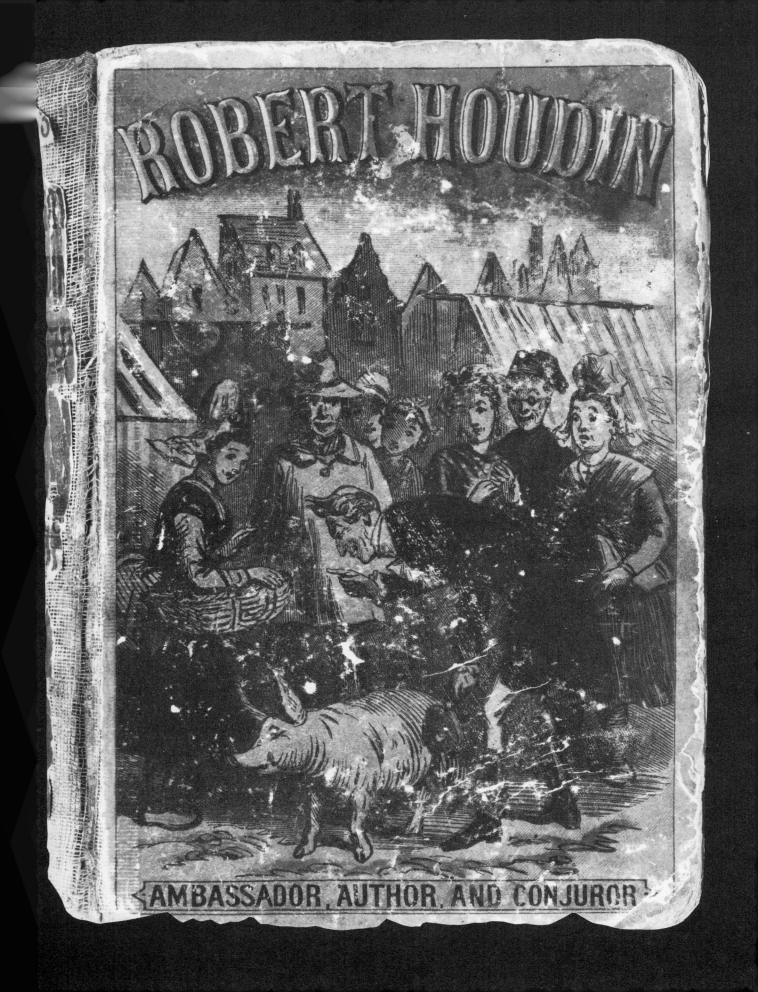

ROBERT HOUDIN

AMBASSADOR, AUTHOR, AND CONJUROR

pected. The lesson was valuable to Harry. He learned, "early in the game, to make myself expose-proof," he said.

From that time on, "Houdini" could almost be said to be the personification of all the clichés of the dime fiction then prevalent: struggling, self-taught, ambitious, and seeking an escape. He was Harry Weiss in the daytime and Harry Houdini at night. He appeared at every booking office and performed for ladies' nights at the local Y.M.H.A. and even for organizations such as the Friendly Circle ("entertainment at Schillerbund Hall"), practicing and refining his talent. As his confidence in his abilities and destiny took shape, he determined that life without magic would be life in an airless dungeon and made his first escape—leaving the employ of H. Richter and setting out on his own as, in his own words, "a professional magician under the name of Harry Houdini."

Thus, early in 1891, after two years as an assistant necktie-lining cutter, Harry Weiss ventured forth into the world as Harry Houdini, with only a letter of recommendation from the company he had served attesting that he was "an honest and industrious young man" and a burning ambition to become a magician. At this time, one of those fortunate Horatio-Algeresque incidents in the youth of one who was to make his mark in the world took place. A down-and-out magician offered the young partners the feature of his act: the trunk trick. They could have both the plans and the apparatus for $25—no small amount in those days, when a roast beef dinner cost fifteen cents and an entire man's outfit, complete with hat, cost $11.90. Harry and Jack somehow borrowed the money and took possession of the heart of their act—the old "One-In-One-Out" trick, or, as they called it, "Metamorphosis."

Metamorphosis, as developed by Houdini and Hayman, was a variation on the old escape from a roped and locked box, first introduced by John Maskelyne as early as 1864, and improved upon down through the years by others, including Robert-Houdin. Houdini's hands were tied behind his back and he was put into a sack, which was tied and placed in a trunk, which, in turn, was doubly tied with rope and locked. A curtain was arranged around the box to conceal it as Hayman announced to the audience, "When I clap my hands three times, behold a miracle." The curtain was then reopened to reveal that Houdini had vanished and in his place was Hayman bound in the same fashion.

Even though with Metamorphosis the Brothers Houdini had a *shtick*, Jack Hayman wasn't happy as a magician and soon left to team up with his real brother as song-

and-dance men. And so, the Brothers Houdini in name became the Brothers Weiss in reality. Left momentarily without a partner, Harry drafted his younger brother, Theo—called "Dash" because of his fondness for fine haberdashery—to take Jack's place, both in the act and in the box. Because Dash was five eleven, three full inches taller than his brother, it made the trunk trick difficult to handle. But continued practice, both on and off the stage, brought the new Brothers Houdini their first real measure of professionalism. It was the only indication throughout 1891 and early 1892 that they were, indeed, professionals.

Harry and Dash encountered many difficulties acquiring bookings, even as "home talent" in the little local clubs, but their mother encouraged their ambition. She sewed their costumes, mended their frock coats, and generally provided all the comfort a Jewish mother, particularly a Jewish stage mother, could muster, hearing their problems and shoring up their resolve to succeed. While her other children had more orthodox ambitions, such as wanting to become businessmen or doctors, she acted as a sounding board to Harry and Dash, alternately exhorting them to practice or to get out and see booking agents, in her mixed German and English dialect. Although she had learned some English, the language continued to elude Samuel Weiss—together with steady employment. The rabbi's small Hebrew school had collapsed, and he was again reduced to looking for work as a part time *moyel* and *shocket*. Jobs were none too plentiful.

As summer turned into fall in 1892, the prospects for the Brothers Houdini turned colors like the trees—from a rosy red to a dark and despairing black. Without bookings, Harry and Dash were forced to remain at home most of the time, there to watch the bedridden remains of their sixty-two-year-old dying father. With no past to speak of and no future, the erstwhile rabbi could cope with a debilitating illness no better than he had coped with life. On his deathbed, he is supposed to have called to Harry and asked him to carry on the torch, renewing the oath that his son had taken on a Torah six years before in Milwaukee, that he would always provide for his mother and "never let her want."

On October 5, 1892, Rabbi Samuel Mayer Weiss went to the only reward he had ever earned, leaving Cecilia Weiss and seven children without a husband and father. Houdini's resolve to succeed as a magician was newly strengthened by his obsession to replace his father as patriarch of the family and for the first time to give them a true breadwinner.

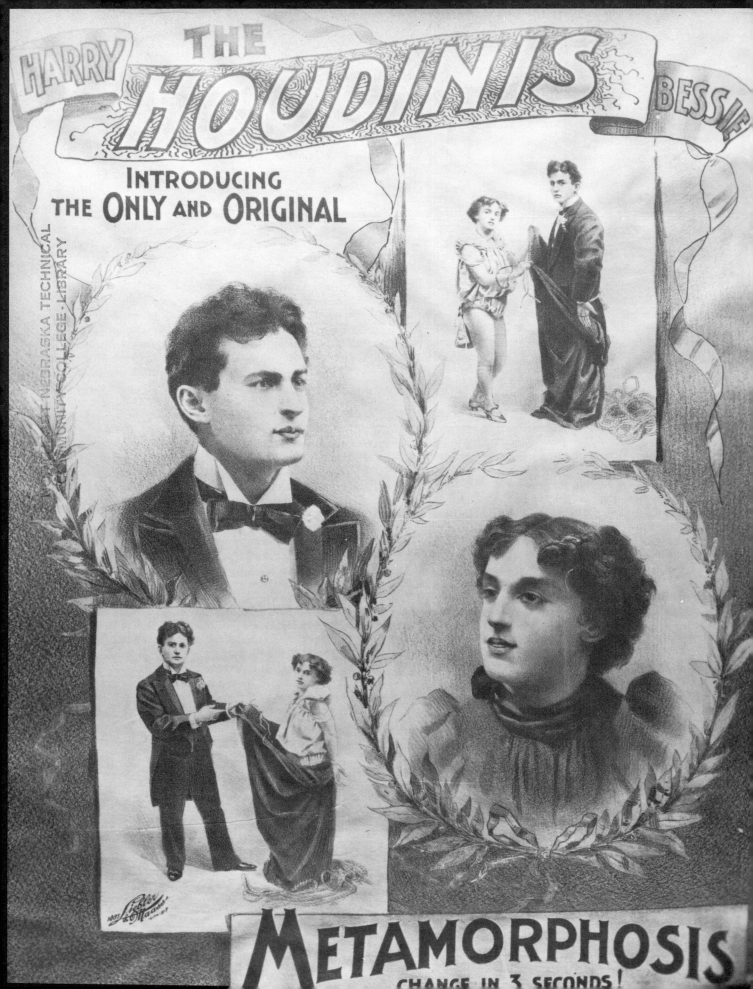

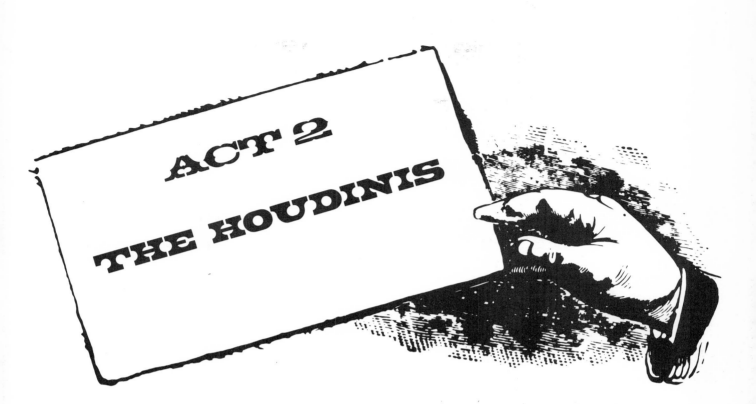

ACT 2
THE HOUDINIS

In the words of one of the Sweet Caporal cigarette buttons then being worn by some of the so-called gay blades, the year 1893 "just has to get better, 'cause it can't get worse."

And if that was the rallying cry for the Brothers Houdini, it also was for the country as a whole, for the United States was suffering through its second depression in twenty years, this time complete with millions out of work and the first bread lines in American history.

The hardest-hit areas were those with large numbers of unskilled laborers, the East Coast in general and New York in particular. So the Brothers Houdini, following the admonition attributed forty years earlier to New York *Tribune* editor Horace Greeley to "Go West"—although he really meant Erie County, Pennsylvania— took their act west, in the general direction of Chicago and the Columbian Exposition.

The 1893 World's Fair, called the Columbian Exposition to celebrate the four hundredth anniversary of the discovery of America by Columbus, opened one year late. But no one seemed to mind. Opened on May 1 when President Grover Cleveland touched an ivory and gold key to start the machinery, turn on the fountains, and unfurl the flags of the "White City," it was re-

nowned for the great Ferris Wheel, invented by George Washington Ferris, who had answered the challenge sent out by the promoters of the fair for something that would rival the Eiffel Tower, built in Paris to commemorate the exposition of 1889. The fair had cost $32 million and had taken 10,000 workmen three years to complete (one of these was Walt Disney's father, Elias, who had worked as a carpenter for a dollar a day). But it was neither the Ferris Wheel, rising 250 feet above the fair and carrying over 1,000 passengers, all scared stiff by the winds that blew in from Lake Michigan, nor the Palace of Electricity with the colored globes in the pillar of light flashing out ever-changing patterns that captured the imagination of the millions who attended. Nor was it the special display of the first locomotives or the fleet of ships that had sailed in from Spain, called Columbus Caravels, that held the public spellbound. It was the Midway Plaisance, across the Illinois Central Railroad tracks from the main exposition grounds, that was the best remembered by those who attended. There one could see Sol Bloom's Egyptian Village, with dancers who were really corn-fed American girls with dark eyes and a little special training, dancing the "hootchy-kootchy." By May 2 the entire country had heard about Little Egypt, the lead dancer, and the other "naughty" delights to be experienced along the Midway—including the hookah, a Turkish water pipe, which any American girl who went to the fair and felt like doing something deliciously wicked could sample. And it was on the Midway that Florenz Ziegfeld first became known as an entrepreneur, running an all-girl show, and where Theodore and Paul Dreiser worked as pitchmen. And at a little side show, if anyone recalled, could be found the Brothers Houdini doing their wildly enthusiastic but not highly skilled magic act, with Metamorphosis as its signature.

From the standpoint of experience, it was a success. The inquisitive Houdini visited most of the other attractions along the Midway, gleaning all of the tricks of the trade that were available to the bush-haired youngster with the strange-sounding name. It was here that he was reputed to have picked up the secret of the East Indian needle trick he was later to incorporate into his act. But, alas, one of the common but often sad facts of performing life is that events never work out as planned. For if the Midway and its Egyptian Village were resounding successes, the Brothers Houdini were far less so. Within a month they were back in New York seeking employment.

On July 31, Harry and Dash ingratiated themselves into New York's Huber's 14th Street Museum at the magnificent sum of $12 a week. They performed down in the basement next to the freaks. While hardly the "big time," it was a step up and gave Harry and Dash their first real taste of the semiorganized world of show business. There, according to the Houdini legend, J.H. Anderson, the manager, took an instant liking to Harry and his desire to absorb as much as he could. The manager taught him everything he knew about escaping from ropes and handcuffs. And Houdini, who had always been fascinated by restraints—whether made of rope or iron—became a willing student in the art of escapology. The future "Master Magician" became, for the first time, the master of his own destiny.

Prior to Phineas Taylor Barnum, American museums had been "a place for the muses" and little else. They were places for scholarship, filled with stuffed birds and beasts, while theaters housed amusements. Barnum started to transform museums from places for instruction into amusement centers. He first added attractions, or, as some observers called them, "hoaxes," and then live shows to his American Museum in New York. He then built the most magnificent of all museum-variety houses, the Hippodrome, completed the same month Houdini was born—April 1874. His overall contribution to American theater is still open to debate, but what is not debatable is that Barnum single-handedly brought attractions to the masses—equestrian, fire eaters, midgets, conjurors, sword swallowers, jugglers, and "curiosities" (the forerunners to freak shows).

It was this world of museums and their offshoots—aptly named dime museums—that Harry Houdini and Dash now canvassed, seeking bookings for their act. Sometimes Harry was able to get engagements without Dash. On one of these occasions he was booked into Kohl and Middleton's Dime Museum on Clark Street in downtown Chicago just prior to the fair for $12 a week. But museums, even dime museums, were far beyond the skills of Harry and Dash at this point in their professional development, and they were reduced to taking jobs, any jobs, in beer halls, saloons, and cabarets.

There, amid the din of clinking glasses and noisy patrons, the Brothers Houdini performed their "dumb" act, with very little patter, trying—and mostly failing—to get and hold the attention of the patrons.

It was during this frustrating period in his life, while he was playing at a Coney Island casino, that another act changed Harry Houdini's life. Once he had been a part of the credulous audience watching the world-famous Harry Kellar, the scholarly-looking illusionist who was the standard by which all magicians were measured. Performing one of the wrist-ties he had learned while serving as a publicist for the Davenport Brothers—the famed spiritualists of the seventies—Kellar had announced to his volunteer, "I challenge you to tie up my wrists with this rope so that I cannot extricate my hands." This bit of derring-do provided that one spark of inspiration that Houdini was later to use to propel him into the public limelight—the dramatic public challenge.

This time it was not a magician who captured his imagination. It was a girl. Not a woman, but a girl, who stood less than five feet tall, weighed all of ninety pounds, and had pigtails, a sylphlike figure, and a girlish voice. She was part of another act on the bill—the Floral Sisters, "Neat Song and Dance Artists"—and was singing "Rosabelle" when Houdini first saw her. The words, very appropriately, went: "Rosabelle, Sweet Rosabelle, / I love you more than I can tell, / Over me you cast a spell, / I love you, my sweet Rosabelle." For the man who had just set out to conquer all obstacles the world over was himself conquered—for the first and only time in his life.

The slip of a girl was Bess Raymond, or so it said on the bill. Her real name was Wilhelmina Beatrice Rahner, but it made no difference to Houdini. It also made no difference that he saw her later that same night in the company of his brother. Dash had set Harry up with another of the Floral Girls and they double-dated. The diminutive Bess had already changed his life, and Houdini, in the same impetuous manner he was to exude the rest of his life, had lost his heart to a girl he knew very little about, except that at eighteen she was two years younger than he, came from Brooklyn, was a gentile and responded to his timorous infatuation with a worldliness beyond her years. Perhaps it was his directness, perhaps it was the rapt attention he paid her, or perhaps it was that as a little girl without a father she longed to have someone look after her and reciprocate by mothering someone

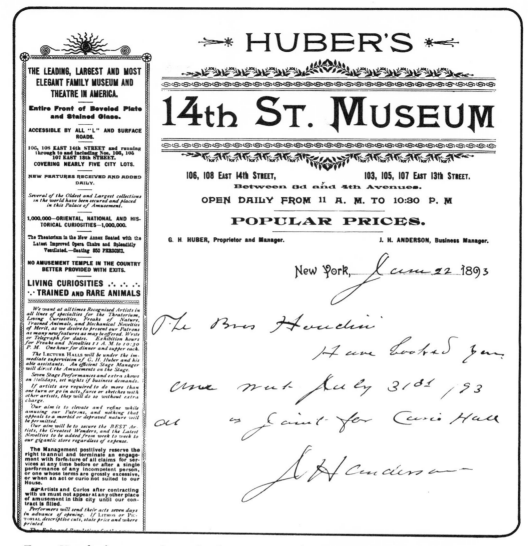

From Houdini's personal scrapbook: a contract dated June 22, 1893 for the Brothers Houdini. Note the amount to be paid has been cut out, probably by Harry in later years.

who believed in himself and in the only profession she knew—show business. Whatever it was, it was love.

According to one romantic account, their whirlwind courtship and marriage was the direct result of some liquid that spilled during Houdini's water-to-ink trick. Both the Brothers Houdini and the Floral Girls were performing at a girls' school, and the "water" soiled Bess's dress. Professing apologies, the embarrassed Houdini had his mother make a new dress for the young lady, who came to Houdini's house to pick it up. She agreed to a walk around the block with the young magician. The story had it that as they passed City Hall, Houdini blurted out, "Let's go in and get married." Of such stories legends are made. Dash remembered that Houdini met Bess on the double date and, while walking with her, heard the taunts of a patron concerning "fakers and fake box

tricks." Quick to take offense in the manner he was later to become famous for, Harry supposedly shot back, "In de presence of me lady fred' I'll say nothing. But I'll do youse dirt when I git back!" He challenged his detractor from the stage to duplicate the trick and placed him in the box from which the heckler pleaded for help after ten minutes.

Two weeks later, on June 22, 1894, over the objections of both mothers, Harry Weiss and Wilhelmina Rahner were married by a justice of the peace. The wedding was repeated one month later by Reverend G. S. Louis of Brooklyn in a Catholic ceremony at the behest of the bride's mother, and once again by a rabbi at the insistence of the bridegroom's mother. Bess was later to say, "I was the most married woman in the world—by a justice of the peace, a priest and a rabbi." In later years Houdini

"The RANNERS" America's
Greatest Comedy Act.

Not Professional Picture

1ST YEAR MARRIED LIFE,

would say, "Mrs. Houdini is the only handcuff I never escaped from—or tried to escape from."

While the wedding brought together one team, it effectively broke up the Brothers Houdini for all time. Dash, bitter at his brother for deserting him, dissolved the partnership and went out on his own as "Harden", a name he selected because of its similarity to Houdini. Harry made Bess his partner in the act and billed them as the Houdinis. He printed up playbills advertising "their marvelous mystery, Metamorphosis, The Greatest Novelty Act in the world!" performed by "Mons. Houdini and Mlle. Houdini."

By the 1890s America was changing from a nation of performers to a nation of spectators. Professional entertainment was everywhere, big-time, small-time, anytime, to fill out the idle time created for the workers with their half-days on Saturday and their newfound standard of living. One of those typically American phenomena that helped to take entertainment to the people was vaudeville, known as "variety" entertainment in England and "vaude" by the entertainers. It was made up of music, singing, dancing, and skits, given in a series of short, independent acts. If it was designed for family entertainment, it was vaudeville; if it had a broad ribald flair to its comedic and dance routines, it was burlesque. But whatever it was, it was entertainment for the masses, and the Houdinis sought to become a part of it.

Vaudeville theaters sprang up throughout the country, replacing museums and dime museums as the primary source of entertainment for the people. The first American vaudeville house was Benjamin Keith's Gaiety Museum, which opened for business in a deserted candy store in Boston in 1883. Theaters across the United States numbered almost two thousand by 1894, all of them thriving.

There were so many gradations to vaudeville that when promised a spot on one of the bills, one entertainer inquired, "Which one is it—small-time, medium small-time, big small-time, little big-time, medium big-time or THE BIG TIME?" The anchor theaters of such chains as Keith, Orpheum, Pantages, and Proctor were the proud homes of the two-shows-a-day, aristocratic showcases of the art. Around them, like a gigantic pinwheel, revolved a network of the other, lesser vaudeville theaters, offering four, five, or even six shows a day.

Vaudeville was important to America and to the Houdinis. Some theatrical historians have even traced the total history of vaudeville by the professional life of Harry Houdini, who held center stage for almost its entire life.

A typical bill opened with a "dumb," or silent, act—animals, acrobats, magicians, jugglers, etc., all playing in the worst position—the opening, or "set up," act, while latecomers rustled coats, programs, and refreshments and searched for their seats, distracting those already in the theater. Then came a single act—the mon-

ologist, ventriloquist, boy-girl dance team, or song-and-dance man beating out a rhythm dancing on sand or with the old soft shoe. Next came a comedy team with fast patter or a sister act. And then intermission, an opportunity for the hawkers to sell their wares. After intermission came an elaborate act, a tableau set out usually in some patriotic, biblical, or contemporary theme, and finally, at the top, perched the star act. Through hard work, the headliner or headliners had usually worked their way up from the bottom of the bill, spending as many as twenty years polishing up ten minutes.

Finally, winding up the entire program, much like the sweepers after a glorious parade, came the "getaway" act, similar to the "set up" act and performing the function of providing those anxious to depart early with a chance—if not a reason—to do so.

It was this vast grab bag of performing arts and whatnots, this cornucopia of talent with a scrambled format all providing an abundance of activity and variety, that Harry Houdini sought to conquer, much as a climber attempts to conquer a mountain. In fact, he sought to become the first "dumb" act to reach vaudeville's top rung.

Although Houdini aspired to the top rung, he could barely grasp the bottom one, as bookings became harder and harder to get for the Houdinis' novelty act. They were glad to take whatever they could get—beer halls, dime museums, anything! Alternately traveling to some small city to hook on with a Ten, Twent', Thirt' show—ten or more shows a day, twenty dollars a week, up to thirty cents admission—and living at home with Mother Weiss and surreptitiously being clothed by Bess's sister, the Houdinis had humble beginnings indeed.

John Stuart Mill said, "One man with a belief is worth ninety-nine men with an interest." Houdini now set out with a vengeance to realize that belief and make something of himself. He first determined to escape from the bonds he was locked into by his less-than-perfect speech. A "dese" and "dose" speaker, Houdini never had the benefit of formal schooling or even teaching at home—where the dominant languages were Yiddish and German. In a comprehensive program of self-help, he repeatedly enunciated all of the syllables of every word he would ever speak on the stage for hours on end. He practiced his newfound delivery throughout the nights and into the early mornings.

Billed as "the master Monarchs of Modern Mystery," the Houdinis drew scant attention playing curio stages at dime museums up to twenty times a day—when they could get a booking. They took bookings in small-time "vaude" houses in Newport News, Memphis, and other cities in the South for the remainder of 1894. A long way from the big time, or, for that matter, even the medium-small time, it was, nevertheless, a tottering step in the right direction.

One morning during that tour Bess woke up to read an ad in block type that caught her eye. It said: "Challenge!

I, the undersigned, have deposited with the manager of the Theatre One Hundred Dollars ($100), which I will forfeit to the person who can handcuff me so I cannot escape." The undersigned was Harry Houdini, to which he had added a new superlative, "Handcuff King." One hundred dollars! At a time when she was putting together "trick" decks from the used playing cards Harry cadged from social clubs and gambling halls to sell for enough extra money to keep them going, the sum of $100 was frightening to Bess. It was more than they had ever seen in their whole lives.

Houdini's faith in his ability to free himself from any pair of handcuffs was not unfounded. Whether he had learned this strange skill as an apprentice locksmith back in Wisconsin or during his runaway year when the sheriff manacled him in Kansas, Harry Houdini had become fascinated with handcuffs and adept at freeing himself from them. Handcuffs were to be his passport from oblivion, his Open Sesame to stardom. Every town he and Bess played presented another opportunity for Harry to continue his education by visiting the local locksmiths. He learned how to open some locks by giving them blows

in a certain spot; for others he secreted a picklock somewhere on his person. It was even rumored that Houdini could compress his hands smaller than his wrists in order to slip the cuffs.

Another childhood holdover, his fond remembrance of days spent at the vacant lot next to the railroad tracks in Appleton watching the touring circuses, was also put to use. Houdini decided that if the opportunity to get into vaudeville wasn't going to knock at his door, he would seek a place for the Houdinis in his first love: the circus.

So, in the spring of 1895, Harry and Bess signed on with the Welsh Brothers' Mighty Cavalcade and Giant Attraction, a circus without animals headquartered in Lancaster, Pennsylvania, "for $200 a year over my bed and board." Houdini was later to add, "I would like to take note of the fact that the meals which were furnished to us by this circus were the best I have ever eaten."

"Mrs. Houdini and myself first of all had to give a free performance in front of the side show to attract the crowds. Inside, I then lectured upon the curiosities, gave a magic show, worked the Punch and Judy show, and with the assistance of Mrs. Houdini finally presented a

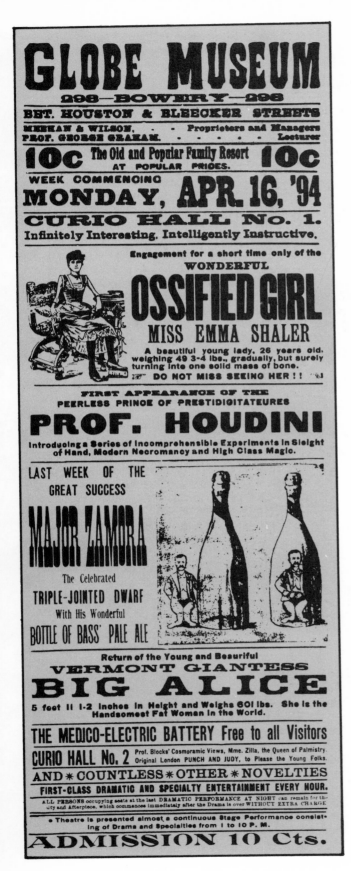

second sight act. In the main concert, Mrs. Houdini acted as a singing clown while later on we presented our
specialty, which consisted of the trunk trick."

Even Metamorphosis had changed. At some point during their tour they had substituted an actual trunk for the
old box Harry had purchased when he first started the
Brothers Houdini. Traveling every day necessitated a
trunk to house their meager belongings, so the trunk saw
double duty. And so did Harry!

One of the come-ons in the small towns the Welsh
Brothers' entourage visited was a gigantic sign heralding
a "ferocious Wild Man." There was no wild man, only a
sign. No one seemed to miss him until, as Bess told the
story, a crowd of young toughs demanded to know
"Where's your wild man?" After hasty consultation, the
circus owners approached Harry and asked him if he, in
accordance with his contract to perform "other duties"
when asked, would fill in for the missing aborigine. In an
improvised costume of sacks and with his kinky, long,
bushy hair disheveled, Houdini climbed into an old
wooden box. He gave every indication of being the
"Wild Man from the depths of the Java jungle." He was
fed raw meat and cigars, which he would "devour" by a
sleight-of-hand gesture, secreting them down his gunnysack costume.

Even though the work was hard and the pay low, it
was the first regular job Harry and Bess had had in show
business. By watching every penny and making do, they
were able to send $12 home every week to Mother Weiss,
the first installment on Harry's pledge to his father that
he would take care of his mother.

When not performing or making extra money selling
necessities to his fellow performers or tricked decks to the
customers, Houdini was roaming the grounds of the circus trying to absorb all the color, lore, and stories that
were to be had. He was befriended by a member of a Japanese balancing group. In exchange for English lessons
from the less-than-fluent Houdini, the Japanese taught
him the yoga principle of muscle control and the art of
swallowing and regurgitating objects.

Seeking additional money, Harry offered his handcuff
act to the Welsh Brothers for $5 extra per week, but it
was rejected. By his own account, "Eventually, I offered
to clown the bars, collect lithographs and do my handcuff show for $3 extra per week, and it was also refused.
In fact, several managers later on refused to allow me to
do handcuffs, and it was only persistently presenting it
every once in a while like a trick in several museums, that
I eventually was allowed to do the act steadily, and only
after I had become known to the managers."

The handcuff act ultimately propelled Houdini to stardom. In 1895, neither the world nor the Welsh Brothers' circus was ready for such a novelty act, preferring
that Houdini stick to prestidigitation and sleight-of-
hand, with occasional appearances as a wild man and
Punch and Judy operator thrown in. Houdini, who had

not quite brought his handcuff act to the high state of art it was to become, employed it only occasionally, alternating handcuffs when doing Metamorphosis, and waiting for his big break to come.

Finally it came. While playing New Orleans, the Houdinis got a wire from an agent they had previously visited, informing them they were booked to play Tony Pastor's in New York in October. Tony Pastor's! A gleaming, spotlighted vaudeville showcase on East 14th Street, infused with an aura of glamour, both for the patrons and the entertainers. Houdini could barely believe it. But there it was—"due to open October 12, 1895."

It wasn't quite as glorious as it sounded, for the couple billed as "the Great Houdinis—Harry and Bessie" were the "getaway" act, sixteenth out of sixteen on the bill. Furthermore, the engagement was only for one week. What a blow to Houdini's self-esteem! His ego at this time was described by one who knew him as "so large that, like Gaul, it could be divided into three parts."

Nevertheless, Harry accepted the booking. He took pains to preserve the playbill, pasting it in his personal scrapbook and altering it so that others could see him, not as he was, but as he wanted to be seen: elaborated, embroidered, and enlarged by his own hand. He carefully cut it in two and circled his position on the bill. In cutting it in half he had changed his position from sixteenth, just above the final double lines, to eighth, or—as he intended to show—the last act before intermission. There *was* no intermission! By looking at the back of the clipping one can see that the order of the players was also rearranged, and that Houdini extended his deception and misdirection even to himself in his own scrapbook. But if he was deluding himself momentarily, he also sought to delude future generations, wanting to be more famous than he thought he might ever be.

Even Houdini's legend-building genius couldn't help him. Their engagement was not extended and they had to scramble for work again.

With the money they had saved from their stint with the Welsh Brothers' circus, Harry and Bess were able to purchase a small equity in a traveling burlesque show on the brink of bankruptcy, the American Gaiety Company. The star act was the American Gaiety girls, a buxom assortment of seven girls corseted in the best fashion of the nineties. Houdini served as a combination midwife, publicist, and performer, sometimes venturing away from the stage to generate publicity for his own show. The Gloucester, Massachusetts, *Times* of November 22, 1895, carried a story about how a young man with the Gaiety Company had visited the local constabulary and invited them to handcuff him, and, to their amazement, had released himself from their official restraints. This was Houdini's first newspaper publicity, and it set a pattern. Throughout his professional life he would shill for his show through the medium of the local papers by effecting releases from handcuffs, jails, crates, or straitjackets

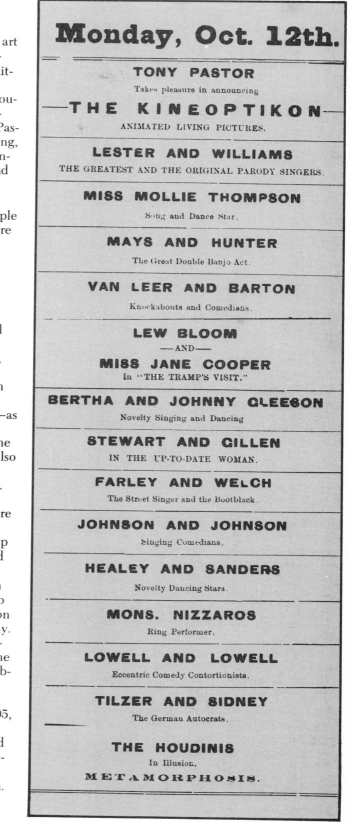

First appearance at Tony Pastor's in New York.

35

while submerged under water. The boy who had been Harry Weiss had determined upon a course of temperance in his youth, a course he was never to deviate from: the only liquid he ever sought in abundance was printer's ink, and his self-promotional genius took care of supplying him with plenty of that.

Unfortunately, a fate befell Houdini and his American Gaiety Company that was all too frequent in those pre-Equity days, when ticket managers weren't bonded. The general manager misappropriated the show's funds. When he was arrested in Woonsocket, Rhode Island, it brought an end to Houdini's dreams, his promotional plans, his money, and his "baby," the show.

They were able to find a few bookings in the Midwest by dealing directly with the managers of the theaters. One such appearance took place in Grand Rapids, Michigan, where they appeared at Smith's Opera House on March 28, 1896. Bess did double duty, performing as Mamie Rile in the opening minstrel number and as a "descriptive vocalist, introducing Major LeVoy's most beautiful song story 'Nobody Speaks His Name.'" Then, after a quartet, a Negro impersonator, and the overture, "the Mysterious Couple, Harry and Bessie Houdini," reappeared "in an entertainment consisting of Psychrometic Letter Reading and Fooling with the Spirits." Their act, if not their future, was taking on dimension.

Harry also had handbills printed up proclaiming:

NOTICE TO MANAGERS
A Startling Feature—Time of Act, 15 Minutes
Our Act Has Been Featured In
Maskelyne & Cook's Egyptian Hall, London,
Oxford—Cambridge
and
Robert Houdin's Paris
We Will Forfeit $1000 if Any Detail of Our Act Given
Herewith Is Misrepresented

Harry and Bessie Houdini

Houdini's challenge to managers was not just an attempt to magnify his importance; it was intended to gain more bookings and it also represented his first covert attempt at building his own legend. But had any manager pointed out the patent falsehoods in the handbill, they would have had trouble collecting $10, much less $1,000, from the impoverished Houdinis.

That summer the Houdinis hooked up with an itinerant magician and part-time church organist from Hartford named Edward J. Dooley, who billed himself as Marco the Magician. An admirer of the satanic-looking Herrman the Great, Dooley invested his life's savings in a magic show styled after Herrmann's production. Together the Houdinis and Dooley toured Nova Scotia, playing to sparse crowds in obscure places. Every evening Dooley would announce that he was on his farewell tour and introduce "my daughter and son-in-law, the Houdinis, my successors." Even the usually surefire gambit of a fare-

well tour failed to bring out the citizenry, and Houdini soon found out why. The previous summer another magician, unfortunately also named Marco, had come through the province and burned the people badly, performing pitiably and ruining the territory for any other magic show, especially one with a Marco in it.

Dooley saw the futility of continuing and returned to his chosen profession, organ playing, leaving everything—locks, stocks, and props—to his "son-in-law," Harry Houdini, who for the second time in a year was left in the uncomfortable position of having to escape from disaster.

Houdini attempted through publicity, advertising billboards, and other means available to keep the show going, but to no avail. Soon he and Bess found themselves once again playing in beer halls for "throw money," a galling experience for anyone, but especially one named Houdini, who believed himself already to be a legend. Hobbling along to New Brunswick, Houdini pursued his dream of succeeding as a magician with a single-minded tenacity that gave him the strength to overcome. In his most recent misfortune, he was able once again to take advantage of an incident that would have eluded a lesser man. He chanced to meet a local doctor, Dr. Steeves, who invited Houdini to accompany him on a call to a local asylum for the mentally ill. Watching through the small barred window of a padded cell, Houdini viewed one of the inmates tossing and turning, desperately attempting to free himself from a canvas and leather restraint with no openings in the sleeves, which were bound across the middle with straps. The sight, coupled with the doctor's remark that only a madman would attempt to effect a release from what was known as a "punishment suit for the murderously insane," provided Houdini with an idea and a new vehicle.

Houdini possessed an incredible amount of energy. He accepted any challenge or dare and worked with scarcely any rest, seemingly charged with an inexhaustible force. So it was on this night. Back in his room, Houdini stayed awake analyzing the scene he had witnessed. Just at daybreak, in a manner reminiscent of Archimedes hollering "Eureka!" Houdini awoke Bess to tell her that he had solved the puzzle of the straitjacket and that he could get out of this seemingly inescapable contraption. He borrowed one from the doctor and spend the entire week practicing.

Drawing on his experience as a contortionist back in Appleton, where he had gained the "ability to twist my body and dislocate my joints, together with abnormal expansion and contraction powers," coupled with his careful observation of contortion acts, Houdini was able to master the "art" of freeing himself from a straitjacket.

But merely discovering the method to free himself from the straitjacket was only half the battle, like opening one cuff but not the other. Houdini still lacked a sense of drama, a sense of impact, a sense of climax. His stage presence was as deficient as his funds. His act was more notable for effort than for total achievement.

This was illustrated by Houdini's first public exhibition of his new straitjacket escape, made in front of a few theater-goers in St. John, New Brunswick. Hidden behind the curtains, he twisted and contorted his body until he obtained the necessary slack to unbuckle the straps through the canvas with his fingers; then, shedding the straitjacket, he stepped out front—to a marked lack of enthusiasm. The cynical citizens of New Brunswick merely assumed that Bess or someone else had sneaked behind the curtains and unbuckled him. Some years before, his brother, now called Hardeen, had taught him that the straitjacket escape should be played live before the audience for maximum impact. The indifference shown by the St. John's audience plagued Houdini. He and Bess were soon forced to sell the props and sets for whatever money they could get and make their way back to the States. They found a boat leaving from St. John's for Boston, and Bess, partly because of her theatrical training and partly because of the pitiable situation the Houdinis found themselves in, was able to plead with the captain to take them aboard in exchange for entertaining the paying passengers. Even this ended disastrously, for Harry became violently seasick. Finally the passengers passed a hat to provide the couple with eating money.

Back in New York the defeated pair were once again forced to move in with his mother at 221 East 69th Street. Facing the crucial decision of whether to stay in show business or take a legitimate job, the twenty-two-year-old Houdini made a choice that was difficult but necessary if he wanted to remain in the field even peripherally. If he couldn't earn a living being a magician, he would earn one teaching others to be magicians.

Obtaining the New York distributorship for a line of magic tricks put out by a Chicago manufacturer, he printed up a catalogue called "Magic Made Easy," offering Professor Harry Houdini's "Hints for Amateurs" and "Magic Tricks, Illusions, Second Sight Acts, Secrets of Money Making, Etc., Etc." for sale by mail. "The exponents of the Art" were counseled to "first, practice, second, practice and practice before a mirror," and "borrow all the coin you can and forget to return it. That's one way of making money." But "Professor" Harry's method of making money was selling the secrets to a number of tricks, including "the Jesse James Tape Trick," "the Needle Trick," "Vivisection Act," and "Carafe of Water and Vase of Ink, performed by Houdini and Kellar." For the first time Houdini, who created few tricks but innovated several, merchandised and sold tricks, something he would become increasingly proficient at in his later career.

But even at selling magic tricks, including some of his own to the local papers for as little as $20—marked down from their prices in the catalogue—turned out disastrous.

By the end of 1896, Harry Houdini was a defeated man, a man whose love for magic was totally unrequited.

Thomas Huxley said "There is the greatest practical benefit in making a few failures early in life." Harry Houdini seemed to have cornered the failure market.

With his resiliency and hopefulness tempered by desperation, he wrote to the Kohn and Middleton Dime Museum in Chicago, the same museum he had played as a single just before the World's Fair, three years earlier. He was looking for a "week or two," and true to his luck, not only did he get the booking but the museum wired him railroad fare.

That winter, out of work, out of funds, and out of sorts, without even the basis of their act (the trunk and its contents of handcuffs were in hock), the Houdinis were forced to live by their wits. They made do with what little food Harry could pick up, even if it was by some sleight of hand at a neighborhood grocery store and what Bess's culinary skills could make of his pickings. At the coldest point of that St. Louis winter, Houdini found a crate with which to make firewood to keep the home fires going. Again an unfortunate situation took a fortunate turn. According to Houdini, "It was while in St. Louis that I formulated the basis for my method for performing my packing-box escape and it happened in this wise: The winter was a bitterly cold one and I had no money with which to purchase wood to start a fire to warm my room. So seeing a discarded packing-case in front of one of the large dry-goods shops, I thought I would take it home for firewood.

"I knew I would make myself too conspicuous by carrying so large a case through the streets and further knew that no police officer would permit me to break it apart in so crowded a thoroughfare, so I conceived a method of taking it noiselessly apart." So was born another one of Houdini's own ingenious creations—the packing-box escape. There is something in a man's fate that compels him toward a goal. Had Houdini, in his younger days, always had enough money to buy complete magical acts—as he did when he purchased the Metamorphosis—he might never have become the Great Houdini. Being unable to purchase the paraphernalia used by conjurors, he had to compensate by improvisation. No entertainer ever approached his profession with more fervor, more serious study, more hours of relentless work, more of a need to be accepted and admired. This was to be his destiny, his passion. Possessed of miraculous deftness of muscle and brain, Houdini conquered seemingly insuperable bonds and created a whole new genre. No longer would he be just a magician. He was now an escapologist.

For the moment, however, future conquests were beyond the sight of the Houdinis; their immediate goal was to get a job, get money, and get their precious trunk out of hock. Without the props he needed to be a magician,

Harry was able to convince the manager of the Escher Music Hall to book the pair as a comedy act. So "the Rahners" played the Music Hall as a comedy team, with Harry doing an improvised baggy-pants tramp routine and Bess doing her little-girl song-and-dance skit. The $30 they were paid was welcome, even if the former "Professor" Houdini had to swallow his pride, something he had learned to regurgitate along with material objects. The pair signed on for a second week, at a reduction in salary. With the money they accumulated, they were able to pay the freight office the $20 they owed and redeem their trunk. They were held over for a third week, but this time Houdini was billed as the King of Handcuffs.

Back on the circuit, the Houdinis next played Harry's second home, Milwaukee, where a music hall manager shorted them out of their weekly pay. Once again they wired their old standby, the Kohn and Middleton Dime Museum in Chicago, for a week's engagement and train fare.

Chicago had been a jumping-off point for Harry Houdini before, and this time it was no different. As 1896 turned into 1897, he took the path that Eugene Field, James Whitcomb Riley, and Theodore Dreiser had taken; he joined up with an old-fashioned medicine show. These itinerant peddlers honeycombed the Midwest, selling such cure-alls as Cholera Balm and Wizard Oil, relieving—never curing—practically all ills, including catarrh, asthma, tubercular consumption, bronchitis, gout, deafness, diphtheria, carbuncles, rheumatism, eczema, tumors, boils, and that most famous of all catch-alls, nervous and physical collapse. It was a golden age of quackery that was to end with the passage of the Federal Pure Food and Drug Act in 1907.

The Houdinis joined the California Concert Company, a high-sounding name for a group of traveling pitch doctors. The head man was "Doctor" Thomas B. Hill, an impressively bewhiskered man who looked like John Brown and who had gone through the same Kansas Territory that the California Concert Company was now crisscrossing some forty years later. Kansas was suffering through a drought, and many of the covered wagons streaming back east in the 1890s read "In God We Trusted, In Kansas We Busted." Undaunted, the little troupe toured the countryside. Harry and Bess provided entertainment to attract and hold an audience, which was treated to a lecture by Dr. Hill on the virtues of his elixirs at carefully calculated intervals throughout the show; much in the same manner as later radio and television programs broke for commercial messages. While Bessie sang several numbers, Houdini, Dr. Hill, and his sidekick, "Doctor" Pratt, another nonmedical pitch doctor, alternately passed through the audience handing out bottles and crying "All sold out, Doctor!" On other occasions Houdini would mount the stage and release himself from all manner of restraints while Bess joined in selling bottles in the audience.

Many magicians and conjurors have traversed the thin line between natural and supernatural feats, particularly when broke. Houdini, who had performed "psychrometic" reading as far back as 1896, was broke enough to work the other side of the line. For four days Houdini visited every graveyard in Galena, Kansas, studying inscriptions; he read everything he could in the local library, visited the town gossips, and worked his way into the locals' houses as a Bible salesman so he could read the inscriptions in their old Bibles. By Sunday night he was imbued with the town's history.

With Bess as his "control," the blindfolded Harry performed a mind-reading act, correctly "guessing" what she held in her hand. It was a setup. Bess verbally coded each object by mentioning something white just before it. They performed all the psychic feats, as advertised—every night. Bess even came up with a minor miracle, a psychic phenomenon that bordered on the supernatural. When asked by someone in the audience where to find a long-lost relative, Bess answered without hesitation, "In New York City," and further fleshed it out with an address: East 72nd Street. Wonder of wonders! The relative had been the owner of a little candy store near the Weisses' apartment all along.

Leaving the "theater of quackery," Houdini next essayed another turn-of-the-century American entertainment phenomenon, the touring stock company. He starred in one of the morality plays then blazing across the prairies, *Ten Nights in a Bar-Room*. In it, he portrayed Jim Morgan, who falls on hard times after drinking a potion similar to Dr. Hill's elixir for "the cold weather." Remarking on its "warm after-effect," the hard-working mechanic-father downs another glass of "Old Morrison's remedy," and another, and another, and still another. True to the morality play's theme, in as short a time as it took to stage the production, Morgan's life is in ruins. He loses his job and his belongings and soon is on the brink of losing everything when his daughter, played by Bess looking like a little girl and speaking in her little-girl voice, pleads with him, "Father, dear Father, come home with me now."

But medicine shows and morality plays were not what Houdini sought. He was a miracle worker, a magician and escape artist, and nothing short of that could satisfy him. "I therefore started to play one more tour of the Dime Museums to fulfill my expiring contracts, and it was this tour which made Houdini, the Handcuff King, famous." So, after another stint with the Welsh Brothers' circus, he took Bess back out to his second home, Kohl and Middleton's in Chicago. From that day in the fall of 1898 on, Harry Houdini never again had to act in a morality play or a medicine show.

It had been seven years since he had left the employ of H. Richter's determined to be a magician. All he had to show for it were letters of recommendation and a minor

*Early bill featuring Bess as "Mamie Riley," and the
Houdinis together in a spiritualist act.*

reputation as "Dime Museum Harry." Intent now upon both eradicating that reputation and attaining some real recognition, he hit upon a scheme for which he was to become as well known as for anything he was ever to do; one which he had already employed to a minor degree as publicity manager of the American Gaiety Company. He would escape from jail. But this time not to publicize a stock company but to publicize himself!

The first step in the campaign was to make friends with some newspapermen, an important stratagem from that time forward in Houdini's ceaseless publicity seeking. Next, he got one of them to arrange an introduction to a top police official, Lieutenant Andy Rohan, chief of detectives and an aide to Chicago's chief of police. On the two previous occasions when Houdini had mounted a challenge to the police, he had merely walked in and announced himself. But then, Holyoke and Springfield, Massachusetts, weren't Chicago, where clout counted as much in the 1890s as it does in the 1970s. Newspapermen were necessary both to gain access and to cover the story.

On their first visit to Rohan's office at the city jail, Harry showed him some card tricks and then Bessie struck up a conversation in order to keep the 260-pound detective occupied while Houdini prowled around the cells studying locks. After a second visit Houdini announced to the press that he would escape from the city jail after allowing himself to be handcuffed and locked in a cell. The newsmen were intrigued, and Rohan—himself a publicity-conscious cop—also showed more than casual interest in the proposition, assuming that should Houdini fail—and there was no reason why

he should succeed—all the publicity would be his.

Rohan personally oversaw Houdini securely trussed up in handcuffs and leg irons and locked in a cell. Moments later, the magician reappeared at the door and strode triumphantly into the room. The chilly reception was not unlike that given him by the audience in St. John's, New Brunswick, when he emerged freed of his straitjacket. The newsmen were totally unenthusiastic, almost to the point of apathy. The coolness, Houdini found out, was attributable to the fact that Rohan had told the newsmen that Houdini had been hanging around the jail for days. They merely assumed that he had obtained a pocketful of keys, so the "miraculous" escape was hardly news. Houdini responded in the usual Houdini manner—he issued a challenge! "Suppose you strip me and search me before you lock me up!" he directed the newsmen. Moreover, he suggested they lock his clothes in a second cell and tape his mouth. This they did quickly—though not without a few wisecracks—and retired to the same outer room to wait. This time Houdini sauntered jauntily in fully clothed within ten minutes. To make it an even better show, he entered by the street door. Now, that was news!

The next morning, the Chicago *Journal* carried a front-page story about a dime museum performer who had "escaped out of all their handcuffs, leg irons, insane restraints, belts and straitjackets." While he hadn't actually freed himself from all that, the Houdini legend was already beginning—and growing even then in the telling. Harry Houdini had found that publicity was the new magic, a force for hypnotizing and misdirecting

To Whom it may Concern 1898

We can cheerfully recommend Harry and Beatrice Houdini with their unique and mysterious act called "Metamorphosis" as being the strongest drawing card of its class in America. Their act is totally unlike others and always creates a profound impression upon their auditors. They were the especially engaged feature of our employ during the tenting season of 1895 and also the past season (1898) for a period of twenty five weeks. They are artists of the first line as further a lady and gentlemen in all that the term implies and can always find room with any of our amusement enterprises.

We will be pleased to play them at any time. The Houdinis are truly great people.

Yours Very Truly
Welsh Bros
Mgrs & Prop. Welsh Bros Shows

Lancaster, Penna.
Monday Oct 8th 1898

Letter of recommendation from Houdini's last stint with the Welsh Brothers Circus.

people as much as anything he ever did on stage.

As a result of the write-up, he was offered a coveted spot on the bill at the Hopkins Theatre in Chicago, the next-to-the-closing act. Bess, however, was not feeling well, so Houdini tried to postpone the engagement by demanding start billing and $100 a week—quite a bluff for a next-to-closing act. But the manager gave in to his request, and for one week the Houdinis—with Bess well enough to participate—played the Hopkins.

After their second brief taste of vaudeville, the Houdinis returned once more to Kohl and Middleton, but they had had enough now to know where they belonged.

They soon set out for St. Paul and what was to prove their last engagement at a dime museum. There, while Harry was cramming in all of his repertoire, much like writing the Lord's Prayer on the head of a pin, they were "discovered." Not discovered in the classic show business sense of being found in a drugstore like Lana Turner, but up on the stage performing sleight-of-hand, card tricks, and illusions, interspersed with escapes from all manner of restraints. In the audience that first night with a party of managers was Martin Beck, the booking agent for the fast-growing Orpheum Western Circuit. He was, as always, on the lookout for new talent. Intrigued by Houdini's mastery over restraints, particularly handcuffs, he "perhaps more in a joke than sincerity, challenged me to escape from one of his handcuffs . . . and sent them up onto the stage." Unknowingly, in accepting the challenge and escaping from Beck's handcuffs, Houdini also escaped from the obscurity of small-time dime museums forever. It was, according to Houdini, "the first chance I ever had."

Signed by Beck to the Orpheum Circuit, Houdini's entire act was structured for the first time. No longer would he have a free-form act, with pigeons appearing from nowhere one minute, silks the next, handcuffs the next, and then cards before Metamorphosis. Now, under Beck's direction, the act took on shape and built to a climax. It consisted entirely of handcuffs and Metamorphosis, accompanied by music to heighten the suspense and excitement.

As their act gained form and substance, so did their salary. Originally booked at $60 a week, they asked for and got raises to $90 a week and then $125 a week, half of which, true to his promise, he sent home to Mama.

The reviews were also rewarding. At the Orpheum in Los Angeles, the act was described as "one that is entirely unique, and one that is likely to keep the guessers guessing for some time to come." Houdini invited officers of the Los Angeles Police Department to come up on the stage and place at least four pairs of regulation handcuffs on him. After this added touch of authenticity and authority, Houdini "retires to a cabinet and reappears after a lapse of time no longer than it took to fasten the 'darbys' on him, freed thereof and with the gyves locked into each other, showing that his hands have not slipped out." The review in the Los Angeles *Times* adds, "It is too much of a mystery for the novice's unraveling."

The *pièce de résistance* was—as it had been from the day Harry and Jack Hayman first purchased it—the Sub trunk, or Metamorphosis. This time a new element had been added. Prior to his being bound and placed in the trunk, Houdini took one of the police officer's coats "bearing the officer's star." After being tied in a sack he was locked in the trunk. Then, as "Mme. Houdini claps her hands three times," he emerges from the trunk in his shirtsleeves and "Mme. Houdini is found inside it wearing the officer's coat." This was their new act, and it was received by those in the audience—and in the press—as "a big success."

With some small measure of success, some bookings, and some money, the Houdinis had come a long way from the days when they had to scrounge for bookings and sell secrets. Harry challenged the police in every city, and as he escaped from handcuffs, shackles on his boots, and even an Oregon boot—a 15-pound leg iron secured by a wrench lock—he began to accumulate press clippings and signed testimonials from police chiefs certifying that he had freed himself from whatever they had secured him in, all written by Houdini himself.

But even good things come to an end, and the Or-

pheum tour ended in the fall of 1899. Harry thereupon printed broadsides heralding his triumphant tour. Theater managers throughout the East were soon bombarded by someone named HARRY HOUDINI! whose hyperbolic notices proclaimed: "Who created the biggest sensation in California since the Discovery of Gold in 1849? WHY! HARRY HOUDINI! The ONLY recognized and Undisputed King of Handcuffs and Monarch of Leg Shackles."

Although he did manage to obtain a few engagements in the East, Harry knew his own personal El Dorado lay elsewhere. And so, as a new century dawned and a new spirit spread throughout America, Harry Houdini, with the same cocksure confidence that typified the nation, took the biggest gamble of his life.

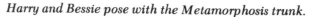

Harry and Bessie pose with the Metamorphosis trunk.

ACT 3
RISING STAR OVER EUROPE

According to the Bible, a prophet is not without honor, save in his own country. Magicians are similar. The very first magician born in North America, Jacob Meyer, toured Europe to gain fame as Philadelphia Philadelphius, in honor of his native city. Down through the years, many magicians, such as Nelson T. Downes, the "King of Koins," have been praised and feted abroad as major acts while still ranked as minor ones at home. This was to be the curious lot of Harry Houdini, who sailed from New York on May 30, 1900.

So confident was Houdini of his ultimate success that he had only enough money for one month abroad—and no bookings. This purely speculative trip was both the reflection of Houdini's great need for recognition, which still eluded him at home, and part of an overall plan to capture and hold national, and international, attention by gaining the sorely needed prestige of a successful European trip.

Harry's first mission, then, after putting Bess up at an actors' boarding house, was to search for bookings. His still-skimpy book of clippings and certificates from police chiefs failed to impress the booking agents, however. While canvassing the booking agents, he found a sympa-

thetic ear in the person of young Harry Day, who was filling in for an old agent who was out to lunch. Day not only became interested in the ambitious Yank as a client, but even arranged an audience for him with the manager of the Alhambra Theatre, the English equivalent of Pastor's. The manager, C. Dundas Slater, gave Houdini a trial, but was not impressed with his handcuff act, having witnessed these tricks as far back as 1871, when Samri Baldwin, the "White Mahatma," performed them. What interested him, though, was Houdini's innovative addition of the "challenge" to the audience. Knowing that other challenge acts had not lived up to their promise and possessed little audience appeal, Slater suggested that Houdini try the stunt he had so effectively employed in the United States, adding, "If you escape from handcuffs at Scotland Yard, I'll sign you up." Encouraged by this first show of interest he had elicited in England, Houdini challenged Slater to join him that very moment, and the trio immediately made their way to New Scotland Yard on the Thames Embankment.

One of the Yard's officers, Superintendent Melville, stretched Houdini's arms around a pillar, placed a pair of English "darbies" on his wrists, and remarked, "Here's how we fasten Yankee criminals who come over and get

43

into trouble." Then he invited Slater and Day to join him in the office while the American, behind a screen, tried to escape from the supposedly impregnable cuffs. Before they had reached the door, they heard a clatter and turned to see an unmanacled Houdini standing away from the pillar shouting, "Here's how Yankees open the handcuffs!"

And so, less than two weeks after he had landed in England, Harry Houdini was signed to a July opening at the Alhambra at sixty pounds a week. The two-week engagement was extended to eight as Houdini captured the imagination of British audiences, who loved the "unsophisticated energy of the daring child of nature."

Mathematical and physical laws are permanent; once proved they are accepted for all time. But Houdini's law of escape had to be proved to everyone at least twice a day. The British flocked to see this man who could escape "gaols, cuffs and manacles" challenge the laws and the audience twice a day.

One member of the audience who challenged Houdini was a man who called himself the Great Cirnoc and fancied himself the original handcuff king. One night, when Houdini asked for challenges, Cirnoc leaped up on the stage and proclaimed that he was the original and that, moreover, Houdini was a fraud. Not only was he not an American but he had never been in America. Another member of the audience, Chauncey M. Depew, chairman of the New York Central Railroad and senator from New York, immediately identified the magician: "The young man is an American. I also am an American and I saw him several years ago doing the handcuff act." Houdini now sought to regain the initiative and bade his wife fetch the outsized cuffs, "the Bean Giant." Bess was dressed as a page, having been relegated more and more to a minor role in the act. Houdini challenged his detractor to solve the secret of the cuffs and offered him $500 if he could escape from them. Cirnoc declined the challenge, demanding first to see Houdini free himself. With that, Houdini had himself locked into the "Beans" and retired to his little "ghost cabinet," made of pipe racks and curtain to allow the audience to keep the magician in view at all time and assure them that he had no accomplices. In a moment, he emerged free of the Beans. Now he challenged Cirnoc, who reluctantly accepted. Houdini graciously gave him the key to the manacles, knowing full well that it was a sheer impossibility to apply the key to the lock. After twisting and turning for a long time, Cirnoc gave up and asked to be released, while Houdini received the ovations.

It was after this performance and in accordance with the custom of these gaudy times that Houdini began to call himself "the Handcuff King." In later years, after he had become world-famous and outgrown his dependence on handcuffs alone, Houdini would try to live it down. But for now he was known to Britons as the Handcuff King, and sandwich boards were carried all over London advertising his stay at the Alhambra. The stay was notable for his continued escapes from jails of every conceivable type and willing authorities who aided and abetted the entertainer in gaining his desired ends—publicity and testimonial letters averring his escapes. He broke out of cells built by Oliver Cromwell to hold Puritan prisoners, murderers' cells, and the cells of famous jailbreakers. He soon became known as "the World's Champion Gaol Breaker and King of Locks," a title he had immodestly chosen for himself.

Harry Day next booked Houdini into the Central Theatre in Dresden, Germany, where he was to appear for the month of September 1900. Suspicious of reputations made in England, the theater director, Gustav Kammsetzer, approached the man billed as *Der König der Ausbrecher* before his first performance and told him, in his best broken English, "If der public vistle, you don't finnish der act. Now you vork; I vatch." Herr Direktor then retreated to the wings to listen for that most dreaded of all German reactions to an act—a boo or a whistle. "This manager had brought me to the continent with a contract which enabled him to close me right after my first performance if I was not a success, and I was not aware of that fact until just before going on." Houdini, who had "never addressed an audience in German before," stepped forward and managed to give a more-than-adequate speech in the language he had heard his mother and father use since infancy. Starting his act with his staple, the handcuffs, he then freed himself from leg irons and manacles brought to the theater by the Mathilda Gasse Prison. As he stepped forward, not knowing what to expect, the crowd rose "in a solid mass," cheering the *Ausbrecher*, and the Herr Direktor was "shouting like a madman. He ran to the middle of the stage and applauded. He took off his hat and applauded. I knew I was going to stay my full engagement."

Not only did Houdini play the full engagement, but he also closed down an act at an opposition theater that was advertised as exposing his secrets (Cirnoc again). He became so popular that Herr Direktor Kammsetzer wanted to keep him over for another month. The Houdini who couldn't get bookings anywhere in the United States just two years before was now in such demand that theaters fought over his services!

In Dresden Houdini chanced to meet Franz Kukol, a former Austrian officer, who would serve him for the rest of his life as a dedicated assistant. In honor of Kaiser Wilhelm II, Kukol wore a black moustache fashioned after the emperor's. The Austrian spoke many languages and was an accomplished musician. He also signed a lifelong pact never to reveal Houdini's methods or secrets.

Friendly with the German *Polizei*, Kukol sought permission from a ranking officer for Houdini to jump from one of Dresden's bridges spanning the Elbe River while fully manacled. Word came down that such a jump was not punishable by German law and was therefore coun-

London England
July 1900.

H Houdini

tenanced by the police. The publicity stunt was the product of much careful planning by Houdini, plus much practice, some of which dated back to his youth, when he spent many a free summer's day swimming nude in the East River. Throughout the years Houdini had developed his strong lungs as a long-distance runner for the Allerton Athletic Club in New York. By practicing in the bathtub, he had extended his powers of breath retention to the point where he could hold his breath for almost four minutes

On the day of the announced jump, hundreds crammed the banks as Houdini, fully laden with handcuffs, leg chains, and irons, jumped off the bridge and resurfaced to cheers from the crowd. Upon emerging from the water, he was arrested—for trespassing on the grass! Houdini followed up one publicity success with another, challenging the Royal Saxon Police to chain him so he couldn't escape. When he did, they attested in a statement written by him, translated by Kukol, and placed in every newspaper in Dresden by Harry Day.

With the publicity titillating the crowds and the theater packed to overflowing every night, Kammsetzer appealed to the management of Berlin's Wintergarten to

postpone Houdini's engagement there. Herr Direktor wanted the act he originally had been hesitant to let go on for still another month. The Wintergarten, having heard of the success in Dresden, refused. So in October 1900 Houdini opened at the famed Wintergarten as the headline act.

If Houdini was successful in Dresden, he was sensational in Berlin! Every night Europe's largest theater was packed with latecomers pushing and shoving for the last precious standing-room tickets.

One look at German handcuffs had been enough to tell Houdini they were nothing like the simple American and English cuffs he had worked with. There were many variations, and Houdini found that "cuffs are 1,000 times harder here than in America." Moreover, he discovered that "keys are out of the question" and so apprenticed himself to a Berlin locksmith, spending from six to ten hours a day in the shop learning to pick locks. As before, his total dedication made Houdini a success until there wasn't a single type of lock used in Germany from the time of Theodoric he couldn't master.

The Wintergarten, which had denied Dresden's request for an extension, made its own request to Roana-

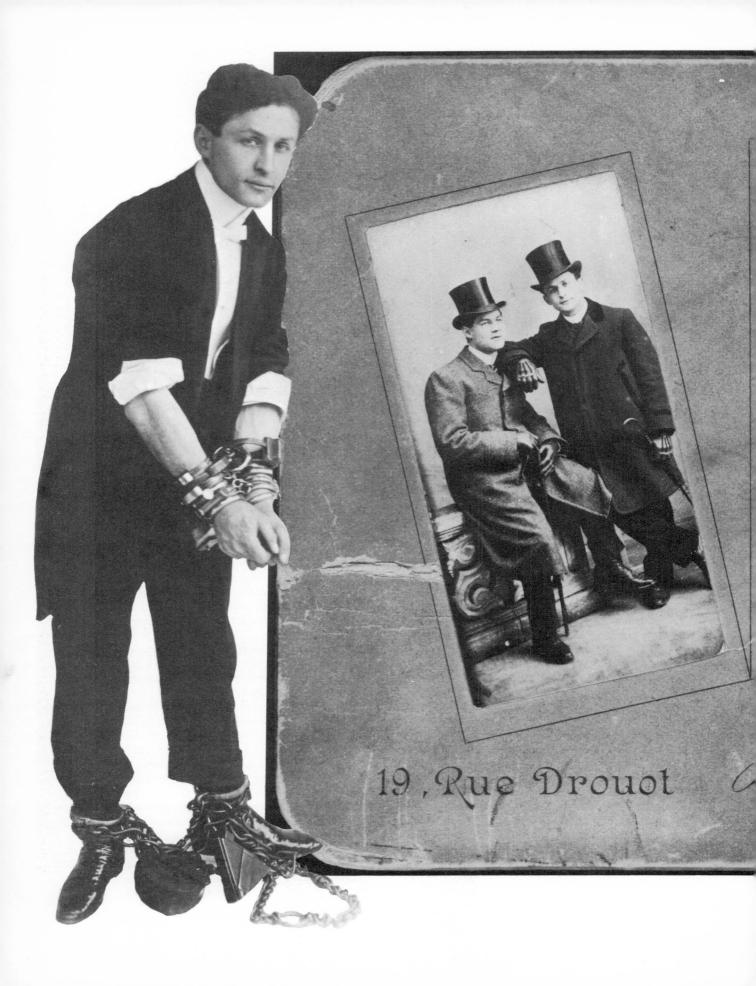

19, Rue Drouot

Harry and his brother Dash (later known as Hardeen) in Europe, circa 1901.

cher's Theatre in Vienna and paid them a forfeit of 4,000 marks, or $1,000, to extend the *Ausbrecher* through November.

If he was in sufficient demand to have theaters fighting over his bookings, then there had to be room for two Houdinis. Believing that the surest way to pre-empt competitors from usurping his position as King of Handcuffs was to create a second show, Harry cabled his brother, Dash, to "come over, the apples are ripe." Dash was now called *Hardeen*, having added another letter to his professional name in the manner popular among leading magicians like Herrmann and Kellar. The Great Hardeen booked passage on the first available boat the minute he received the money to pay for the transatlantic voyage from his brother. When they met in Berlin, Houdini immediately set to work providing Dash with all the trappings for a traveling Houdini show and gave him his hand-me-down acts, much as an older brother would give his kid brother his secondhand clothing.

If one thing distinguished Houdini the toast of the Continent from Houdini the dime-museum performer, it was his delivery. From the day Martin Beck had given form and fabric to his act, he had chosen to excel in his own field of magic. He had devoted himself as much to his stage presence as to his magical presentation. An important feature of his act was his voice; once punctuated with the gutteral sounds of a street urchin, it now had the bell-shaped tones of an orator addressing the last row in the balcony. The electricity he radiated when he came on the stage to "Land of Hope and Glory"—a tune befitting his king-size ego—was something no member of the audience would ever forget. Years and years of playing to American dime-museum and medicine-show audiences were paying off in Europe with a level of excitement and drama that only superior showmanship could produce.

During his triumphant two-month engagement at the Wintergarten, Houdini escaped from police straitjackets and even from the Berlin Police Headquarters, adding another official letter of verification to his files, and the name "*Augsgebrochen Aus der Polizeizehe*" to his own.

By the time he returned to the Alhambra in London for the second part of his engagement in December 1900, just over six months since he had first landed in Europe, Houdini's stature had grown to the point where he was a legend-in-the-making. He found himself featured at the Alhambra above the famed ballet, and was particularly proud to see a dozen sandwich boards carry the message along Pall Mall: "Houdini—Alhambra." It was a satisfying blend of London's modern media and Houdini's medieval magic.

While England mourned Queen Victoria in January 1901, Houdini longed for his beloved mother. He had not seen her since sailing for Europe almost a year before. Walking aimlessly on the streets of London during the week of mourning, Houdini chanced to pass one of the finest shops in London, which displayed a gown

made expressly for the Great Queen. As Houdini stared at the gown, he estimated that the late queen's size was approximately that of his mother and determined to buy the gown. He approached the proprietor, who was shocked by the idea of anyone buying the belongings of the queen. But the persistent Houdini soon made the shopkeeper an offer he could not refuse, fifty pounds. With the stipulation that the dress must never be worn by anyone in Great Britain, the merchant reluctantly agreed to sell it. Houdini later said, "As I walked out with that dress in my possession, I would not have exchanged places with any crowned head in the world."

Prior to departing for the second round of engagements Harry Day had set up for him in Germany, Houdini wrote his mother urging her to join Bessie and him in Hamburg that February and hinting at a "pleasant surprise."

Houdini crisscrossed Germany, playing to full houses at the Apollo Theatre in Düsseldorf, the Crystal Palace in Leipzig and the Orpheum in Frankfurt. Managers battled not only to keep him longer than they had originally booked him for, but also to keep their headline act at the introductory prices Day was charging them back in July of 1900.

Harry and Bessie met Mama Weiss at the dock in Hamburg and took her directly to the A. M. and Hansa Theatre, where that night Houdini was performing a special benefit. Mrs. Weiss was given a special seat to view her son. It was in a box overlooking the stage and it was the only place in the packed house where an extra chair could be wedged in.

Before his next engagement in Hanover, Houdini gave his mother part of her "pleasant surprise," taking her back to her old home in what was now called Budapest. The surprise started out in a less than ceremonious manner, with the always frugal Houdini booking them on a second-class coach for their trip to Hungary.

In the twenty-seven years since Mama Weiss had last seen Budapest, much had changed—and nothing had changed. The glittering Budapest of 1901 was a proper setting for her triumphant return. The most glittering of all the sights in the Budapest of 1901 was the Royal Szalloda, the deluxe Royal Hotel which was built in 1896, with its famed English courtyard, enclosed by a glass ceiling and enveloped in a luxurious palm garden. The most famous gypsy band in all of Europe provided entertainment. Although short of cash, as usual, Harry sought to engage the courtyard for his mother's return reception, but the management refused. His precious courtyard, the traditional meeting place of Budapest's artistic society, would not be available without a substantial rental fee. "After listening patiently to his remonstrances," Houdini later recalled, "I revealed my plot to crown my mother and allow her to be queen for a few, fleeting hours. He immediately consented to become my confederate, for the scheme appealed to his sportsmanship and the scene was set."

Everybody—uncles, *tantas*, distant relatives, and people too far removed in relationship even to be called distant relatives—came to see Cecilia and little Erik.

The highlight of the evening was Cecilia's donning of Queen Victoria's dress, the other part of Houdini's "pleasant surprise." "If happiness ever entered my life to its fullest," Houdini remembered, "it was in sharing my mother's wonderful enjoyment at playing queen for a day. The next morning, after having lived two ecstatically happy days, I escorted the Fairy Queen Mother en route to America." Houdini then returned to fulfill the remainder of his German engagements.

During an engagement in Hanover, Houdini visited Count von Schwerin, the chief of police, who demanded he give a private performance of his straitjacket escape. "He was determined to prevent my escaping from the strait-jacket which he and his court had selected, and commanded his henchmen to adjust it in such a manner that it was a constant source of physical torture to me every minute that I was in it," Houdini recounted many years later. "So great was the pain that I was unable to work with any degree of speed and it was 90 minutes before I finally freed myself." But free himself he did, and the newly acclaimed *Ausbrecher* went on to Essen an der Ruhr after his virtuoso performance at the count's court. It was while at the Colosseum in Essen that Houdini first experimented with the "packing-box" escape, a trick that had its genesis in St. Louis five years earlier. He described the packing-box escape and its connection with his own resourcefulness: "A challenge was issued to me, more in jest than in earnest, by one of the employees of a large linen factory which I visited while in *Essen an der Ruhr*. One of the men, packing a case of linens to send to America, recognized me and knowing I had just escaped from the local jail, laughingly said, 'If we nail you in this packing case like we do linens, you would never be able to get out.' Jokingly, I replied, 'Oh, that would be easy,' and proceeded on my way, thinking the incident was closed. The next day, on reading the morning newspaper, to my astonishment, I found that the packers had publicly challenged me to escape from one of their packing cases, into which they proposed to nail and rope me. My thoughts flew back to the year long gone by when I secured firewood to heat my room and I determined to accept their challenge, meaning to escape by using as a basis the method I had employed in securing my firewood years ago." The method, simply stated—if anything ever is when referring to Houdini—was the use of cut or short nails to allow one of the boards to swivel inwards and allow him to escape.

The results? "It was a sensation and has been the means of putting a few solid stones in the foundation of my reputation." So spoke the man who had come to believe everything he read about himself in the papers, up to and including the articles he himself had planted!

The remainder of 1901 was one triumphant performance after another: he was locked in complicated handcuffs made by the Krupp armament works; he was manacled with specially constructed hand and leg fetters. Always he escaped, to the ovations of standing-room crowds everywhere. At the age of twenty-seven Houdini had conquered the Continent; he had theater managers fighting over him and had so many bookings he could share them with his alter ego, his brother, Hardeen.

Booked into the Folies-Bergère in Paris, Houdini made a pilgrimage to the tomb of his namesake and idol, Robert-Houdin. This was the first of many visits he was to make to the graves of dead magicians, a fascination that bordered on obsession and was to continue throughout his remaining years. He placed on the tomb of Robert-Houdin a wreath bearing the inscription "Honor and respect to Robert-Houdin from the magicians of America," while a conveniently placed photographer took pictures for posterity and Houdini's scrapbooks.

Discovering that the widow of Robert-Houdin's son and his daughter were both still alive and living in the environs of Paris, he determined to pay homage to them, too. Neither would receive him. One was too ill and the other too preoccupied. Houdini, never one to forget a slight, swore a personal vendetta against the very name he bore. By now he possessed all three of the essentials for a prototypical performer, the unholy trinity of egomania, pettiness, and paranoia. His hurt at being snubbed brought about his most petty act. He wrote a book entitled *The Unmasking of Robert-Houdin* dedicated to proving that his illustrious namesake, "instead of being known as the King of Conjurers, was in reality the Prince of Pilferers." All the book accomplished was to show that Robert-Houdin had not invented some of the tricks he claimed credit for—a charge that could also be made against Houdini.

But if Houdini's vanity was hurt by the failure of Robert-Houdin's heirs to receive him, his very career was threatened by what happened upon his return to Germany. During his tour the previous year, a police official, Schutzmann Werner Graff, had written in the *Rheinische Zeitung* that Houdini was a charlatan, and charged that he had engaged in false advertising when he claimed he could escape from any manner of police restraints. Once again, the famous Houdini ego, unable to take either bad press or—worse yet—being ignored, flared up. He rose to the challenge by suing Graff. Houdini's response arose from the belief that if the slur went unanswered his career would suffer.

Engaging the best lawyer in Cologne, Herr Rechtsantwalt Dr. Schreiber, and exuding his famous confidence, Houdini instituted criminal libel charges in the Cologne *Schaffengericht* in February 1902. Graff told the judge and jury that he was prepared to protect the German people and prove that Houdini was misrepresenting his talent, and further, that he, as an expert,

The Imperial Police of Cologne slanderously libeled HARRY HOUD[INI] stating his advertised tricks were swindles!

HOUDINI answered them by sueing for "An Honorary Public Apolo[gy]" The Police lost the case in the three highest Courts, as they were unable [to] fetter or Chain HOUDINI in an unescapable manner. He was even success[ful] in opening a special lock that they had constructed which after it had o[nce] been locked could not be opened!

FIRST TRIAL "Königliches Schöffengericht" in Köln. Feb. 26. 19[..]
SECOND TRIAL "Königliche Strafkammer" in Köln. July. 26.19[..]
THIRD TRIAL "Königliches Oberlandesgericht" Sept. 26. 19[..]

Having lost the case in all three trials the Police were ultimately compel[led] to publicly advertise "An Honorary Apology" and pay all costs of the tr[ials]

BY COMMAND OF KAISER WILHELM. II. EMPEROR OF GERMANY

would fasten the magician so that he could not release himself. After looking at the lock, Houdini permitted himself to be chained by a policeman named Lott, and to show how easy it would be, he offered to free himself in full view of the judge and jury, with all outsiders excluded. He freed himself, more by slipping out of the chains than by unlocking the lock.

After a four-day trial, Houdini won the lawsuit, and the Cologne police were fined and ordered to publicly apologize to Houdini "in the name of the Kaiser." Graff

immediately appealed the case to a higher court. At this trial the Cologne police presented a keyless lock specially manufactured by a master mechanic named Kroch, which, once locked, could never be opened, since it had no keyhole. Houdini was allowed to retire, manacled by a short piece of chain and this special lock, to the privacy of an adjacent room selected by the jury. In four minutes he emerged and handed the fetter to the judges. The court reaffirmed the lower court's ruling.

Now the Cologne police appealed to the highest court

in all of Germany, the Oberlandesgericht. There Schutz-mann Graff charged that although Houdini had opened handcuffs and fetters, he had also represented that he could open safes. Since no safes had been opened, this then was false advertising. According to the embroidered version Houdini was to tell many times, one of the judges showed Houdini the safe in his chambers and then closed the door, telling him to summon them when he had conquered it. Houdini's fabled luck stayed with him. The door to the safe had not been locked. It opened easily when he yanked at it. After a proper period of waiting to build up the suspense—a lesson Houdini said he never forgot in his subsequent escapes—he reentered the courtroom.

Whatever the circumstances, Houdini's verdict was upheld. Werner Graff was fined thirty marks, ordered to pay all costs of the three trials, and compelled to publish a public apology in the name of Kaiser Wilhelm II, the emperor of Germany. Houdini, anticipating the high court's decision, had already printed flyers of his own. At the very minute the decision was handed down on September 26, 1902, these were being handed out on the streets of Cologne and other German cities.

Houdini had met the challenge. The man who lived by his acts, both on and off the stage, had turned potential disaster into an epoch-making event, outwitting and humbling the German state. Only a man with the strongest confidence in his own skills could have done that. Or an egomaniac. Or both.

Houdini had also established an important precedent, not in the courts of law, but in the laws of human relations. From that day on, competitive entertainers saw the wisdom of avoiding any legal entanglement with Houdini.

While the German case dragged on to its finale over a period of eight months, the homesick Houdini made his first trip back to the United States in over two years to visit his mother. Then he returned to Europe to join the Circus Corty-Althoff, which was touring Holland. Houdini first saw the stately windmills there as a tourist attraction, and then as a ready-made setting to publicize his appearance with the circus. He would tie himself to windmills and escape as they turned. However, when he was tied on to the arm of a windmill, the supports gave way, hurling him to the ground. Though physically unhurt, his pride had been damaged, for his escape had not failed him so much as his publicity coup. No matter. Even his disaster was a success as crowds flocked out to see the crazy foreigner who tied himself to windmills.

Although imitation is reputed to be the sincerest form of flattery, Houdini didn't see it that way. In his mind's eye, he was the *only* escape artist. In the wake of his success many imitators sprang up, among them Oudini, Miss Undina Kleppini, and even Madame Houdini. But in his competitors' hands their magic wands became clubs; their handcuff and straitjacket escapes were mere

shadows of the great escapes Houdini effected, and he accepted their imitation, not as flattery, but as a challenge.

One such escape artist was Engleberto Kleppini, then appearing with the Circus Caesar Sidoli in Dortmund, Germany. In bold type Kleppini advertised that he had escaped from all of Houdini's handcuffs while leaving Houdini standing helpless on a public stage securely fastened in his. This was tantamount to throwing down the gauntlet. Taking a five-day leave of absence from the Corty-Althoff Circus, Houdini took the first available train to Dortmund, dragging along a grip brimming over with the most maniacal manacles he could get his hands on. Donning a false wig and moustache and affecting the walk of an old man, Houdini went to the circus to see his competitor.

During his opening speech, Kleppini recounted his besting of Houdini. At this point Houdini jumped up on the stage and, tearing off his disguise, cried, ''*I* am Houdini! I dare you to let me lock you up!'' Producing an enormous bankroll, he said, ''Here are 5,000 marks if you can escape.''

Kleppini wouldn't accept the challenge, so Houdini made his way back through the crowd to his hotel, leaving an arena filled with jeering fans, disappointed at seeing the man who only moments before had bragged of his mastery of Houdini in a handcuff duel now evade an immediate trial of skill before their eyes.

That night the manager of the Circus Sidoli came to Houdini's hotel room to attempt to arrange a challenge match. Houdini accepted his terms, and posters were printed announcing the challenge duel the next night. In the morning the manager reappeared and insisted upon inspecting Houdini's collection of cuffs. Houdini indicated that Kleppini could take his choice of more than a dozen cuffs in the grip. A French letter cuff, opened by a combination of five letters on the five cylinders, attracted the manager's attention. Suppressing his interest, he tried, in a tone of indifference, to find out what combination of letters opened the cuff. Houdini, playing him along, wouldn't tell him until he had his word that he would not pass the information on to Kleppini. Thus apparently assured, Houdini let him in on the secret that if the cylinders were spun to form the word *clefs*—French for ''keys''—the cuffs would open.

That night when Houdini reached the circus and offered Kleppini his choice of cuffs, the pretender—not surprisingly—chose the French letter cuffs. Kleppini immediately rushed into his cabinet with the unlocked cuffs and returned just as quickly with an assured air. ''I will open these cuffs,'' he announced, ''and challenge Houdini to lock them on me.'' Houdini experienced some difficulty in getting the cuffs back in order to inspect them before he put them on Kleppini's wrists. Once the cylinders were spun, Kleppini made directly for his cabinet, shouting to the crowd that he would be out in seconds.

As he did so, Houdini announced, "Ladies and gentlemen, you may all go home. I do not lock a cuff on a man merely to let him escape."

For the next few hours, the once enthusiastic crowd whistled derisively. Finally they grew disinterested and then impatient and then disgusted and started wandering toward the exits. The furious circus manager told the stagehands to remove the cabinet, with Kleppini still in it, from the stage. Kleppini sent his wife to find Houdini and beg him to come and release him, but Houdini refused to do so unless there were newspaper witnesses. Finally, in the presence of witnesses, Houdini told the manacled man, "Didn't you guess I would change the combination when you handed me back the cuffs?" and proceeded to turn the five-letter combination until "a good American word," F-R-A-U-D, fell into place and the cuffs opened.

Returning to England for the third time, Houdini introduced a trick he is reputed to have learned at the Chicago World's Fair, known as Ovette's Original Needle Trick. However, in keeping with his heritage of being named after Robert-Houdin, the man who called his namesake "an imposter" for "claiming original inventions as his own" soon turned it into the Houdini Needle Trick, adapting it to a more majestic and visual illusion than Ovette had ever imagined possible. The effect was, in Houdini's own words, that of a "performer [who] invites a committee to step on the stage and examine a pack or several packages of needles, thread and to thoroughly inspect his mouth. Performer taking the needles lays them on his outstretched tongue and swallows them, drinking water to 'wash' them down. Performer unwinds a length of thread and swallows that also. Several grimaces are made after which performer reaches into his mouth and securing hold of the thread withdraws it slowly and it is seen that the needles are threaded on the thread. The mouth once again shown as empty." Ovette only withdrew his needles to an arm's length, but Houdini, the master entertainer, had a member of the "committee" slowly draw one hundred threaded needles out the length of the stage, with the threaded needles perfectly spaced out and tied on the withdrawn thread so that even those in the very last row of the balcony could see the needles gleam from the stage lights. From that day on, it was part of his act.

Adding constantly to his repertoire of acts, both in magic and in escapology, Houdini now looked for new worlds to conquer. Harry Day found one, booking Houdini into the Establishment Yard in Moscow for four weeks.

Theodore Roosevelt had called Tsar Nicholas II of Russia "a preposterous little creature who ruled one hundred and fifty million people with more firmness than ability." Reigning over a political system that had clearly lived beyond its time and was on the threshold of imminent disintegration, Nicholas couldn't comprehend fully the events that were moving his country closer to chaos.

The medieval structure of Russian society was crumbling. The people had had enough of harsh taxation, uncontrollable land hunger, low standards of living, and repressive police measures. Every act of terror or organized pogrom by the secret police brought with it counterterrorist acts from the people.

The Moscow chief of police, Lebedeff, was all-powerful. Not only did he perform all of the functions in a police state normally delegated to the chief of police, but also he had approval of other extraneous matters, such as theater advertising and performers. And "should he take a dislike to you, he could compel you to leave Moscow inside of twenty-four hours," Houdini was to remark upon his return from Russia.

Before his engagement began, Houdini went to Lebedeff's office and challenged the police chief to lock him in one of his escape-proof *carettes*, used to transport political prisoners to Siberia. The dreaded *carette* was a steel safe on wheels with a six-inch-square window with four bars in the entrance door. The vehicle's lock was thirty inches below the window with a padlock. The only key that could open it was reputed to be in the possession of a policeman on the Siberian border, a twenty-one-day journey from Moscow.

Lebedeff willingly obliged Houdini to the great merriment of the other officers. First they subjected Houdini to their own search, Russian police style. They laid the stark naked Houdini on a table, and one man started at his head and worked down to his feet while another proceeded in the other direction, searching every orifice. Then they turned him over and repeated the process. Next they twisted his resilient body in every way imaginable, looking for picklocks and keys in the same manner they used to "work over" their thousands of political prisoners.

The nude Houdini was then handcuffed with two iron bands secured by a metal bar, his ankles encased in steel fetters, and he was half led, half carried outside into the prison yard, where he was locked into the *carette*, which was then wrapped with two chains and padlocked. The only concession that Houdini had won from the less-than-willing Russians was that the van was to be backed against the prison wall, so that he could work in secret—a classic case of misdirection.

His assistant, Kukol, was removed from the yard by the suspicious police. They had seen him drop his match box to get a look at the underside of the van and they wanted to make sure that Houdini received no help from anyone. What they hadn't bargained on was Bess.

For the first six years of their marriage, Bess had been an integral part of their act, performing in the old one-in-one-out, or Metamorphosis, and assisting him in other numbers in the act. But now, after mortgaging her own identity to that of her husband, she was no longer part of

Промотional bills from Houdini's Russian tour.

Гарри Худини,
всемірно-извѣстный таинственный человѣкъ,
прозванный «Королемъ цѣпей».

СЕЗОНА!

Третій выходъ таинствен наго человѣка прозваннаго

КОРОЛЕМЪ ЦѢПЕЙ И КАНДАЛОВЪ

ГАРРИ ХУДИНИ.

Г. ХУДИНИ передъ отъѣздомъ на Нижегородскую ярмарку давалъ представленія въ Москвѣ въ театрѣ „Эрмитажъ". Г. ХУДИНИ былъ одѣтъ въ сумасшедшую рубашку, связанъ цѣпями по рукамъ и ногамъ, затѣмъ онъ былъ посаженъ въ карету Московской пересыльной тюрьмы. По прошествіи трехъ минутъ г. ХУДИНИ легко освободился изъ своего заключенія и былъ встрѣченъ восторженными аплодисментами публики.

Начало въ 9 час. вечера.

From The Moscow Courant, Moscow Russia

the act and was reduced to helping him more off the stage than on. One of those occasions when her help was needed off the stage was during his escape from the prisoner's van, and she acted out her bit part perfectly.

As the van was turned to the wall and Kukol was unceremoniously escorted away, Houdini shouted out that he wanted to speak to Bess. Callous to parting scenes in the *carette*, Lebedeff granted the request, much as he would a condemned man's last wish. Bess went up to the small barred window. There she whispered to her husband and gave him a long, lingering kiss; so long in fact that she had to be forcibly pulled away in an hysterical

scene. But she had done her job. She had passed two miniature tools to Houdini—a coil of spring steel with saw-tooth edges and an apparatus that operated on the principle of a can opener. Even as the seemingly remorseful Bess was led away, blubbering about Houdini's potential failure, her husband was beginning his escape—not through the door, as one diarist recounted, and not by bribing the guard, which another biographer suggests, but by cutting through the zinc underbelly of the van. Accounts of this event are all surmise, and nobody knows exactly what happened.

Less than forty-five minutes after he had been incarcerated in the Siberian prison van, Houdini was out. Instead of the applause he had been accustomed to hearing, he received a different type of response: he was seized and searched again. The Russian secret police found nothing, but in return they gave him nothing, not even the treasured letter of verification he always sought after every prison escape.

Even without a testimonial letter, Houdini soon became the sensation of Moscow because of his escape from the hated *carette*. His stay was extended from four weeks to three months at three of Moscow's leading theaters, and his salary was doubled. Once again Houdini had transcended national boundaries by performing an act that is universally understood—escaping. Nowhere did the public appreciate or identify with Houdini's art more than in Russia, where everyone yearned to escape.

The triumphant magician proceeded next to St. Petersburg, where the Grand Duke Sergius invited him to give a special performance at his palace. According to Bess, "At the conclusion of his acts the Grand Duke announced that for over a month he had had the best locksmiths trying to unlock one of his safes. If Houdini really had power over locks, he could open the chest." Houdini agreed to the challenge under three conditions: first, that he be allowed to inspect the safe; second, that he be stripped and subjected to a complete search before he attempted to open it; and third, that the lights be extinguished for thirty seconds before the attempt. After he had inspected the safe and allowed himself to be searched, he approached the safe. The lights went out and thirty seconds later blazed back on to reveal Houdini standing beside the open safe. "There is one place where ordinary people do not think to look," Houdini later recounted. "I had my picklock fastened to the sole of my left foot with surgeon's cement."

His performance before the grand duke, coupled with his week in St. Petersburg, brought him $1,500, a record for any performer in Europe. At the relatively tender age of twenty-eight, the Hungarian Jew from Appleton, Wisconsin, was the toast of Imperial Russia.

Just as he had overcome the challenge of the safe, he had broken through the reserve of the circle around the tsar. "The supersititous court went mad about me," the immodest magician later boasted. "The Empress, with her love of mysticism, refused to believe that there was a scientific and natural explanation for my magic. She begged me to stay and to give her the benefit of my gifts, but I refused. Wine was served at the court function and it so happens that I am a teetotaler. I did not know the elaborate court ceremony. It seems that a refusal to touch the wine served by the Emperor is an insult to Russia. I promptly lost my standing at court. And so there ended my chance to take Rasputin's place in history." Or so he claimed. He later added, "I sometimes wonder. Certainly I could have out-magiced and out-spiritualized Rasputin if I had wanted to."

Whether Houdini could have taken Rasputin's place in the House of Romanov or whether this was just a daydream of a man who was fast becoming part man, part myth—even in his own mind—will never be known, for Houdini was a good-natured deceiver, both on and off the stage.

The remainder of Houdini's successful Continental tour was marked by his adoption of an avocation—collecting. Possessing more money now that he had ever had before and more time as a result of his two-a-day status, he began frequenting secondhand shops, seeking the ephemera of his interests. Coming from a long line of scholars, his naturally inquisitive instinct turned into an acquisitive urge.

Returning to England with his press notices preceding him and his purchases trailing behind him, Houdini continued his unabated assault on the psyche of the public. In the days of innocence immediately after the turn of the century, the public was most susceptible to a combination of his feats and the publicity they read in the newspapers. A devout believer in the magic of publicity created by the papers, Houdini had learned to fan the flames once they started. Now he sought out the *Daily Illustrated Mirror* in London for a tie-in.

If it was to Houdini's benefit to seek an alliance with a paper, it was just as much to the paper's profit, for the British press in 1904 was made up of hotly partisan papers, and lots of them. The addition of the *Express* in 1900 had given London over thirty papers, all clamoring for attention and readership. Just as Pulitzer and Hearst used circulation-building devices in America, the newspaper moguls of Fleet Street were also given to such promotions and gimmicks when news alone was not enough to sell papers.

The mutually beneficial promotion began during Houdini's performance at the London Hippodrome on Saturday night, March 12. In response to his challenge to "anybody to come forward and successfully manacle him," a representative of the *Mirror* stepped up on the stage. The match was set for the following Thursday afternoon's matinee. According to the *Mirror*, "Not a seat was vacant in the mighty Hippodrome when Harry Houdini, the 'Handcuff King,' stepped into the arena and received an ovation worthy of a monarch." Acknowledging the mighty roar of the 4,000 patrons, he said, "I am ready to be manacled by the *Mirror* representative if he is present."

The *Mirror's* "representative" was a journalist who had "encountered a Birmingham blacksmith who had spent five years of his life in devising a lock 'no mortal man could pick.'" As the reporter came forward with the handcuffs, Houdini called for a committee of volunteers from the audience to insure fair play.

The journalist then placed the handcuffs on Houdini's wrists and, with an effort, turned the key six times, securing the bolt. "Ladies and Gentlemen," Houdini ad-

Chief of the Secret Russian Police LEBEDOEFF has HARRY HOUDINI stripped stark naked and searched then locked up in the Siberian Transport Cell or Carette, May 10/1903 in Moscow and in 28 minutes HOUDINI had made his escape to the unspeakable astonishment of the Russian Police.

HOUDINI in Russia.

dressed the audience in his strange, mesmeric voice, elaborating each syllable, "I am now locked up in a handcuff that has taken a British mechanic five years to make. I do not know whether I am going to get out of it or not, but I can assure you I am going to do my best."

At precisely 3:15 P.M., accompanied by a stirring tune played by the Hippodrome orchestra, Houdini retired to his curtained "ghost house" to attempt to get out of the cuffs 'no mortal man could pick.' But, then, to the Hippodrome audience Houdini was no mortal man.

Twenty-two minutes later Houdini's head emerged

from his curtained cabinet to cries of "He is free! He is free!" But it was only to get a good look at the handcuffs in the light and then to retire once again back into the "ghost house." Thirteen minutes later Houdini stepped out from behind the curtains with perspiration pouring down his face and explained to the audience, "My knees hurt. I am not done yet." The journalist, pacing on the stage nearby, sent an attendant to get a large cushion. This he presented to Houdini with the statement "The *Mirror* has no desire to submit Mr. Houdini to a torture test, and if Mr. Houdini will permit me, I shall have

Harry lost no time in having a poster created heralding his Russian exploits (left), and (below), a bill announcing his visit to Sheffield, during his British tour in 1904.

HIPPODROME

THEATRE OF VARIETIES.

MIDDLE STREET, BRIGHTON.

Proprietors - - - Messrs. BARRASFORD & SMITH
Managing Director - - - Mr. THOS. BARRASFORD

HOUDINI

THE FAMOUS HANDCUFF KING AND PRISON BREAKER.
Direct from a Record Success at the London Hippodrome,

Will be presented during the

Matinee Performance

On

SATURDAY, May 14th

by the "DAILY MIRROR" with a

Solid Silver Manacle

a fac-simile of the one from which he so
marvellously released himself in

62 MINUTES

at the London Hippodrome.

This Manacle took Mr. N. HART, the
Celebrated Safe-Lock Maker, of Birmingham,
FIVE YEARS TO MANUFACTURE. There is a
standing

Reward of 100 Guineas,

to any Locksmith who can open this Manacle
with both hands free and the use of any
instrument in the

SAME TIME AS HOUDINI.

Saturday, 2.30. Prices as usual.

W. E. NASH, Printer, 205, Western Road, Brighton.

great pleasure in offering him the use of this cushion."

Another twenty minutes passed, with the band playing one song after another. The Handcuff King once again emerged from his chamber, still handcuffed! He approached the man from the *Mirror* and asked if he would remove the handcuffs for a moment, "in order that I may take my coat off?" The journalist, aware that opening the handcuffs under Houdini's watchful gaze would provide the escapologist with the visual picklock he needed to solve the cuffs, would have none of it. He declined, saying, "I am sorry to disoblige you, Mr. Houdini, but I cannot unlock those cuffs unless you admit you are defeated."

Houdini, not to be stopped by so small a thing as a denial, took a pen knife from his pocket and, opening it with his teeth, proceeded to cut the coat—which was now turned inside out over his head—to pieces. Having created a diversion to pacify the waiting audience—which responded in wild enthusiasm—he went back into the so-called "ghost house" for a third time.

After ten more minutes, or a total of one hour, the man the *Mirror* called the "Mysteriarch" called out for Bess and asked her to get him a glass of water.

At this point the descriptions of the great confrontation between Houdini and the *Daily Illustrated Mirror* provide room for reasonable speculation. Houdini, who had always set himself up in a never-fail posture, had certainly more than met his match. To him, any failure meant failure to his entire career. So he probably employed Bess's talents in histrionics, as he had in Moscow. He directed her to try anything to get the original key from the journalist, or else he feared his career was at an end. Hesitantly, Bess approached the reporter.

The early 1900s was a time when achievement counted for more than failure, when the success of Tom Swift and Horatio Alger was salable. The journalism of the day reflected this optimism, and the *Mirror* representative may have rationalized that it would not be much of a story if Houdini—then the largest attraction in all of England—failed to escape. Gallantly, he succumbed to Bess's pleas and turned over the key, which she had somehow smuggled to Houdini as she brought him a glass of water.

However it happened, ten minutes after the water was given to him, Houdini bounded from the cabinet with hands aloft holding the handcuffs for all to see. He was free! The crowd erupted. They bore him around the stage on their shoulders, triumphantly exulting in his conquest of the *Mirror's* handcuffs, while Houdini, visibly shaken, wept.

The reporter bestowed accolades on Houdini and, surprisingly, on Bess. He called her "a fair, cultured, beautiful American lady, petite, fascinating and clever." It may just have been this cleverness that enabled Houdini to escape from what he was later to call "one of the hardest tests I ever had."

Although he subsequently escaped from the inside of a safe the first time he tried, the *Mirror* challenge was one of the most difficult and one of his last in Europe—a coda for his entire tour. Within a month he contracted pneumonia and returned to America to recuperate and to see his beloved mother, to whom he had written every day during his four-year absence.

Harry Houdini had conquered the heart and imagination of a continent—but it was not America. This naturalized American passionately sought the adoration of his own country. Now he prepared for that conquest.

When Harry Houdini returned to New York in the spring of 1904, thirty years after he had first arrived in America as immigrant Erik Weisz, he became again one of the hordes who were knocking at the Golden Door. Although not an immigrant in the strict sense, he would nevertheless suffer much of the same disillusionment and ridicule they did. But his would be at the hands of xenophobic theater managers, who looked down on anything "European."

He rested for a time at a house in Stamford, Connecticut, until he was fully recovered from an illness that had forced him to cut short his tour. Then he started to make the rounds of American theater managers. With his bulging scrapbook under one arm and Bess on the other, he visited office after office offering proof of the standing-room audiences he had generated as a European draw. The news clippings, printed challenges, and letters of verification in his scrapbook had been preceded by a bombardment of letters and clippings he had sent to any and all vaudeville managers from his different European stops. But even though America was ravenous for entertainment—any entertainment—it had little enthusiasm for a top-billed act based on handcuffs and escapes. The hurricane force he had loosed on Eu-

ropean audiences and managers failed to create even a minor stir in America.

While his professional affairs were in a state of limbo, Houdini turned his attention to personal ones. For the ten years he and Bess had been husband and wife, they had never really had a home life, or, for that matter, a home. Houdini now remedied that by purchasing a huge brownstone at 278 West 113th Street, which would become fondly known simply as "278." He promptly moved his mother in, along with crates and crates of all his belongings, including his recent purchase of the mammoth collection of the retired magician Henry Evanion.

The brownstone would be more than just a home; it would also serve as Houdini's library, laboratory, and warehouse. While he catered to Bess's whims and put in bathroom tiles reading *B* and *H*, he was also constructing an outsized bathtub for practicing underwater feats and an elaborate system of wiring in the walls so that a voice from one room could be heard in another, enabling him to perform mind-reading "miracles" for visitors. The basement served both as a laboratory for developing complicated, precision-made escape apparatus and as a storehouse. Here he kept all the pamphlets and booklets

he sold in theater lobbies throughout his career—a side-line that more than paid for his traveling expenses while, not incidentally, spreading the gospel of Houdini according to Houdini.

"278"—called by Houdini his "homequarters"—was the scene of whatever little domesticity the Houdinis ever had. Here the couple, who were both admittedly "quick-tempered and arbitrary," instituted a ritual to avoid domestic quarrels. It was a system of signals, not unlike the system they had used in Galena, Kansas, in their mind-reading and second-sight performances. Harry would raise his left eyebrow three times to tell his wife to be quiet when she was irritating him. "Doubtless Houdini used it more than any other signal in our code," Bess was to admit many years later. Harry also developed a novel way to end their petty quarrels. "Whenever I got angry," Bess recounted, "he would leave the house and walk slowly around the block. In a few minutes, he would open the door and toss his hat into the room. If it was not thrown out again, he would enter. If the hat was thrown out, he would go away for another few minutes."

If 278 was the scene of little touches of domestic life, it also was the scene of one of Houdini's most memorable exhibits of high life. On their fourteenth anniversary, Houdini bought Bess a bouquet of roses and delivered them by scaling the outside of the house with the roses in his teeth. But instead of waiting on the balcony like the proverbial breathless bride, Bess was heard frantically hollering at her husband, "Watch out, Harry! You're going to fall."

In the winter of 1905, 278 was the scene of a reconciliation. The always-frail Bess had fallen seriously ill and sought the comfort of her mother, whom she had not seen since the day she married the non-Catholic Houdini. In the same intense manner he approached everything, Harry went to his in-laws' house in Brooklyn and prevailed upon Mrs. Rahner to accompany him back to 278 to be with her daughter. Overcome by Bess's illness and her son-in-law's determination, Mrs. Rahner accompanied Harry back to 278 and effected a reunion between daughter and mother and a reunion between the Rahners and the Weisses.

The pulsebeat of the house was on the second floor—Houdini's library. It was a reflection of his intellectual aspirations and his desire to be accepted as a savant, as well as of his need to be accepted as an American. Much of his money went into this pursuit. He bought books, illusions, and secrets everywhere and from everyone, often from down-and-out magicians whom he desired to help. He acquired over 5,000 books, which he insured for over $350,000. He crammed them into his li-

At 278 West 113th Street, New York, Harry poses with Bessie, her sisters, and Mrs. Rahner (in window, left).

brary with all the other lifeless scraps of history that held appeal for him and activated his emotions and memories: every corny joke he had ever heard in vaudeville; complete files of newsclips on Sarah Bernhardt and Robert Ingersoll, the fashionable agnostic of his time; handcuffs and manacles; oil paintings; playbills and posters; autographs of all the signers of the Declaration of Independence (except Button Gwinnett); the largest collection of Lincoln letters in a private collection; the original Martin Luther Bible; material about circus freaks and anatomical anomalies; Bess's cookbooks; and a complete collection of magicana. When Arthur Conan Doyle visited his library to view his collection of books, he objected to the lack of walking space. "Who cares to walk about in a library?" demanded Houdini. "It's a place to read, isn't it?"

But the pride of the Houdini collection was a little lap desk once owned by Edgar Allan Poe. The famous author had written several of his works on it. The acquisition of Poe's writing desk was fitting because Poe had not only perpetrated one of the great hoaxes of the nineteenth century—the supposed balloon flight of Mr. Monck Mason in 1844 from England to America—but had also uncovered the secret of Maelzel's chess-playing automaton. Not unlike Houdini, he exposed illusions with as much imagination and energy as he used in creating them.

Harry's neurotic desire to collect and own anything and everything was well known, and he kept open accounts with every major dealer throughout the world. For many months after his death, rare books, playbills, pamphlets, and other articles for which he had left standing orders continued to arrive at 278, and the posthumous charges for these additions amounted to well over twenty thousand dollars.

Having chosen his living site, he now sought a burial site. He found it at Macpelah Cemetery in Cypress Hills, bordering Brooklyn, "the borough of churches and cemeteries." Mahpelah had been the burial cave of the patriarchs, Abraham, Isaac, and Jacob, and the Cypress Hills version was now to become the burial ground of the patriarch of magicians. Houdini immediately transferred the remains of his father and his half brother Herman to the new family plot, opening both caskets and remarking that "Herman's teeth were in excellent condition."

This fascination with death was but another part of the intricate mosaic of the man called Houdini. He was known to take long walks in graveyards, and admitted that he had "found the graves of Robert Heller, Bosco, Houdin and searched for the resting places of Cagliostro and Pinetti." Far from proving, as one magician later commented, "that the only magicians Houdini liked were dead ones," Houdini himself indicated that these sepulchral tours would "make interesting reading and bring forth strange items."

Unable to find bookings to his liking, Houdini sailed back to England in August of 1904 as a premier perform-er. He was determined to continue in the rarified atmosphere of a headliner, even if it meant returning to Europe. He had come to believe that the Europeans appreciated and understood his art better than his own countrymen.

Playing Glasgow, Newport, and Paris, he pursued the publicity tie-ins he had pioneered earlier. He visited tradesmen in the area—particularly builders, hardware store operators, and carpenters' unions—and invited them to enter into the spirit of things by challenging Houdini to escape from their own cabinets, boxes, and crates. Their business would reap the benefits of the publicity, and they would be able to display the containers in their windows or plant. Furthermore, they would get as many free tickets for the performance as Houdini could make available.

Houdini, who couldn't get the salary he thought he deserved in America, was making over 150 pounds a week in England. Then Harry Day was able to negotiate a percentage contract, and Houdini soon began clearing over $1,000 a week. The week of February 18, 1905, he made, as he noted in his diary, "$2,150 clear salary."

As they had done for the past five years, Houdini played in one town and his brother, Hardeen, played almost the identical show in another. Hardeen, now billed as the "World's Greatest Handcuff Manipulator," employed all of his brother's stock-in-trade routines. He peremptorily dismissed challengers with handcuffs that were unknown to him by throwing them off-stage and declaring their cuffs "not regulation"—a throwback to the time in Chicago when Houdini had been tricked by a pair of cuffs filled with slugs which couldn't be opened. On those days when no genuine challengers came forward, he laced the audience (as did his brother) with his own plants, who furnished challenges from his own private collection as if they had originated with the audience. And, like his brother, Hardeen arranged beforehand to keep all handcuffs from which he escaped, accumulating a collection second only to Houdini's.

But Hardeen also put something back into the pot, making one important contribution to their act. Believing that part of the reason the straitjacket escape had never met with the expected response of the audience was because no one believed he had done it without the assistance of an associate, he began doing his escape in full view of the audience. The audience reacted with appreciative roars of approval in direct proportion to the amount of his twistings and turnings. Hardeen thus made the straitjacket escape a dramatic participatory act in which the audience now invested itself in the escape and responded accordingly. Houdini quickly adapted it for his own show, and once again the brothers' acts mirrored each other.

During his tour, Houdini received a cable offering him $5,000 for a six-week period at leading eastern theaters back in the States. He declined, for the moment, cabling

back that he was booked through the fall of 1905. But once the tour ended, he immediately made preparations to go back to America as the headliner he always knew he would be.

The Colonial Theatre at Broadway and 63rd Street was more than just fourteen years and many miles from the day he had walked out of H. Richter's to become a magician. When he opened at the Colonial on October 2, 1905, it was, to Houdini, the realization of a lifelong ambition.

Although Houdini was a headliner on the Orpheum circuit, he was discouraged because the big-chain bookers did not appreciate his true worth. His agent "tried to convince those men that they ought to multiply his salary by ten at the very least. But finally I compromised when they agreed to pay him a thousand a week. I think perhaps the most precious thing I got out of that contract was the gratitude of his mother."

But if his mother was grateful, Harry was still incensed over the initial refusal of the bookers to give him the money he asked for. Taking an ad in the Christmas edition of the theatrical trade paper, crammed with the traditional "Season's Greetings" messages from other entertainers, he let loose with his own greeting in the famous

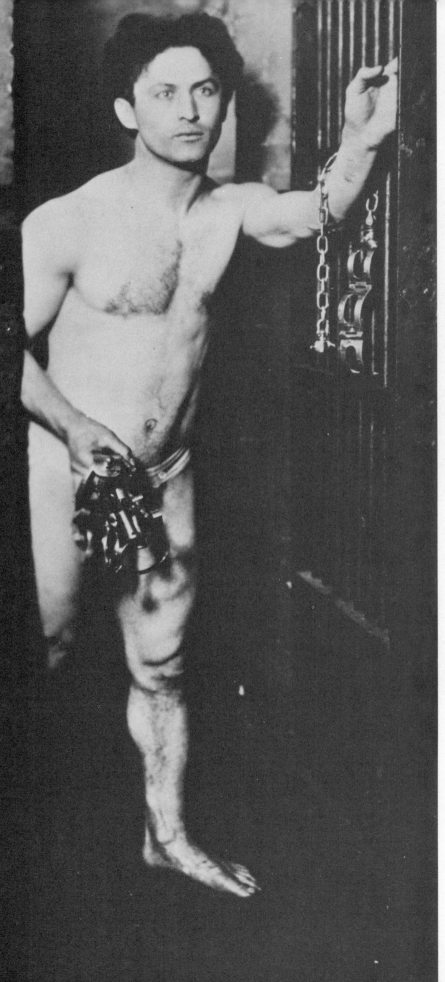

Typical display in a theater lobby (above) to generate interest in Houdini's impending arrival.

Houdini the jailbreaker (left) emerging from a cell after a successful escape, naked but triumphant!

Manacled with the balls and chains that almost caused him to drown after jumping off the San Francisco Bay Bridge (right), and performing the Mail Pouch Escape (far right).

Houdini tradition: "I TOLD YOU SO!!! When it was discovered that Houdini, 'The Prison Defier,' had been brought back to America at a salary of $1,000 weekly all the wisenheimers and Society Know-it-all fellows polished up their hammers, saying 'Gold Brick!' It has now been positively proven beyond any contradiction that Houdini is the hardest working artist that has ever trodden the vaudeville stage!! He is worth more than the salary he is booked for!!!"

One critic, Alan Dale of the New York *American*, took exception to "the offensive manners of the man." He wrote, "The 'famous' Houdini is a clever manipulator of handcuffs who appears to suffer in the very worst way from that terrible and baffling disease—the swollen head. Houdini devoted the greater part of his 'turn' to talking about...what a hard time he had of it in England, how they hated to see him earning money over there, how cruelly jealous they were of him...but that he'd go back there and get more money."

Houdini was fast becoming famous, but not fast enough for the man who, at the age of thirty-one, viewed his stature as substantially larger than his actual five feet eight inches. Playing B. F. Keith's Theatre in Washington, D.C., in January 1906, Houdini sought once again to capture the imagination and press of America by escaping from jail—not just any jail, but the Unites States Jail in Washington. Sure, he had broken out of jails in the United States before, but the only publicity he had engendered was local. This time he sought national attention by escaping from a federal prison.

During a break on the afternoon of January 6, 1906, Houdini went down to the United States Jail and solicited the cooperation of Warden J. H. Harris. He challenged the warden to lock him in the very cell that had once housed Charles Guiteau, the assassin of President James A. Garfield. While Harris considered the challenge, Houdini traded quips, gave out tickets, and had his picture taken. Finally, Harris agreed to the challenge, somewhat dismayed at the sight of the newspapermen Harry had thoughtfully brought along. He stripped Houdini of his clothing and locked him in cell number two in the south wing, the middle chamber of a row of three heavily barred cubbyholes, walled in solid masonry. Houdini's clothing was locked in another one of the three cells. The unabashed nudity of anyone, even a performer, in those days when newspapers spelled *naked* "n----," was risqué—and it was news.

While Warden Harris and a crowd of deputies, visiting police officials, and newspapermen retired in Harris's office, Houdini began attacking the door. The door to the cell was sunk three feet into the brick wall and fastened by an armlike bar that projected out into the corridor and slipped over a steel catch with a spring that held the lock. The lock could be opened only by a key and had five tumblers. Within two minutes Houdini was out of his cell and into the corridor. There he was struck by a whimsical

idea. In the cells lining the corridor were eight other prisoners—two condemned murders, four men under indictment for murder, and two incarcerated for other crimes. Opening their cell doors, he moved each of the startled prisoners to another cell and locked him up again. After opening up the cell where his clothing was imprisoned, Houdini opened the corridor door and marched into the warden's office. All in twenty-one minutes!

The escape, coupled with the game of musical cells, captured the imagination of the correspondents, and Houdini was news—big news—for the very first time in the United States.

Two months later he escaped from a second-tier cell of the Boston city jail in twenty-three minutes. This time Houdini had added still another twist: he had escaped from the cell and the jail and called the superintendent from his room backstage at the Keith Theatre, some five miles away.

Houdini and escapes were fast becoming synonymous. During the remainder of his tour in 1906 and 1907, he escaped from witches' cages in Chelsea, Massachusetts; tarred ropes in Toledo; a large paper bag in San Francisco; a government mail pouch in Los Angeles; a giant pigskin laced with a chain and padlocks in Philadelphia; and a silk fishline and an iron-bound wicker hamper, both in Boston. And of course, his staple, handcuffs—everywhere.

Houdini's genius in sculpting material, ideas, and promotion to mass taste was calculated to increase the public's awareness of him. It was difficult to ignore him. In almost every town he hit, he would either jump off a bridge manacled by hand and leg fetters in the warm months or escape from a jail in the cold months. Employing his promotional genius, he would try new approaches to old shop-worn tricks whenever possible. This included adding a seventy-five-pound iron ball chained to his ankle in San Francisco—a trick he never tried again—or jumping into the frigid Detroit River in his fabled Bell Isle Bridge jump.

In later years Houdini reflected on his underwater submersions and gave them some of the typical Houdiniesque flavor. "I have to go into training for such exigencies as submersion in frozen rivers, while chained and handcuffed. I have, for many years, bathed in icewater to make myself immune from the effects of my professinal submarine activities," he said. Embellishing a story in the telling, he added, "I once had an entire meal served to me while seated in a tub full of floating cakes of ice."

But as he conquered every type of container the ingenuity and versatility of man—with the help of Houdini—could devise, his escapes became accepted. The public, once amazed, now came to expect him to escape from anything. No longer intrigued, they began to tire of escapes. Houdini, who just two years before had been the

headline act, now was told bluntly by theater managers that the public had grown apathetic to his continued successes and that his public appeal was slipping. Worse yet, in St. Louis and in Cleveland, another act appeared above his on the marquee.

Houdini was profoundly hurt when audiences didn't respond to his art. He had foreseen the time when his heroic stature and popularity would be eroded and his theatrical welcome worn out. Now facing the biggest challenge of his professional life, Houdini sought a new *shtick* to capture the public's consciousness.

His first problem was that the success of his challenge handcuff act had generated imitators by the score. Houdini had always thought that once he did a trick, he owned it, and that anyone else employing it was riding his fame. But even personal challenges to competitors and threatened suits hadn't deterred the host of imitators who were calling themselves handcuff kings. And so the galled Houdini, knowing full well that handcuff escapes were a dime a dozen, dropped the act that had originally made him famous.

Houdini became a one-man laboratory, dedicated to

discovering a new trick that would once again propel him to the center stage of public attention. Together with his assistants, Franz Kukol and James Vickery, whom he had hired three years before in London, he developed a new escape, one which wed the traditional escape from a locked enclosure with a new element—water. The result was billed as a "death-defying mystery," from which failure to escape meant "a drowning death."

On the night of January 27, 1908, Harry Houdini stepped to the front of the stage of the Columbia Theatre in St. Louis and in a voice that sounded like a cross between H. V. Kaltenborn and William Jennings Bryan, announced, "Ladies and Gentlemen, my latest invention—The Milk Can. I will be placed in this can and it will be filled with water. A committee from the audience will lock the padlocks and place the keys down in front of the footlights. I will attempt to escape. Should anything happen, and should I fail to appear within a certain time, my assistants will open the curtains, rush in, smash the Milk Can and do everything possible to save my life... Music, Maestro, please!"

Clad in a one-piece bathing suit, the well-muscled Houdini turned toward a thirty-inch galvanized can.

He wedged his body down through the narrow mouth of the can as water sluiced over the top. Then, as the committee secured the padlocks that held the top in place, the orchestra struck up "Asleep in the Deep" and the committee drew the curtain over the can.

The audience, having been told by Houdini that he could stay under water for only a short period of time before he would be "deprived of life-sustaining air," held its collective breath as if part of the act, which they were. As loud exhalation followed loud exhalation and the minutes tolled by, Franz Kukol took his place next to the curtained cabinet holding aloft a fire ax, obviously ready to "rush in, smash the Milk Can and do everything possible to save" Houdini's life.

But it wasn't necessary. Just as Kukol lifted his ax, as if on cue, Houdini parted the curtains and, streaming water and shaking his long hair out of his eyes, walked out to the tumultuous applause of the audience. Just three minutes had passed since his head had gone below the neck of the can, but those dramatic three minutes had changed Houdini's career. There, for all to see, was the milk can, with all the locks still intact and the water obviously still inside. The public's apathy had been changed into excitement. He had put new wine into old bottles without bursting the bottles or spoiling the

wine, and was back on top again as a headliner.

The Milk Can Escape now became part of his act, and the audiences never seemed to tire of it. He was ready to take his freshened act back to Europe for another tour, but before he left, Houdini had some loose ends to tidy up.

One of these was his writing. Houdini had finished his first book, *The Right Way to Do Wrong*, in 1906; it was a 94-pager, dedicated to exposing the tricks of con men, counterfeiters, fake spirit mediums, pickpockets, and thieves, which he sold at a concession stand in theater lobbies for "traveling money" or gave away in each new town "to advertise myself." In 1906 he also started *Conjurers' Monthly Magazine*, a 32-page publication whose reason for being was more to ventilate Houdini's pique and serve him as a soapbox than to be a source of news or information. The pages were filled with self-serving, disparaging jabs at competitors and

With the milk can (far left), and a familiar sight of that era: Houdini manacled and jumping into a river for the thousands who turned out to watch the spectacle.

those who had snubbed and criticized him. He even included a column written by his brother under the name Herr N. Osey, covering activities in Europe, especially those of Hardeen and Houdini. A competitor viewed Houdini's literary effort as that of a writer who was "swelling out his chest like a pouter pigeon, protruding his abdomen like a cormorant and dropping calumny from his lips...." By 1908, stung by the refusal of the Society of American Magicians to adopt his "house organ" as its official publication and pressed for time because of his impending European trip, Houdini brought his magazine to a blessed end.

The Houdini entourage set sail for Germany on August 10, 1908—Harry, Bess, Kukol, Vickery, and a newly hired assistant, Jim Collins, a former magician, master mechanic, and cabinetmaker. Collins doubled in brass—as did everyone in the retinue—not only taking Houdini's rough ideas and bringing them to workable fruition, but also serving as a member of any impartial committee called up from the audience to "insure fair play." Bess functioned in almost as many capacities, serving as comptroller, liaison between her husband and his assistants, and wardrobe mistress—which also meant fussing over Harry to "look decent" and getting him to clean his dirty fingernails, replace his scrubby shoes with the turned-up toes, and put on a clean collar.

Houdini's mind wasn't focused on his appearance off-stage. Instead, it was on matters he considered of utmost importance, such as planning his acts, improving his German in order to perfect his patter, seeking out more and more collectibles, conniving to get more newspaper space for his publicity efforts, and jotting down new "challenge" handbills on scraps of paper.

For the rest of 1908 and into 1909, the Houdinis and their entourage moved from town to town in Europe. They traveled in two private railroad cars. One carried baggage, props, and Houdini's specially constructed library, built to house his artifacts and books and the "shop," where Collins made keys and challenge devices. The other carriage carried "the family"—Harry, Bess, Kukol, Vickery, Collins, George Brooks (another assistant added for the European tour), and Little Charlie Dog, a Russian Pomeranian, supposedly given to the Houdinis by the grand duke of Russia and to whom the childless couple were devoted.

The only alteration in his act, besides the absence of the familiar handcuffs, was the introduction of restraints used by insane asylums. Discarding the straitjacket for "crazy cribs," an oysterlike rocking apparatus used for the violently insane and those suffering from delirium tremens, and "wet blankets," soaked linen bandages designed to render the captive totally helpless, he imparted a new sense of showmanship to make even his escapes from these restraints dramatic.

The rest of the trip through Europe was uneventful, except for a visit from both mothers-in-law and the death of Little Charlie Dog. Uneventful, that is, until Hamburg.

While playing at the A. M. and Hansa Theatre in November 1909, Houdini heard of an aviation exhibition at a flying field adjoining a local racetrack. From the moment he saw the French Voisin biplane, a new passion entered his life. Gone were all thoughts of art, paintings, and lithographs. The only thing that mattered was the delicately frail flying machine comprised of boxed wings, three strutted bicycle wheels, and an English E.V.N. 10.80-horsepower engine. It was a challenge, not just to own but to fly. Houdini instantly believed he could add the conquest of space to his earthbound conquests.

He watched the pilot soar into the air, circle the field, and come in for a perfect landing. He was like a little kid with his nose pressed against the candy shop window. The minute the plane landed, he was running ahead of the pack to ask the pilot questions: What was it? How much did it cost? And, of course, how could he get one?

Houdini moved with his usual impetuosity. Within a week he had bought a similar plane for 25,000 francs directly from Voisin. He hired a mechanic, rented a makeshift hangar at the nearby Hufaren parade grounds in Wandsbek from the German army, in exchange for his agreeing to teach some of the officers to fly, and immediately added his own touch. He painted the word *HOUDINI* on the rudder in red block letters.

Every morning at dawn he would motor out to the parade grounds for flying lessons from his French mechanic, Brassac. He would sit behind the controls of his grounded machine, with his cap on backwards in the seemingly reckless pose all aviators assumed, while the mechanic taught him how to use the controls, how to get the plane aloft, how to catch the breeze, and how to land. Houdini the student absorbed everything Brassac taught him and then asked questions. Time and again, Houdini would be driven out to the parade grounds, anticipating his solo flight, only to find that the biting winter wind and snow flurries had once again limited his training to on-the-ground instruction.

Finally the weather broke and it was time to put his textbook learning to use. He got the flimsy plane aloft, and then boom! "I smashed the machine. Broke propeller all to hell," wrote the momentarily discouraged aviator in his diary. But the unhurt Houdini was undaunted. He had been challenged, and he responded as he did to all challenges: he would overcome.

On the morning of November 26, 1909, Houdini climbed into the pilot's seat, clutched the wheel, and nodded to Brassac, who yanked at the wooden propeller, setting it in motion. The engine fired and Houdini raced it. He gave the thumb's-up motion and the mechanic removed the wheel chocks. The fragile aircraft slowly lurched forward. It began to pick up speed, bumping along the less-than-even parade grounds, and finally the Voisin was airborne. Houdini was flying! Climbing to a

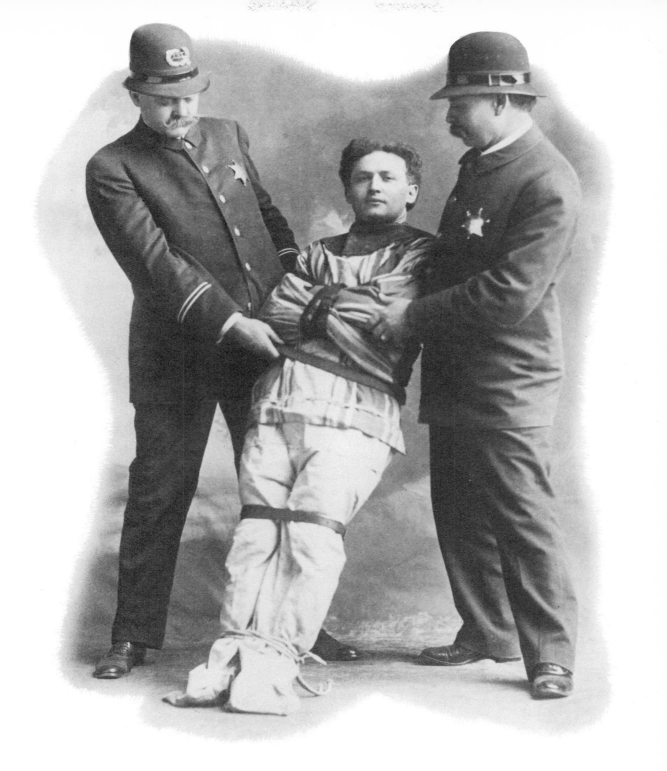

height of over fifty feet, he cleared the treetops and flew over the parade grounds two, then three times, banking in wide circles. Finally, after a few minutes, he made his landing approach. It, too, went as smoothly as the takeoff and maneuvers aloft. As he taxied to a halt in front of Brassac, Houdini felt the same exhilaration he had felt when he first conquered the straitjacket and the packing box. He had conquered gravity!

During the rest of his two-month stay in Hamburg, he spent his mornings at the Hufaren parade grounds, flying his Voisin for as long as ten minutes at a time. Now as an accomplished aviator he made good his promise to the young officers stationed in the area, and began to teach them the rudiments of flying, just as he had learned. At a

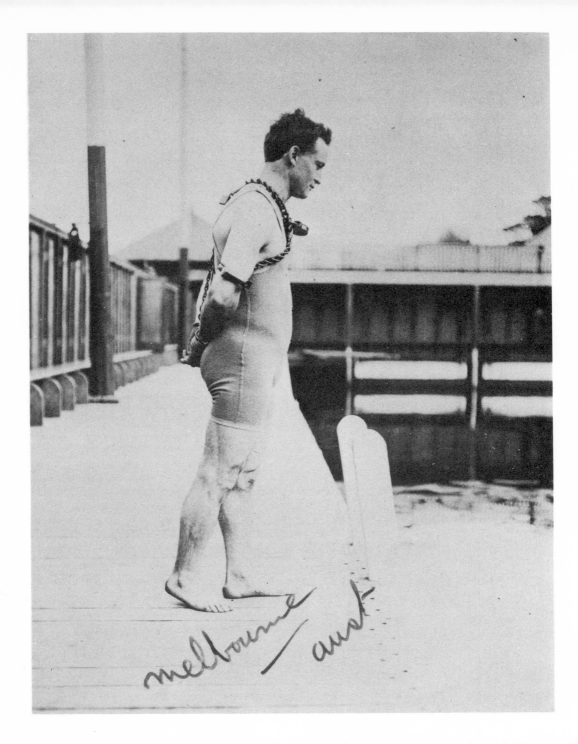

bond rally during World War I, Houdini was to say, half in shame and half in mock appreciation of his talent, "And to think I taught all those Germans how to fly."

On January 7, 1910, Harry Houdini set sail for Australia, having demanded, and received, "full salary while on board the steamer." Houdini had proudly noted in his diary that he got "paid twelve weeks for resting and twelve for working. This is the only condition I would go all that distance." The management of the New Opera House in Melbourne heralded him as "Absolutely the Greatest and most Sensational Act that has ever been engaged by any manager."

In the hold of the *Malwa*, along with his theatrical props, was the dismantled Voisin, and the Houdini family was further expanded to include Brassac, the French mechanic. Houdini had determined to take his new, albeit expensive, hobby along with him.

After a twenty-nine-day journey, during which the constantly seasick Houdini lost over twenty pounds, they arrived in Adelaide. Houdini's first order of business was clearing the Voisin through customs, a privilege he paid a duty of 154 pounds for. They next made their way to Melbourne, where he was the stellar attraction at the New Opera House—"The Talk of the Town in Train, Tram and Taxi," as the ads proclaimed. Houdini opened his act with films of his jumps and escapes from the Friederichstrasse Bridge in Berlin, from the roof of the Morgue in Paris, and from bridges throughout the United States. He followed up with vintage Houdini escapes, including the straitjacket and the milk can.

But it was his bridge jumps that had captured the imagination of the Aussies and of impressario Harry Richards. And so, less than two weeks after opening at the New Opera House, Houdini planned one of his patented bridge jumps off the Queen's Bridge spanning the Yarra River in downtown Melbourne.

Ever since he had made his first bridge jump ten years before in Dresden, it had been one of Houdini's favorite publicity stunts. In his mind's eye, he not only created it—he owned it. There was hardly a river or harbor in Northern France, Germany, or England into which

Houdini had not jumped with his hands and feet manacled, as thousands of onlookers cheered his efforts. But his success begat imitators, and just as he used it to publicize his shows and stimulate record houses wherever he went, others now tried to duplicate it, although not always with the same success. Alburtus had attempted it in Atlantic City and had had to be saved by lifeguards from drowning. Menkis had been brought up in an unconscious state when he tried it. And an entertainer named Ricardo had jumped handcuffed from the Luippold Bridge in Landshut, Bavaria, just the previous April and drowned.

Fifteen thousand Aussies, intrigued by the derring-do of the Yank, crowded the banks of the Yarra to watch the manacled Houdini leap into its chilly waters. As Houdini jumped into the water, a corpse from a recent suicide jump from the very same bridge floated to the surface, dislodged by the impact. Most of those in the crowd thought it was Houdini. When the self-liberator came to the surface, he was so shaken by the experience of seeing a dead body floating close by that, in the words of one of

the Melbourne papers, he "froze" and had to be assisted to the nearby boat.

The rest of Houdini's stay down under met with a similar lack of success. The impatient Aussies refused to sit still for the necessary half-hour while Houdini struggled with a challenge device inside the curtained cabinet, and Houdini was forced to cancel engagements in other cities on the Australian continent, but not before making an 89-foot jump from a Sydney bridge, hitting the water at a wrong angle, and bloodying his mouth and nose.

But his lack of stage success was counterbalanced by the success he had in his new avocation—flying. Uncrating the component parts of the Voisin on February 22, Houdini and Brassac took them to a field called Digger's Rest twenty-five miles outside of Melbourne. There they reassembled the aircraft. The Enfield 80-horsepower engine was overhauled, and by March 1 the craft was ready. But the treacherous winds that buffeted the airfield kept both Houdini and a Wright plane that had been brought in for the first air flight grounded. Houdini slept with his passion, racing from the New Opera House to the airfield after every performance in a motor car he had just learned to drive.

On March 16, 1910, Harry Houdini strode out of the tent that served both as hangar and sleeping quarters, threw a scarf jauntily around his neck, and settled into the pilot's seat as Brassac had the Voisin wheeled into takeoff position. Within minutes Brassac had engaged the motor and removed the moorings, and Houdini was ready. He nodded to his mechanic, set his jaw firmly, and took the 11,000-pound aircraft up. Getting the speed up to over fifty miles an hour, Houdini circled the field for over three minutes, becoming the first man ever to make a sustained flight on the Australian continent. Once again Harry Houdini was news, even if the magazines couldn't quite decipher his reason for flying. One of the leading magazines wondered aloud, "Here is Houdini, who is an amateur, a beginner. He has taught himself to fly here amongst us, and he has shown us what his machine can do. He may be doing it for advertising or he may be doing it for love of adventure." But, the article concluded, "The reason doesn't matter." Hailed by the Aerial League of Australia with a winged trophy set on a mahogany plaque for "the first aerial flight in Australia," Houdini was positive that future generations would remember him best as a pioneer airman. He wrote to one of his correspondents, "Even if history forgets Houdini, the Handcuff King, it must write down my name as the first man to fly here." Then he added characteristically, "Not that it will put any jam on my bread."

When Houdini left Australia on May 11, 1910, on the *Manuka*, he left behind several unfilled engagements, a new record as an aviator and his desire ever to fly or drive a car again.

Rochester N.Y. 1908

The first decade of the twentieth century still retained one vestige of the nineteenth—the sentimentalizing of that sacred institution known as motherhood. Men sang "M-O-T-H-E-R, a word that means the world to me" with moist eyes and commemorated motherhood in pictures by Whistler and poems by Kipling.

For although it may have been a man's world, a woman had her world too. But her world was her family. Her mission on earth was to find a husband, obey him, make him happy, and replenish the human race with children—lots of them. A woman's entire domestic satisfaction was wrapped up in her family. And her family reciprocated. Whether it was a backhanded chauvinism which deified their position or the adoring view of sons and daughters who idolized those who bore them, mothers were worshiped by all.

But no one worshiped his mother more passionately than Harry Houdini. Ever since that day on his twelfth birthday when his father had made him swear on the Torah to take care of his mother, Houdini had more than fulfilled his pledge. As the country sang "I Want a Girl Just Like the Girl that Married Dear Old Dad," Cecilia Weiss's adoring son sought to be with her whenever he

could, most especially on that second Sunday in May 1912—a day then gaining nationwide observance as Mother's Day.

While playing at Hammerstein's Victoria Theatre in New York in 1912, Houdini asked Willie Hammerstein for his weekly salary in gold. Hammerstein acceded to his odd request and gave Houdini a heavy canvas bag laden with one thousand dollars in gold coins. Then, after having his assistants polish the "double eagles," he entered his mother's room at 278 and is said by Bess to have cried, "Mother, Mother, do you remember the promise I made to father years ago; that I would always look after you? Look what I bring you now! Hold out your apron!" And with that he poured the glittering contents of the bag into his ancient mother's lap. His mother clasped her son to her bosom, and tears streamed down the cheeks of both of them.

The Victoria Theatre stood proudly at Broadway and 42nd Street. Known to theatergoers as Hammerstein's Roof Garden, it combined a theater, smoking room, music hall, billiard room, and Oriental café.—all for fifty cents. The main attraction at Hammerstein's was the Roof Garden, with windows on all sides, a huge onstage tank that held nine thousand gallons of water, and a

moving roof that slowly receded to reveal the stars. Stars also shone brightly on Hammerstein's stage; stars like Will Rogers, Gertrude Hoffman, and Bert Williams. And waiting in the wings to titillate the customers were wrestlers, bicycle riders, men with seventeen-foot beards, Polar explorers, notorious ladies who had just ventilated their lovers, French apache dancers, or—Hammerstein's most famous act of all—the Cherry Sisters, billed as "America's Worst Act." They were so bad that they sang behind a huge net, which protected them from the rotten fruit hurled by the audience. Hammerstein, a latter-day Barnum, also featured hoaxes. Among these was Abdul Kadar (the court artist of the Turkish sultan), and his

three veiled wives. Kadar was in reality a German named Adolph Schneider, and his three veiled wives were his wife, daughter, and sister-in-law, who avoided talking to reporters by falling to their knees and shouting the name of Allah whenever questioned.

It was said by one observer that if Keith and Albee ruled vaudeville, "Willie Hammerstein ruled the heart." This was THE BIG TIME, and Houdini, the first silent act ever to be booked as a headliner at the Roof Garden, den, wanted to make good.

By 1912 Americans had grown blasé about his underwater escapes from handcuffs and manacles. As the self-proclaimed "Self-Liberator," Houdini now sought something more newsworthy to publicize his appearance at Hammerstein's. For over a year the man who was fascinated by graveyards and cemetery vaults had been developing a "buried alive escape." Now he worked on coordinating it with his opening at the Roof Garden, both as a replacement for his jumps into water and as a publicity stunt to break into the New York papers.

For a week prior to his July 1 opening, the passersby at the municipal swimming pool on 80th Street and the East River witnessed a strange daily ritual. A man with his wrists firmly clasped with two pairs of handcuffs and his ankles bound together by a pair of ugly leg irons was nailed up in what appeared to be an unusually strong packing case reinforced by rope and steel bands, and then lowered into the shallow end of the pool by four men. In another minute, they would have seen the man bob up to the surface, free of the manacles. It was Harry Houdini experimenting with a new trick—the packing box escape.

Six days after his opening at Hammerstein's, thou-

The Packing Box Escape, shown here in sequence. Houdini is manacled, nailed into the crate, and lowered

gingerly into the water by a trusted assistant, only to appear smiling at the surface several seconds later.

sands of handbills were passed out up and down Broadway heralding the trick Houdini called "the submersible Iron-Bound Box Mystery." Houdini was to be manacled with leg irons, two pairs of handcuffs, and elbow irons, placed into a large wooden box 40 inches by 22 inches by 24 inches, and then—after the box was nailed in place with thirty-six wire nails and banded with band iron (or, in technical language, "packed for export")—he was to be thrown into the river.

As a crowd of curiosity-seekers and well-wishers, together with members of the press, began to congregate along the sea wall overlooking Pier 6 on the East River, the New York police interrupted the proceedings. But Houdini was equal to the interruption and transferred the scene of operations to the deck of a large barge that was, coincidentally, standing nearby and which he seemingly commandeered. The barge took the party to the dock of the Federal Quartermaster's Department at Governor's Island, far from local police interference.

The handbills had noted that his trained assistants were instructed that "in the event of Houdini's not appearing within three minutes, they are to dive in and get the box with grappling irons and do their utmost to save his life." And the owners of the barge required that he sign a release for all damages in case of accident. But the intrepid performer didn't need any such prophylaxis. His flirtation with death had been carefully worked out. After being shackled hand and foot, nailed up in the packing case, and weighted down with two hundred pounds of lead, Houdini was slowly lowered down a chute into the water—not "thrown in" as announced. Almost one minute later Houdini surfaced, free of all manacles. He had escaped from the box without drawing either a breath or a nail!

The only thing that marred the otherwise perfect stunt was the appearance of two moving picture cameramen, who had forced their way aboard the barge. Houdini demanded they leave immediately, hollering that he did not intend to "do an act for the benefit of moving picture theatres." After much pushing and shoving, the two cameramen were finally removed, but one succeeded in getting aboard a police patrol boat and shooting the escape from there.

Despite this minor altercation, the escape was an unmitigated sensation. For the first time Harry Houdini was news in the Big City—his city. Not only did the escape create such widespread excitement that it made his act at Hammerstein's a success, but it became part of his act. Starting the following week, every night in the pool atop the theater, Houdini duplicated the perilous trick that was now called "one of the most difficult feats that has ever been attempted by himself or any other daredevil artist." Called by Houdini "my challenge to Death," it was soon to replace his much-imitated bridge jump.

Houdini was a one-man band, throwing off

sparks in the form of new acts, publicity stunts, inventions, pamphlets, and press releases. His four-week engagement at Hammerstein's was extended for another four weeks as one publicity stunt followed another. He conceived of leaping from a Wright airplane over New York while handcuffed and releasing himself on the way down in time to pull the parachute's rip cord. But high winds in the cavernous city streets dictated against such an ambitious idea. Instead, he had himself bound by rope to a girder high atop the Heidelberg Building Tower across the street from the Victoria by construction workers building the skyscraper. He escaped with ease and came down to entertain the reporters with a display of exotic knots supposedly used to truss him up. Houdini had captured the imagination of the newsmen and the public, so much so that he commanded more newspaper space than Jim Thorpe's pentathlon and decathlon victories at the Olympics in Stockholm or Teddy Roosevelt's Bull Moose campaign; and more customers than the competing "Passing Show" revue at the Winter Garden or the Ziegfeld Follies at the Jardin de Paris atop the New York Theatre. Houdini the incandescent was the talk of New York!

If his offstage exploits captured headlines, his onstage acts were just as heroic: he escaped from the locked milk can filled with water; from a straitjacket strapped on by asylum attendants; from soaked sheets wrapped about him by a committee of graduate nurses; from a Chinese punishment frame to which he was roped and chained by three Chinese soldiers; from an export packing case; from a solid-leather, copper-riveted punishment suit strapped on by U.S. Marine officers; and from any other devious device the citizens of New York, with the help of Harry Houdini's fertile imagination, could devise for the Self-Liberator.

By 1912 the milk can escape had become old hat. Not only was it advertised in the Mysto Magic Company's catalogue for $35, but escapologists everywhere were even imitating Houdini's dress and his speech. They were now also emulating his success with his "1908 can," as he called it. To counteract their success and the lessening impact he was having with his own invention, he attempted to vary the act. First he filled it with beer, but the teetotaling Houdini almost succumbed to the alcoholic fumes. Next he had the "air-tight Galvanized Can, filled with water" placed upside down in "a hermetically-sealed iron-bound wooden chest," and the lid clamped down and fastened with padlocks by members of the committee called onstage from the audience. "Failure to escape," the playbill exclaimed," means death by drowning," a more grammatical caveat than the poster for the original can.

Nothing seemed to deter his imitators or stop his star from falling. Previously competition had driven the impetuous Houdini to great lengths to eliminate it, whether by facing it in a direct challenge or by instituting legal

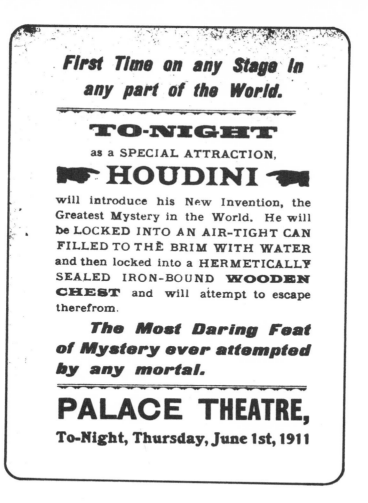

First Time on any Stage in any part of the World.

TO-NIGHT

as a SPECIAL ATTRACTION,

▶ HOUDINI ◀

will introduce his New Invention, the Greatest Mystery in the World. He will be LOCKED INTO AN AIR-TIGHT CAN FILLED TO THE BRIM WITH WATER and then locked into a HERMETICALLY SEALED IRON-BOUND **WOODEN CHEST** and will attempt to escape therefrom.

The Most Daring Feat of Mystery ever attempted by any mortal.

PALACE THEATRE,

To-Night, Thursday, June 1st, 1911

proceedings to enjoin competitors from using his inventions. Now he sought something else, something better.

Looking for that something better, Houdini dedicated himself to discovering new tricks. Up to this point, most of Houdini's escapes had been concealed, accomplished behind the curtains of his "ghost house." In an effort to add showmanship to the illusion—like the suggestiveness of a beautiful female body draped in a diaphanous covering—he began to experiment with visible escapes.

Finally, that something better evolved out of his experimentation with the milk can. The idea of escaping from an upside-down position—from which escape seemed impossible—intrigued him, and together with Collins he worked tirelessly on trying out tanks filled with water in which he was suspended head downward. After many months, Houdini and Collins perfected their idea, known as the Chinese Water Torture Cell to the world and the U.S.D. (for "upside down") to Houdini.

The man who made the impossible possible described the U.S.D. as consisting "of the performer being locked into a narrow Water Torture Cell filled with water while standing on head, ankles clamped and locked above in center of massive cover and escaping therefrom in this upside down position." The walls were made of glass so

that spectators could watch every stage of the incarceration and see him hanging, head down, in the water. This was unconcealed drama. And it was to be the fulfillment of his career and his signature act. Like the mythological phoenix, Houdini was once again to rise from the ashes of his own career!

With an eye toward protecting his secret, Houdini ordered the component parts of the water torture cell from several different manufacturers. Appreciating the scant protection given by the patent laws of the United States, he decided on a novel course of protection. He would apply to the British Lord Chamberlain for a license for a stage play with the water torture cell as an integral part of the play. The play, together with its lesser features, including the Chinese water torture cell, would then gain the protection of the British Crown.

Houdini crated his water torture cell and set sail for Europe. As always, Houdini and his mother embraced tearfully until pried apart and then waved handkerchiefs at each other until the ship had made its turn in New York Harbor and the communicants were no longer visible. The departure of the *Kaiser Wilhelm II* was no different. As it took its famous passenger and his soon-to-be-famous contraption to England, Mrs. Weiss stood sadly at dockside waving to her adoring son, slowly disappear-

This bill gives an excellent idea of what Houdini's act consisted of at the time of his return to Great Britain.

ing into the east.

Harry Houdini then presented his production to the Lord Chamberlain in the form of a playlet. Approval and protection were granted. He immediately sent out letters to all theaters reading, "I wish to warn managers and the profession in general that I invented another sensation, vis-a-vis, the Water Torture Cell, which is the greatest feat I have ever attempted in strenuous career and hereby wish to give notice that I have *Special License from the Lord Chamberlain,* as a stage play and I will certainly stop anyone infringing on my rights."

When the Circus Busch opened in Berlin that September, the featured star was Houdini and the featured act, the Chinese water torture cell. As the expectant audience leaned forward in its seats, the well-built little magician in a tuxedo came to the center of the stage and in halting German tinged with Yiddish addressed the audience:

"Ladies and gentlemen, in introducing my original invention the Water Torture cell.... Although there is nothing supernatural about it, I am willing to forfeit the sum of $1,000 to anyone who can know that it is possible to obtain air inside of the Torture Cell when I am locked up in it in the regulation manner after it has been filled with water. I will first thoroughly explain the apparatus, and then I will invite a committee to step upon the stage to examine everything to see that things are just as I represent. The cover is made to fit into the steel frame which prevents it from being opened even if it were not locked. The steel grill acts for the double-fold purpose of condensing the space inside of the Torture Cell which at the same time prevents my turning around even were I capable of throwing both of my feet through the cover. In front, a plate of glass for self-protection. Should anything go wrong when I am locked up, as it's absolutely impossible to obtain air, one of my assistants watches through the curtains, ready in case of emergency, with an axe, to rush in, demolishing the glass, allowing the water to flow out, in order to save my life. I honestly and positively do not expect any accident to happen, but we all know accidents *will* happen and when least expected. The bands of steel form an impromptu cage held together with padlocks that enclose the same. I would like to invite eight, ten or twelve gentlemen to kindly step up on the stage. I assure you I have no confederates, and any gentleman is perfectly welcome. A staircase at your service on this side of the stage, and now is your opportunity. I thank you for your attention."

Then, as his assistants started pouring 100 gallons of warm water into the cell through a hose, Houdini retired to his dressing room to change into a black one-piece bathing suit. Reappearing, he lay on the floor as the stocks were fitted around his ankles and his hands were cuffed. Then the entire apparatus was raised and Houdini was slowly lowered head down into the water-filled cell. "The Justly World-Famous Self-Liberator" was then padlocked in, visible for all to see through the glass and the horizontal bars of the cage. A curtain was dropped over the entire cell, and as the orchestra struck up "Asleep in the Deep," Kukol and Collins took their places, with their fire axes poised for the moment when they might be needed. This was all high melodrama, and the audience responded with claustrophobic gasps and heart-wrenching shrieks. And then, a little over two minutes later, just as the axes were raised for the impending moment of truth, the curtains parted and a wet and smiling Houdini came out to the erupting roar of the German audience. The Chinese water torture cell with all its padlocks was still intact, but minus Houdini.

This twenty-five-minute act was a resounding success not only with the first audience, but with all audiences who saw it for the next fourteen years. It was to become, in Houdini's own words to his friend and fellow magician Will Goldston, "a marvelous success, and is without doubt the greatest spectacular thing ever witnessed on the stage."

But Houdini was so obsessed by the thought of someone stealing it that, once he went on stage, any performer still backstage was locked in his room until after the act.

As Houdini took the Chinese water torture cell, "His Own Original Invention; The Greatest Sensational Mystery Ever Attempted in this Or Any Other Age," from European city to city, he no longer had to worry about novelty escapes. His greatness had been achieved. He was the greatest escape artist of all time.

Houdini interrupted his successful European tour during the spring of 1913 to return home. He took a two-week engagement at Hammerstein's Roof Garden in order to be at the side of his failing mother. Both Willie Hammerstein and Cecilia Weiss were elated. Hammerstein would have his top attraction back for two weeks at the height of the season and Mother Weiss would have her son back to help celebrate her seventy-second birthday.

Remembering the dramatic stunts Houdini had concocted to publicize his opening the previous season, Hammerstein's press agent attempted to see him and raise him one. He contacted the captain of the famous convict ship *Success*, which had been raised from the bottom of Sydney Harbor and was now anchored at 79th Street and Riverside Drive. The log of the eighteenth-century vessel showed that she had never lost a prisoner. Houdini sought to become the first ever to escape from one of the *Success*'s narrow ancient cells. Demanding only "fair play," Houdini was chained in massive ring bolts in a cell below the water line and locked behind a bolted door. Within an hour, Houdini had got out of the chains and was swimming around in the Hudson River, the massive door left locked behind him.

The publicity generated by Houdini's escape, coupled with his return as the stellar attraction of the Roof Gar-

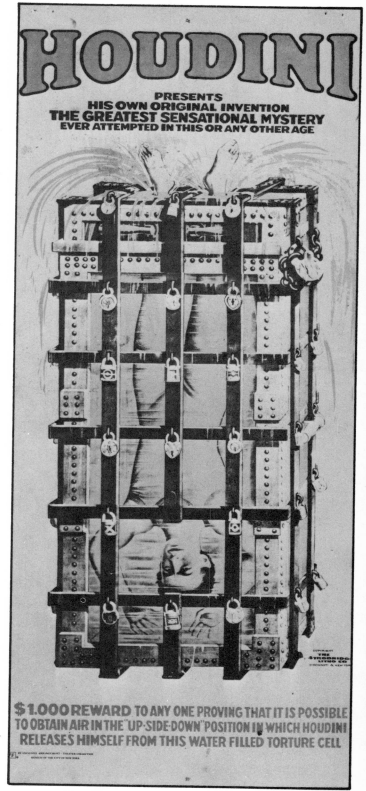

A poster for the Water Torture Cell Escape.

den, made for a successful two-week appearance. Houdini's act consisted of the milk can placed inside an iron-bound wooden chest, his Hindoo needle trick, and, eventually, the American introduction of the Chinese water torture cell. Both the audience and the formerly impervious New York press were ecstatic. A newly won-over critic wrote of Houdini: "One follows his entrances and exits as breath-batedly as if he were pushing himself through the small and hindermost entrance of a Yale lock. And he would get himself out of there—that's the wonder of the man."

After the close of his two-week engagement, Houdini repaired to 278 for three weeks. There he began cataloguing his disorganized collections and books, now thrown about in utmost confusion; answering his mail; filing as many as seven copies of his correspondence away for himself and posterity; and attending to his mother. Even though he pampered her and even threw a birthday party for her seventy-second birthday on June 16, it was obvious that she was suffering the infirmities that attend advancing age. Prior to his sailing for Copenhagen, where he was to open July 18, Houdini made arrangements with his brother Hardeen, then playing in Asbury Park, New Jersey, to look after Mama.

On the morning of Tuesday, July 8, the dockside scene next to the *Kronprinzessin Cäcilie* was a strange one. Any bystander who stopped long enough to take note would have seen a grown man in a rumpled black suit and porkpie hat clinging to a little woman dressed in black silk, capped with a black bonnet. They were embracing and kissing each other in as sentimental a leave-taking as the West Side piers had ever experienced. Asked if there was anything he could get for her, the ancient woman answered, *"Nicht vergess' nummer sechs"* ("Don't forget, slippers, size six," referring to a pair of night slippers she wanted.). Then the man went up the gangplank, only to return time and again to embrace her and repeat the entire ritual all over. The woman was heard to murmur *"Ehrich, vielleicht wenn du zuruck kommst bin ich nicht hier"* ("Perhaps I shall not be here when you come home"). Finally, pried loose by the petite woman, who hurried him up the gangplank just before it was drawn up for the noon sailing, he said to those standing nearby, "See, my mother drives me away from her." As the

moorings were released and the anchor hauled up, the man stood at the railing with hat in hand and—partly in reverence to the little old lady on the pier and partly so she could more readily identify him from a distance—threw paper streamers at her. The last sight he had was of her holding a paper streamer while he leaned far over the railing holding the other end.

Cecilia Weiss was never to wear those slippers. Hardeen was appearing at the Lyric Theatre in Asbury Park, and Mama Weiss went down to be with him and his wife, Elsie. On the night of July 14, Cecilia suffered a paralytic stroke in her room at the Imperial Hotel. Two days later she died trying to form the words of a message to her son Ehrich. Hardeen immediately dispatched a telegram to his brother in Hamburg: "The almighty has called for darling mother." Houdini had just left for his next engagement. The cable was relayed ahead. According to Houdini, "I had just arrived in Copenhagen, Denmark, and on reaching the station, my chief assistant handed me the cablegram, which had arrived 20 minutes before the train."

Houdini was a man in a trance. Bess had to take over. She packed and made plans for their immediate return. They caught the first train back to Germany and booked passage on the very same vessel on which they had just arrived. In Bremen, the bereaved son bought that pair of slippers, "nummer sechs," as a fond remembrance of his mother's last wish.

Houdini had left Denmark in such haste that he didn't have time to communicate fully his personal crisis to the manager of the *Cirkus Beketow* in Copenhagen. In the manager's eye, the contract had been broken, an act so serious in Denmark that it subjects a man to imprisonment. The authorities promptly arrested the loyal Houdini aide, Jimmy Collins, who had successfully impersonated his boss, and placed him in jail. Houdini, meanwhile, made his way back to America, reaching New York on Tuesday, July 29, in time for his mother's interment at Machpelah Cemetery the next day. Just before her body was laid to rest beside her husband's, the inconsolable Houdini placed the small woolen slippers in the casket as a small token of his pledge always to care for her.

Houdini's mother waving goodbye from dockside, as he was leaving for Europe in 1913. It was the last time he saw her.

ACT 5
SORROW, STRAITJACKETS, AND VANISHING ELEPHANTS

The sound that had died on Cecilia's lips resembled the word *forgive*. Hardeen guessed what the message meant; so did Houdini, though in a later communication to his brother he admitted, "Time heals all wounds, but a long time will have to pass before it will heal the terrible blow MOTHER tried to save me from knowing." At the time of Cecilia's death, six of the seven Weiss children were still alive, only Herman having predeceased her in 1885. The oldest surviving son was Nathan, or "Nat," who owned a restaurant down by the old Madison Square Garden at Madison Avenue and East 26th Street. The Toots Shor of his day, Nat went to sporting events all over the world and drank more than his share. High living finally caught up with him, breaking up his marriage and, in the vernacular of the day, forcing him to go into the soda-pop business or on the wagon. Houdini's youngest brother, Leopold, an X-ray technician, first comforted Nat's wife, the distraught Sadie, and then ultimately married her. Nat had expected it and accepted the marriage between Leopold and Sadie as a good thing. Everyone else in the family also accepted it—everyone except Houdini, who was obsessed with his duty to hold the family together. He had looked after his young brother, put him through medical school and even provided him with laboratory facilities at 278. His high moral standards had been compromised, his name defamed. No matter what the message had said, the Great Houdini couldn't forgive Leopold for his breach of those standards and for besmirching the family name. His sense of morality was absolute. From the day he learned that Sadie had left Nat for Leopold, Houdini had not talked to his kid brother; nor would he for the rest of his life. The man who had spent his life flouting the laws of society now demanded they be obeyed with slavish attention—particularly by his own family.

In the weeks that followed his mother's death, the depths of Houdini's despair knew no bounds. He would wake from fitful sleeps and walk for hours on end, usually winding up in a graveyard—any graveyard. His discussions were distracted and filled with morbid undertones. He read and reread his mother's precious letters and every day he visited his mother's grave and poured out his heart to her, trying to communicate and pierce the thick darkness of futurity in both English and German. For the remainder of his life, his very first act on arriving in New York and his last act before leaving New York was always to visit the grave of Mama.

Harry Houdini
June 22/1913
New York U.S.A.

CECELIA WEISS
BORN STEINER
JUNE SIXTEEN 1841

GONE TO HER ETERNAL REST
JULY 17 1913
She lived for others.

In memoriam

IF GOD IN HIS
GREATNESS EVER
SENT AN ANGEL
ON EARTH IN
HUMAN FORM, IT
WAS MY MOTHER

HARRY HOUDINI.

Nothing could salve the heart of the adoring son. He lost interest in his work and, according to Bess, "also in his manifold collections and his professional contacts."

His mother's death was the watershed in Houdini's life. From that moment on, the youthful quality that had carried Houdini to success after success in the face of life's challenges disappeared. At thirty-nine, the graying man no longer possessed that delicious little-boy quality he had always had. He mellowed perceptibly. For Harry Houdini, his mother's death marked the beginning of his attempt to solve what he called "the Great Mystery"—communication with the dead.

The moody and dazed Houdini stayed cloistered in his house on West 113th Street for two more months. Then he tried losing himself in his work. He booked another tour of Europe for the remainder of the 1913 season and into 1914. But it didn't work. He walked through his act, merely reciting his now-static patter from memory and going through the motions of escape, much like one of Robert-Houdin's automatons. The old Houdini fire that one critic had described as "intense originality" was gone. On November 22 he wrote to Hardeen, "Dash, its TOUGH, and I can't seem to get *over it*. Some times I feel alright, but when a calm moment arrives I am as bad as ever."

On April 6, 1914, Houdini celebrated his fortieth

birthday in Edinburgh, Scotland, for since "Darling Mother...always wrote me on April 6th, that will be my adopted birthdate."

The world and its institutions were on the threshold of enormous change. Already legions of Serbs, known as "the Union of Death," were plotting the assassination of Archduke Francis Ferdinand, heir to the thrones of Austria and Hungary; an act that would trigger the bloodiest war in the history of mankind. Nothing would ever again be the same. Show business was no different. Houdini would never again play on the Continent.

During his London tour that May, an old magician named Sidney Josolyne visited him backstage at the New Cross Empire Theatre. Josolyne offered Houdini the secret to his "walking through the wall of steel" illusion, which Houdini purchased on May 4 for three pounds. The contract was hastily written on the back of a will which Houdini had in his pocket and which had been made in Hanover, Germany, in 1901, leaving "50% of all monies" to his brother "Theo. Hardeen" and the other 50% to his wife. It was a trick Houdini would further enhance and present the following summer at Hammerstein's.

Wars build high walls between generations. Postwar generations politely turn their backs on the people and the pastimes of the prewar generations. But Houdini would walk through that wall of generations, just as he was soon to walk through a wall of his own making.

Harry Houdini, the man who had escaped from every known restraint, had finally escaped from his own walled-in state of despondency. From his almost-planned decline he now designed his own reemergence to burst on the American—and the world's—consciousness again. For the moment, all his thoughts were on the future and how he could best conquer the challenge of change.

On June 18, Houdini sailed for New York on the Hamburg Amerika Line's *Imperator*. The nine-month trip in Europe had been a tonic for him. Not only had he purchased the "walking through the wall of steel" illusion, but also he had his third straight year at Hammerstein's to look forward to. And in four days it would be his and Bess's twentieth anniversary. He planned a dinner aboard ship to celebrate.

One of his fellow passengers was Colonel Theodore Roosevelt, who had returned the previous winter from the famous River of Doubt in South America. On the second day out of Liverpool, the two men were taking a brisk walk on deck, discussing Houdini's newest obsession since the death of his mother—spiritualism. Even in those days of luxurious transatlantic travel, shipboard entertainments frequently drew upon the professional talents to be found on the passenger list. An officer of the *Imperator* approached Houdini, the most famous entertainer on board, and asked if he would give a performance for the ship's passengers that night. "Go ahead, Houdini," exclaimed the excitable former president,

"give us a little séance."

That evening Houdini began with some card sleights of hand in which Roosevelt was selected to pick the card. "I was amazed," wrote Houdini, "at the way he watched every one of the misdirection moves I made."

Next came slate writing by the spirits in response to TR's request. Slate writing is an old and honorable standby of mediums. The spectator writes a question, which he then conceals on a slip of paper. The paper is enclosed between two blank slates, and the stub of a pencil is usually inserted, with which the spirits are supposed to write an answer. In most cases the medium writes the answer with a thin piece of lead wedged under his fingernail while inserting either the paper or the pencil. But on this night at sea, Roosevelt took great pains to make sure that Houdini neither saw his question nor touched the slate board.

With his back turned to the great magician, Roosevelt wrote, "Where was I last Christmas?" He folded the paper carefully, sealed it in an envelope, and placed it between the two slates himself. When the slate boards were opened to the view of the small party, one slate revealed a many-colored map of the South American wilderness just recently explored by Colonel Roosevelt, with a legend reading, "Near the Andes." Roosevelt's entire itinerary was also outlined on the map, and the slate board bore the signature of W. T. Stead, the English editor and spiritualist who had been lost aboard the *Titanic* two years before, as the "control."

Roosevelt took the slate, looked at it, and asked, "How did you do that? Was it real spiritualism?"

Houdini only grinned at the Colonel and said, "It was just hocus-pocus."

It was, indeed, hocus-pocus, the type Houdini was famous for. As Houdini later related, "When I went to the steamship company to get my tickets, the man at the desk whispered, 'Teddy Roosevelt is on the boat, but don't tell anyone.' As I walked out, I began to think what I could do with the information, as I always give impromptu performances on shipboard. *The London Telegraph* was just beginning to publish the Colonel's story of his trip to South America, so I promptly went over to the *Telegraph* office to see what I could find out. I obtained an unpublished map of the trip, along with various inside information. Then I prepared my slates and was ready for the 'séance.' I found it easy to work the Colonel into a state of mind so that the suggestion of the séance would come from him.

"On the night of the séance I asked the passengers to write any question they wished. Then one question was to be selected from about half a dozen placed into a hat. I had secretly prepared half a dozen of my own, and, of course, intended to see that only my envelopes went into the hat, *all* of which contained the same question: 'Where was I last Christmas?' By a strange coincidence, he asked exactly that question.

Taken on Board the
Hamburg American Liner "IMPERATOR"
In Mid Ocean June 23, 1914.

"Here's how I got his message: The morning of the sé-ance I took two books from a table in the salon into my stateroom and cut them with a razor blade along the edges of the cover. Lifting up the outer cloth binding I inserted a sheet of white paper and on top of this a carbon sheet. Then I carefully glued the cloth binding back on the books, just as they had been, and replaced them in the salon. At the seance, I handed the Colonel a pencil and a piece of paper to write his questions on. As he started to write, with the paper in the palm of his hand, I exclaimed, 'Beg your pardon, Colonel,' and reached over and handed him one of the prepared books to rest his paper on.

"Victor Herbert, the great composer, was standing near Roosevelt, and said, "Turn around. Don't let him it. He'll read your questions by the movements of your pencil.' So the Colonel turned around and scribbled his question in such a position that I couldn't see him do it. But, of course, it made no difference to me! After he had sealed the question in an envelope, I reached over and took the book from him, ostensibly to replace it on the table. But, as I did so, I tore the cover and peeked at the question. Luckily, it proved to be the same question I had prepared for, and I didn't have to resort to sleight-of-hand, but boldly asked him to place his question between the slates himself. While I pretended to show all four

faces of the two slates, by manipulation I only showed three.

"My message from W. T. Stead was already on one slate. The Stead signature was copied from that of a number of his letters picked up in London."

Thus, Houdini's infinite patience, detailed planning, and painstaking preparation—called by him "hocus-pocus"—were the true explanation for this "trick," as they were for so many others the Master Magician performed.

To commemorate the encounter, which had been relayed to New York by the radio operator, Houdini had his picture taken with the Colonel on deck the next morning. Ignoring the many "extras" who crowded in on all sides of the twosome, he cut them out and sent the altered picture to his brother Willis with a see-what-a-celebrity-your-brother-is note: "There's the President and me." This was the Houdini of old, reveling in his self-importance.

Houdini began his third season at Hammerstein's on July 6, at a weekly salary of $1,200 a week. He escaped twice from packing boxes in New York Harbor to put New Yorkers on notice that Houdini was back. But it wasn't necessary. The story about the TR seance had preceded him in all the papers. Moreover, New Yorkers were already talking about Houdini's new illusion, which he had announced from the Victoria stage on opening night.

He promised to "present a feat which has, since the dawn of history, been considered an absolute impossibility. I shall endeavor to walk through a solid brick wall."

Drawing from his experience as a jailbreaker, Houdini embellished Josolyne's trick and substituted brick for steel. On the night of July 13, a steel beam, one foot wide and ten feet long, was wheeled out on the stage. Masons then set to work with bricks and mortar to build an eight-foot brick wall, while Houdini called for volunteers from the audience to serve as a committee. The twelve-man committee then assisted Houdini in laying down a seamless cloth rug which covered the main part of the stage, and over it a muslin sheet. This, Houdini told the audience in his loud and electrifying voice, which sounded in those pre-amplification days as if it were coming from inside a very large tin can, would "insure that no stage traps would be used." Once the bricklayers had completed their twenty-five minute task, and the wall was at an angle perpendicular to the audience, members of the committee were then dispersed to the four corners of the muslin sheet "to prevent any suspicion of trickery." Two three-fold screens were then brought out by Collins and Vickery and placed against the wall, one on each side, leaving only the end of the wall at right angles to the audience and and the top of the eight-foot barrier visible.

Houdini again pointed out to the audience that there could be no trapdoors and that he, obviously, couldn't scale the wall without being seen by the audience or leave the stage without being seen by the committeemen.

Then the music started and Houdini went behind the screen on the right side of the stage and raised his hands above the screen. "Here I am!" he yelled. A drumroll. He shouted, "I'm going... I'm going... I'm gone!" Then a cymbal. And from behind the other screen came the yell, "And now, here I am!" Houdini had walked through a solid brick wall. He had done the impossible.

Some illusions are so good and so fast that the mind boggles at them and after some speculation, gives up trying to comprehend what happened. The "walking through a solid brick wall" illusion was one of them. But this wasn't the reason this illusion was never shown beyond the two weeks Houdini featured it at Hammerstein's. Houdini had always tried to protect the "secrets" to his tricks and illusions. This was impossible with the brick wall illusion. Too many people, including most of the stagehands, could see how the trick was done—a defect that Houdini the perfectionist considered fatal to its continuation.

The trick was a simple but ingenious one. Despite his misdirection, Houdini had gone *underneath* the wall. There *had* been a trick down—but under the rug and the muslin, allowing a "give" in the center that was unnoticeable, even to the committeemen standing on the far edges of the rug and sheet. (In fact, if the men had

not been standing on the corners, the rug and sheet might have fallen in.) Passage underneath was possible only for a man of Houdini's agility. In his own private notes, Houdini described the working of the illusion: "A large trapdoor was set in the center of the stage. When the screens were in position, the door was opened from below. Both the cloth and the carpet, which were large in area, sagged with the weight of the performer's body, allowing sufficient space for him to work his way through, the cloth yielding as he progressed. The passage accomplished, the trap was closed, and no clew remained."

Another problem was that although Josolyne had sold Houdini the "right of doing the mystery," that right was somewhat more restricted than what Houdini had thought he was buying. Subsequent to Houdini's purchasing the right but prior to his introducing it on the stage of Hammerstein's, P. T. Selbit had introduced the illusion, using a brick wall and an agile girl performer, on the stage of the Liverpool Hippodrome. Moreover, Selbit claimed that he, not Josolyne, was the originator of the illusion. (In truth, the illusion dated back to 1898, when the Great Alexander walked through blocks of ice at the Palace Theatre in Dawson City, Alaska.)

In any case, after Houdini closed at the Victoria Theatre in July 1914, he never used the "walking through a solid brick wall" illusion again.

With Europe embroiled in the agonizing aftereffects of the assassination of Archduke Ferdinand on June 28, Houdini next went on a tour of the United States. He turned his attention to mining the rich vein of the American vaudeville circuit, and played cities that had never seen him or his straitjacket escape or his needle trick or his Chinese water cell before.

While he was in Kansas City, Houdini introduced another innovation to his offstage publicity stunts. Ever since that day back in St. John's when Houdini had first seen an inmate of a mental hospital try to get out of a "camisole," or straitjacket, he had been intrigued with its attention-getting possibilities. Hardeen had developed the exposed escape. Now Houdini would add his own touch—one he was to become famous for.

Houdini approached the Kansas City *Post* with an idea for a tie-in. He would escape from a straitjacket atop the Post Building while hanging upside down! The *Post*, also keenly aware of publicity that this would engender, agreed to the stunt and ran a full-page ad reading: "Under the auspices of the *Post*, Houdini, the originator of all his sensational methods of self-liberation, will attempt to release himself from a straitjacket hanging downward from the roof of the Post Building next Thursday at noon."

At noon on September 8, over 5,000 people crowded around the Post Building at Tenth and Walnut to see the man they had only heard about escape from a seemingly impossible position. Houdini and members of the city's detective bureau mounted a specially-built platform, and

100

as the crowd watched silently, policemen laced the escapologist into an infernal-looking leather and canvas contraption. The detectives told a reporter that no one—not even Houdini—could escape from their vise-like contraption, especially hanging upside down.

With his arms pinioned in closed sleeves, Houdini's ankles were secured by a rope attached to a block and tackle which was attached in turn to a crane, and he was hoisted about thirty feet above the sidewalk. An agreed-upon fifteen minutes was given Houdini to "try to escape." But as soon as he was swung out over the street, the trussed-up figure began a series of violent contortions and within a matter of seconds had secured some "play" for his arms. It seemed to those below that the figure twisting above had no bones. Then, as the stunned crowd below craned its neck to look at the flailing shank ham hanging over them, the tight cocoon of canvas and leather began to slip perceptibly downward over his head. A few more violent wrenches and the jacket came free. As it came over his head, he grabbed it with one of his hands, and in a gesture that was to become as famous as the escape, he held the jacket in one extended hand, forming a

crucifixion-like T with his arms. Then he dropped the jacket to the street below, where the cheering crowd fought for pieces of it as souvenirs. Lowered to the platform, the breathless and smiling Houdini was informed by the chief of detectives that he had escaped in just two and a half minutes.

Now the aerial straitjacket escape replaced the bridge jump and all-too-familiar jail escape. He performed it time and again over the next twelve years, in Pittsburgh, Toronto, Boston, Oakland, and always with the same response—thrilled crowds and headlines in the local newspapers that had tied in to the increasingly popular stunt.

Once, as part of the stunt he wanted to publicize his appearance at the Orpheum Theatre in Oakland by having circulars pinned to his jacket which he would throw down to the waiting crowd. Hardeen, who was then appearing at a theater in San Francisco, had the circulars printed for Houdini. When the jacket was removed, the circulars fluttered down to the expectant crowd as planned. But instead of advertising Houdini, they read "Go See Hardeen at the Pantages." The little brother who had been the recipient of a hand-me-down act had

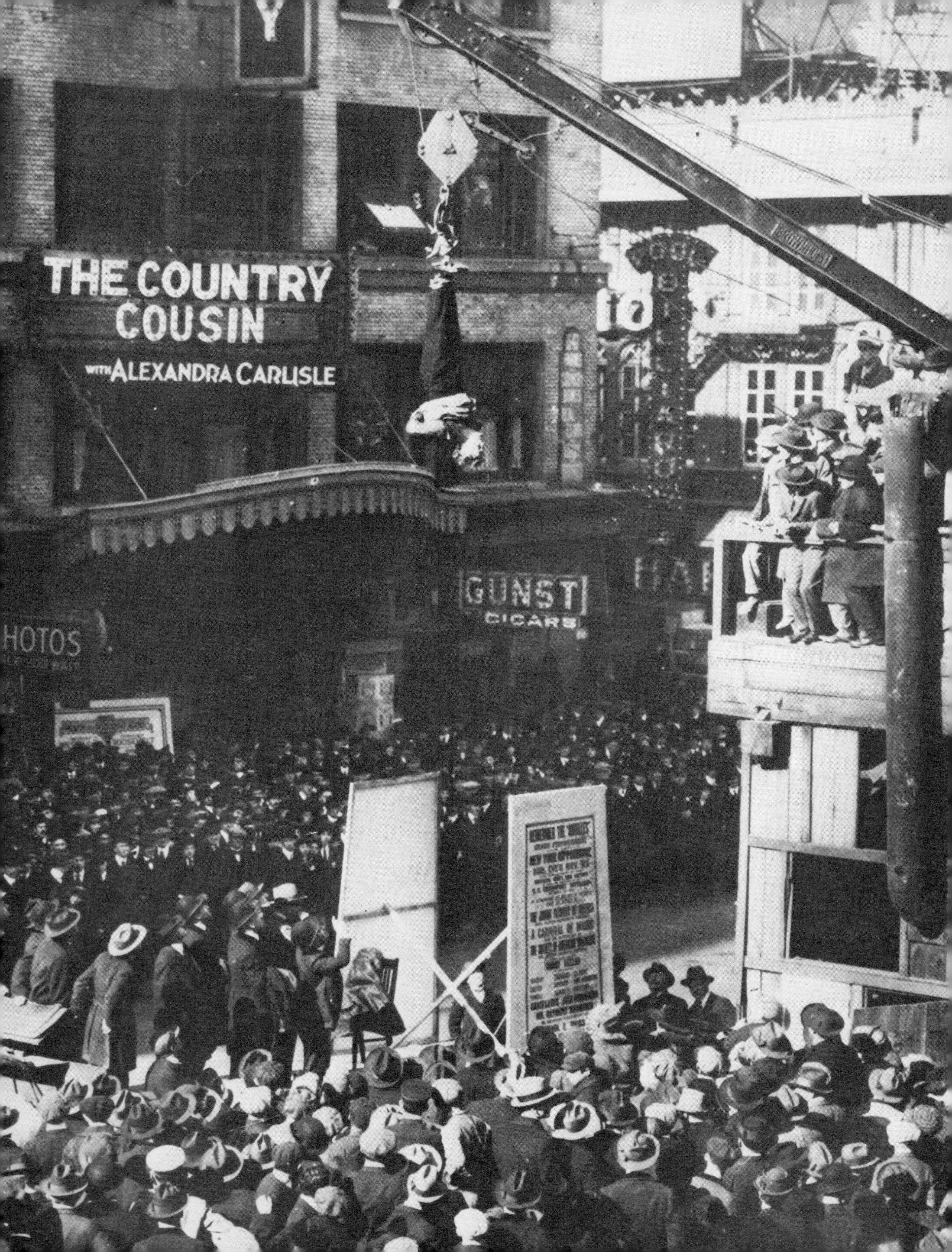
THE COUNTRY COUSIN
WITH ALEXANDRA CARLISLE
GUNST
CIGARS
HOTOS

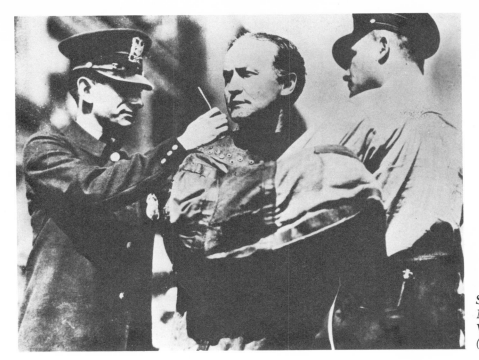

Straitjacket spectacles: in New York (far left), and Washington, D.C. (below).

STRAPPED IN STRAIT JACKET

SECURED IN CASKET

BURIED UNDER SAND AND SECURELY
LOCKED IN GIANT VAULT

HARRY
HOUDINI'S
ORIGINAL CREATION
ESCAPING FROM A QUADRUPLE
SMOTHERING IMPRISONMENT
UNDER TONS OF SAND.

the sea, or when I am buried alive under six feet of earth, it is necessary to preserve absolute serenity of spirit, I have to work with great delicacy and lightning speed. If I grow panicky, I am lost. And if something goes wrong, if there is some little accident or mishap, some slight miscalculation, I am lost, unless all my faculties are working on high, free from mental tension or strain."

But when, as part of his Orpheum buildup, he was challenged by some Los Angelenos to let them manacle him and bury him alive under six feet of earth, he almost lost his ability to conquer fear—and his life.

Just the previous year Houdini had escaped from a casket locked inside a steel burial vault in Salt Lake City. Emboldened by his conquest of this macabre double dare and fascinated by death and the prospect of being able to rise from the dead, he accepted the challenge. His acceptance was predicated on certain conditions being met: that he be interred first one foot deep, then two, and so on, so that he could work his way up—or down—to a six-foot test.

A place near Santa Ana was selected where, as Houdini knew, the soil was sandy. There he experienced no difficulty at all in breaking out of shallow graves, but he had some trouble at the four- and five-foot depths. By that time the challengers were suggesting that the tests had gone far enough. But the Master Magician would not hear of anything short of total promised performance. Accordingly, the extra foot of soil was dug up, Houdini was handcuffed and thrown into the hole and six feet of soil was shoveled over his body.

Then, for the first time, the man who had conquered land, sea, and air had a momentary underground lapse into panic that almost cost him his life. Gruesome fantasies paralyzed his initiative for precious seconds, while his breath ebbed. He pulled himself together by strong concentration of will and proceeded in a molelike fashion to claw, tear, push, and scratch at the earth; but soon even his extraordinary strength began to fail. Then he made an almost fatal mistake: he tried to shout to those on the surface, wasting still more precious oxygen and choking his mouth and nose with sand. Finally, more out of instinct than conscious effort, he resumed his desperate digging and at last burst through into the daylight, where he was pulled from the grave by his assistants, so exhausted he had to spend an entire week recuperating. Houdini in his diary wrote: "tried out buried alive....Nearly (?) did it. Very dangerous; the weight of the earth is killing."

The rest of the world was at war. Names bombarded the public for the next two years with a dizzying rapidity, names that were new and strange: Verdun, Jutland, Gallipoli, Hindenburg, Foch, Joffre, Marne, Ypres, and Lawrence. But as soon as they emerged in newsprint, they submerged almost as quickly. One name, however, was constant and familiar—the name of Houdini. His exploits, always newsworthy, now were a welcome dis-

finally gotten even and had shown up his big brother!

Houdini's Orpheum tour next took him to Salt Lake City, San Francisco, and Los Angeles, where he experienced one of the most noteworthy sidebars of his whole career.

On stage and off, Houdini always believed the key to his success was in his "conquering fear." He told a few intimates, "When I am stripped and manacled, nailed securely within a weighted packing case and thrown into

traction from the tragedy that was engulfing Europe.

Everything Houdini did seemed to make news. When Sarah Bernhardt, "the Divine One," toured the United States in 1916, a group of American actors honored her at the Metropolitan Opera House. Their spokesman, John Drew—a famous light-comedy actor and uncle of Ethel, John, and Lionel Barrymore—presented her with a silver statuette in her own likeness. The seventy-year-old actress graciously accepted the statuette and the plaudits of her fans and friends. Nothing more was thought about the honor until the following January, when the widow of the sculptor presented Madame Bernhardt with the unpaid bill. Responsibility for the questionable gift devolved on the actors and on Drew. For a week nothing was heard from the benefactors and Mme Bernhardt was forced to play the uncomfortable role of accepting something she did not deeply desire, and for which she had no wish to pay. While performers in nearer artistic relationship to the actress hesitated before making a cash expenditure, Houdini, upon hearing of the incident, immediately sat down and fired off a check for $350. Then he sent a quick note to the famed actress asking her to accept the statuette—this time from her friends in American vaudeville. The juxtaposition of the legitimate theater and vaudeville provided the French actress with an "extravagant" delight.

Not only did she accept the statuette, but Houdini's thoughtful act provided him with the gratefulness and friendship of one of the great names of the theater. It didn't matter that one magazine called his act "a bit of advertising," or that the goodwill it engendered could be measured in dollars and cents when the story got out—as Houdini was sure it would!—coast to coast. What mattered was that Houdini had risen to the occasion like a gallant knight and come to the rescue of the fairest-haired damsel in the world of the theater.

Just one year later his kindness was to be repaid in the only way Houdini cared about. After escaping from a straitjacket while hanging by his ankles from high atop a downtown Boston office building, Harry, along with Bess, was called over to a nearby automobile. The occupant was Mme Bernhardt, who was also then appearing in the Massachusetts capital. She first complimented Houdini on his accomplishment ("*très merveilleuse*") and then consented to have a picture taken with the Houdinis. This meant more than $350 to Harry Houdini!

In later years Harry would recount the story of the ride he and Bess had had in Mme Bernhardt's automobile that afternoon. Three years before, the French actress had had her leg amputated ("They can cut out everything as long as they leave my head"), and believing Houdini's powers to be supernatural, even satanical, she had pleaded with him to restore her lost limb. He wrote, "As we were seated in the motor car...she placed her arm gently around my shoulder, and in that wonderful speaking voice with which she was gifted...she said to me: 'Houdini, you do such marvelous things. Couldn't you—could you bring back my leg for me?'"

Houdini's act towards France's foremost celebrity was in keeping with America's actions towards France and the rest of her allies during 1917. France was now a battlefield. American aid to the Allies had increased to the point where nonbelligerency was difficult, if not impossible, to maintain. On April 6, the United States became officially caught up in the conflagration. On that day, President Woodrow Wilson went before a joint house of Congress seeking America's entry in the war, saying, "God helping her, she can do no other." And millions of Americans went off to "make the world safe for democracy."

Although it was the stated belief of many that the war was "knitting us together," an aroused America demanded—and got—conformity and homogeneity from its citizens. Laws that violated the First Amendment were enacted. Over six thousand people were arrested for criticizing the government, the Constitution, and the flag. Americans paraded with signs identifying themselves as "100 percent patriots" and super-Americanism was in vogue. Pretzels were banned from lunch counters and sauerkraut was called "liberty cabbage." Everything European was distrusted—especially anything German or Austro-Hungarian.

Houdini, by birth an Austro-Hungarian, strove hard to be accepted as an American. Refusing to reveal his real last name, he copyrighted and then legally changed his name to "Houdini," embraced Appleton, Wisconsin, as his birthplace, and assumed the day we declared war as his birthdate (a day he had adopted earlier because his mother had always written him on his Gregorian birthdate). He even attempted to enlist, and wrote to one of his fellow magicians, "I register tomorrow for enlisting... HURRAH, now I am one of the boys," But the military wasn't interested in a forty-three-year-old, even if he did have the body of a much younger man. So Houdini's contribution to the war effort was confined to his cancellation of all his engagements for the immediate duration, and the devotion of his time to entertaining the troops and selling War Bonds.

Celebrities by the hundreds appealed to audiences to buy Liberty Bonds and to kids to fill Liberty Books with

twenty-five-cent stamps ("Lick the Stamp and Lick the Kaiser"). Stars like movie idol Douglas Fairbanks donned boxing gloves labeled "Victory" and "Liberty Bonds" and predictably knocked out the Kaiser. Harry Houdini, like Madame Ernestine Schumann-Heink, the famed operatic contralto, who was also born in Austria-Hungary, wrapped himself in the flag and sold more than $1 million worth of bonds.

Houdini's trips to stateside hospitals and bases provided servicemen with a live hero to offset the grimness of the monolithic conflict "over there." Everywhere he escaped from straitjackets and packing boxes fastened to hold him by servicemen. And he revealed his secret of how to get free of "official German fetters" in case "the Germans take it into their heads to manacle prisoners of war." He ended his camp shows with a straight magic act called "Money for Nothing," in which he produced five-dollar gold pieces from the air and tossed them to the servicemen in the audience as souvenirs. It was estimated that Houdini gave away more than one thousand of these gold coins to our boys.

For patriotic reasons, Houdini even gave the government an invention he had developed for a diving suit from which an entrapped diver could quickly escape. (In later interviews, he would admit also to having invented the wardrobe trunk and the double-colored typewriter ribbon.)

But Houdini's most memorable wartime performance was at New York's famed Hippodrome Theatre, in a Charles B. Dillingham revue called "Cheer Up," which opened on January 7, 1918. The Hippodrome, or "Hipp," was described by conductors on the Sixth Avenue El, as they rattled by the entertainment palace that took up the entire block between 44th and 45th Streets, as "the pride of New York City." And to anyone even remotely associated with show biz, it was! Built in 1905, for a then-heady cost of over two million dollars, it was a brick, marble, and steel edifice 110 feet high in the rear and 72 feet high in front, with 5,200 seats and two electric towers that rose 120 feet above the sidewalk and beamed their twin lights across Manhattan. The stage was just as grandiose. The platform was mammoth, 200 feet wide by 100 feet deep, with a 30-foot tank under the stage where the previous year Annette Kellerman had performed. The stage could accommodate up to 600 persons and even 150 horses for some of the indoor circus extravaganzas.

It was only fitting that the keynote of the theater's decor was an elephant's head, for this was to be the theme of Houdini's greatest spectacle, performed at the only supercolossal theater that could handle it—the disappearing elephant.

Magicians have always been able to make pigeons and even ponies disappear. Harry Blackstone performed an illusion in which he'd march a pony into a tent and put on a rear light by which the audience could see the shadow of the pony prancing up and down the wall of the tent. Then the light would be extinguished, the tent would collapse, and the pony would disappear! But no one had ever made an elephant disappear. No one before Houdini, that is!

Houdini, who featured the world's "biggest little mystery feat—the East Indian needle masterpiece," now was to bring the world its largest illusion—the disappearance of a 10,000-pound elephant. Houdini borrowed the elephant for the life of his New York engagement from Clyde Power's elephant show, then also appearing at the Hipp, and claimed she was the daughter of the famous Jumbo. While there was no genealogical proof that his elephant, called "Jennie," was in fact Jumbo's daughter, the legend was undoubtedly created to capitalize on the country's fascination with Jumbo as well as to commemorate Houdini's first appearance at the gigantic Hippodrome—a worthy successor in name to the first "Hipp"

built by P. T. Barnum, the owner of Jumbo.

Houdini described the unfolding of the act after trainer Powers brought Jennie out on the Hipp stage: "The elephant salutes me, says good-bye to the audience by waving her trunk and head, turns to me, lifts up her trunk as if to give me a kiss. In fact, I say to the audience, 'Jennie will now give me a kiss,' but she is really coming to me with her mouth open for sugar, with which I trained her." At this point in his patter, the Houdini who had perceptibly mellowed since his mother's death would do something that the intense Houdini of five years before would rarely have done—he would invoke humor into his act by smiling and saying, "Jennie is the cause of the sugar crisis." And although the line was not the same type of thigh-slapper that Bert Lahr, who was on the same bill, would deliver, it indicated that Houdini was having fun with the audience.

Jennie had, according to Houdini, "a baby blue ribbon around her neck and a fake wrist watch on her left hind leg, so the audience can see her leg until the last possible second, when she enters the cabinet. I say, 'She is all dressed up like a bride'," another humorous aside from a man on a serious mission, but who expects the audience to join with him in his little fun. He waits for the laugh. It comes. "That gets a big laugh for the good-natured beast lumbers along and I believe she is the best-natured elephant that ever lived. I never allowed a hook to be used, relying on block sugar to make her go through her stunt." And Houdini, the animal lover whose love had been requited, added, "She certainly is very fond of me. She weighs over ten thousand pounds and is gentle as a kitten. Everything is in bright light; it is no 'black art' and it is a wonderful mystery for an elephant to be manipulated, they move so slowly."

The act was a sensation. An immense cabinet elevated above the floor on rollers was wheeled onstage, and the elephant shambled in. The elephant cabinet with the 10,000-pound Jennie in it was turned around for seven or eight minutes by a stage crew of twelve men, aided by a special block and tackle. Then it was righted in front of Houdini. Houdini opened the drawn curtains in the front and back of the cabinet, and the animal—pronounced "animile" by Houdini—was gone!

How was it done? Houdini mischievously replied, "Even the elephant does not know how it is done." *Variety* said, "Curtains closed. Curtains opened. No elephant. No trap. No papier-mâché animal. It had gone....Crowds will worry themselves into sleep nightly wondering what Houdini did with his elephant." Not only crowds, but magicians sought to solve the mystery of the vanishing elephant. (This time there could be no traps. The tank of water under the stage apron made that impossible! Such was the continuing mystery of Houdini!

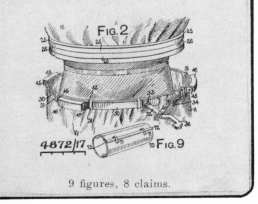

4872. 11 Aug. H. Houdini, New York, United States of America.

Class 82.8.

Diving Dress.

To enable a diver to divest himself of a diving-dress in case of accident while submerged, a manually controlled water-tight connexion is provided between the upper and the lower sections.

The upper section 10 is formed with integral gloves and carries a resilient band 25 having a groove 26 fitted with a correspondingly shaped metallic band, into which fits the waist of a trousers section 11 formed with integral sock portions and provided with a split metallic belt 30, which is tightened by a hand-lever 32 and an adjustable link 34. Removable weights 46 are attached to the belt by screws 45 passing through lugs 31.

Weighted shoes with back stiffening plates are attached to the feet by straps and buckles.

Stiff gauntlets 70 are secured around the fore-arms and the lower portions of the legs to prevent inflating of the extremities.

9 figures, 8 claims.

ACT 6
SILENT MOVIES AND SPIRIT MEDIUMS

The steady drummer of death had swept over the world. The Great War, which had mercifully come to a close, was measured in terms of eight million lives lost, a statistic that deadened the minds and numbed the senses of the survivors. Great Britain had suffered the cruelest loss, 76 percent of all Allied casualties. Her grief was symbolized by a postwar medal: "In peace sons bury their fathers; In war the fathers bury their sons."

The ranks of the survivors were further decimated by the influenza pandemic that ravaged the globe in 1919 and 1920. Twenty million more lives were lost. Bereavement warped the judgment of those who remained, as relatives of the dead sought somehow to assuage their personal tragedies.

Many of the bereaved tried to soften their loss by piercing the darkness and communing with their dear departed in the afterworld, much as Houdini had tried intensely to communicate with his departed mother. By 1919, one out of every three Britons claimed to have contact with the spirit world.

Although as old as human hope, spiritualism as a social movement dated from March 31, 1848, when two sisters, Margaret and Kate Fox, challenged a strange rapping sound in their parents' newly rented house in Hydesville, New York, to repeat the snappings of their fingers. By corresponding raps with letters of the alphabet, they established a dialogue with a spirit source in front of curious neighbors. It identified itself as a traveling peddler who had been murdered by the previous owner and whose body had been secreted in the wall. Subsequent investigation revealed hair particles, teeth, and bone fragments, but no body. (When a cellar wall disintegrated fifty-six years later, a human skeleton was found.) The Fox Sisters made a career out of their mediumship, touring the country under the sponsorship of none other than P.T. Barnum.

Soon other mediums began to receive communications from the spirits of deceased people. The most successful of these were two stage spirit mediums of the nineteenth century, Ira Eratus and William Henry Davenport. Tied up securely in a cabinet that resembled an old-fashioned wardrobe, they produced ghostly music on bells and guitars and caused ethereal hands and strange spectral shapes to appear. Another famous medium was Daniel Douglas Home, called the greatest medium who ever lived. Home was renowned for séances, and although he never accepted payments, he did accept presents from

Houdini holds $10,000 worth of bonds offered to any spirit medium who could perform a "miracle" he could not duplicate.

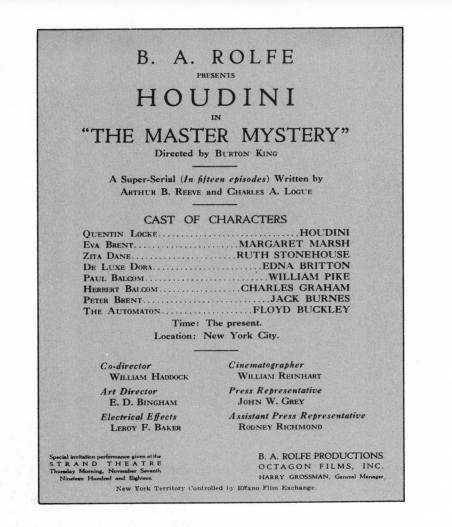

his wealthy patrons, who included Napoleon III, Tsar Alexander, Kaiser Wilhelm I, and the kings of Bavaria and Würrtemberg. At Home's séances, heavy untouched objects moved, well-executed tunes emanated from musical instruments not manipulated by any visible agency, and disembodied hands and faces materialized. Both Home and the Fox Sisters were later exposed as frauds.

Long before the end of the nineteenth century, one could easily find in any city of any size a medium who would produce spirit messages written on slate, ring bells, have unseen visitors "talk" through speaking trumpets, shoot "ghost pictures" of their subjects with spectral personages hovering in the background, and even materialize a frothy substance known as ectoplasm. Intellectuals, including physicians and scientists, as well as just plain ordinary folks, gave serious consideration to such spiritualistic phenomena. Interest in the occult was so widespread that a device known as the Mysterious Oracle Talking Board, invented by two Baltimore toy manufacturers in 1892 and widely known as the Ouija Board ("oui" and "ja" being the French and German for the word *yes*), became a popular craze. Persons sitting across from each other and guiding a little planchette by so-called psychokinetic inference would go into hysterics when it pointed out supposed dispatches from the dead.

It was this world of things that go bump in the night that the now vulnerable and exploitable Harry Houdini turned to in his bereavement, a world he had first become familiar with when he was fourteen.

Communicating with his dead mother became his all-consuming desire. The same Houdini who had given a spiritual séance in Galena, Kansas, and "psychrometic" readings in Grand Rapids, Michigan, now took up spiritualism as an elderly spinster might take up a charitable cause. Those frozen words that had died on his mother's lips still haunted him. He went to séance after séance looking for a way to get through, for any "evidentiary" manifestations of communication from the hereafter. There were none; only rappings and strange noises.

His intensity was rapidly turning to disillusionment.

Bess recalled in later years, "Even after our numerous disappointments, whenever we visited a new medium, Houdini, with closed eyes, would join in the opening hymn, and then sit with a rapt, hungry look on his face that would make my heart ache. I knew the message that he wanted, and sometimes I felt myself tempted to give the medium the word that he longed for. I would be tempted—but I could not betray his trust in me. So the séance would go on—the same guesses, the same trivial nonsense, the usual spook tricks that Houdini could do with his hands tied. The rapt look would fade from Houdini's face." And then Bess added, pathetically, "At his next visit to his mother's grave, I would hear him say, 'Well, Mama, I have not heard.'"

Unable to pierce the veil, Houdini sublimated his disappointment by finding a new passion—moving pictures. By 1919, there were more than 20,000 movie houses, where some 150 million miles of film were shown each week to an estimated 100 million customers. Houdini watched enviously as his coveted final position on the bill was usurped by a single reel of weekly news. The new, impersonal phenomenon threatened to supersede his personal feats of daring.

Unlike many vaudeville stars who waited for vaudeville to come back, Houdini decided to throw his porkpie hat into the nickelodeon ring so that "generations to come could see my feats…and know that I did them." The April 28, 1917, issue of the trade journal *Moving Picture World* announced: "Houdini, hero of thousands of challenges and the creator of many miraculous escapes and inexplainable feats, has been approached for an appearance in motion pictures. The famous self-liberator has accepted the offer of the Williamson Brothers, and will be featured by them in an international drama of thrills in the air, on land, and under water, receiving for his services the largest sum of money ever paid to any

one performer for a single motion picture."

But Houdini was not to star for the Williamson Brothers in his first film. After many conferences, he despaired of getting a fair fee, let alone "the largest sum of money ever paid to one performer," and signed with producer B. A. Rolfe. Houdini had met Rolfe two years before while serving as a technical advisor for Pathe's serial *The Mysteries of Myra*. Believing that serials offered him his "chance for immortality," he immediately sat down and outlined a script he humbly called *The Marvelous Adventures of Houdini, the Celebrated Elusive American*. But Rolfe explained that he had just hired Arthur B. Reeve and Charles A. Logue, who had been the scriptwriters for *The Perils of Pauline*, the fabulously successful serial starring Pearl White. They were writing a scenario for Houdini. The result: a 31-reel serialized potboiler called *The Master Mystery*.

Ever since the first serial, *It Happened to Mary*, made its appearance in 1914, audiences had flocked to witness the archetypical hero or heroine left in a death-defying danger at the end of each week's episode. And when the words *Continued Next Week* flashed on the screen, ending the chapter, audiences groaned, not sure they could wait to see how it would come out. *The Master Mystery* was to be no different.

Houdini starred as Quentin Locke, a secret agent of

B. A. ROLFE PRODUCTIONS
Octagon Films, Inc.
HOUDINI
in
"The Master Mystery"

Rolfe

Episode Six
"THE MAD GENIUS"

B. A. ROLFE PRODUCTIONS
Octagon Films, Inc.
HOUDINI
in
"The Master Mystery"

Episode Six
"THE MAD GENIUS"

B. A. ROLFE PRODUCTIONS
Octagon Films, Inc.
HOUDINI
in
"The Master Mystery"

Episode Fifteen
"BOUND AT LAST"

the Justice Department seeking information on patents that had never been marketed. Locke takes a research job with the firm he is investigating, International Patents, Incorporated. The story contains all the stereotyped stuff of which serialized melodramas are made: a cavernous house with a cellar known as the Graveyard of Genius, and a cast of characters that includes an automaton, which has glaring eyes that "belch scorching flames," makes "a sound as of clanking chains," and looks, in the words of one reviewer, "something like the Tin Woodman in *The Wizard of Oz*"; a beautiful daughter of one of the partners; a doting father, now deranged by "Madagascar madness"; a sinister and oily partner and his son, who is engaged to the beauteous daughter; a lady of the night in love with the nefarious son; and a seedy group of unshaven characters alternately called "thugs" and "emissaries." The exotic locales that flash by in rapid succession include a Chinese joss house, the Black Tom Cafe, a wharf, a boat, a fishing village, the den of a hypnotist, an abandoned warehouse, and Brent Rock, the home of International Patents, with its Graveyard of Genius. Put them all together, and you have *The Master Mystery*.

The story is weird and improbable, but not nearly so incredible as the feats performed by Houdini in it. He escapes from a straitjacket, a diver's suit, an electric chair called the Chair of Death, and a "Madagascar garroting machine," as well as from ropes while hanging upside down over a vat of vitriol, and so on, until it seems that he can't stay out of danger's way. In each installment he battles no less than six thugs and emissaries—at least twice each week—but, to the delight of his fans, he escapes in the nick of time, just when the villains seem to have him in their clutches. In the words of one reviewer, "they hadn't reckoned on his uncanny ability to use his legs, feet and toes as lesser mortals [use] their arms, hands and fingers." In the fifteenth and final chapter, Houdini kills the automaton and finds—for the first time in movie history—a living man inside the robot; saves the daughter; and finds that he himself is the long-lost son of a brilliant scientist. As the chapter mercifully comes to a close, Quentin Locke and the beautiful daughter are married in as touching a scene as Harry Houdini—the man who was frightened of absolutely nothing except women—can manage. The daughter looks up at the heavily made-up Houdini, and the title reads: "After all the things from which you have escaped, dear, I am afraid nothing in the world can hold you." Cut to a close-up of Houdini. His graying jungle of hair darkened by hair coloring, he kisses her wedding ring and the title says: "'Nothing but that band of love' THE END."

The Master Mystery was an unqualified box office success, but Houdini had to sue B. A. Rolfe to get his percentage of the profits. Believing, however, that movies were the wave of the future, he next signed with Rolfe's former partner, now the biggest name in pictures, Jesse Lasky. Together with Cecil B. De Mille and Samuel Goldwyn, Lasky had formed Famous Players, the forerunner of Paramount. He signed Houdini for two features, *The Grim Game* and *Terror Island*.

Houdini arrived in California for shooting early in 1919 and promptly announced to the press, "I am told out here in California, where I am working away at my scenarios and productions, that my act is bound to go well in the movies. Edgar Allen Poe will furnish the first scenarios, as his tales contain the desired amount of mysticism, danger and opportunity for physical exertion." Then Houdini added a characteristic parting sally: "So, if you hear that the Famous Players have made a small fortune during the year 1919, you will know at whose door to lay credit for it." Just as he had done in the serial, Houdini had a heavy hand in the writing and rewriting of several portions of his first feature film. The major rewrite, however, was not occasioned by Houdini, but by a plane wreck that took place during the shooting.

Houdini had previously escaped from a jail cell, from a straitjacket hanging upside down, and from under the wheels of a speeding truck, but the *pièce de résistance* was to be a plane-to-plane transfer that had Houdini leaping from his plane into the pursuing plane of the villain. During the filming of *The Master Mystery*, Houdini had eschewed the use of stunt men and performed all of the stunts himself, in the manner made popular by Douglas Fairbanks and Harold Lloyd. He had had the satisfaction of knowing that at forty-four he could still perform the same mock heroics he had performed as a youth, but he had also sustained a broken wrist and finger in the process. This time, two stunt men were used for the plane sequence, a wing-walker and a stunt flyer who would make the transfer by rope from one plane to the other. Houdini, who had just reinjured his fragile wrist during the jail-escape sequence, stayed on the ground and confined his activities to close-ups. As the two planes came closer and closer together, a sudden wind brought them too close. They collided and tumbled to earth. Luckily neither the pilots nor the stunt men were hurt, and the crash was written into the script. Publicity stories, however, said, "In his latest daring and terrible stunt, the story runs that Houdini has to climb from one aeroplane to another, the ultimate end being that one of the machines actually crashed and he fell 3,500 feet to earth, luckily landing in a peafield, where both he and the pilot were little the worse for their terrible experiences." It was good, albeit fictionalized, publicity, created to take advantage of an *ad hoc* accident, and Houdini and the film both benefited.

Houdini's on-the-screen defiance of death was no different from his real-life flirtation with danger. All the adventure was calculated; most of it was foolproof. Before he had had himself tied to the mouth of an antique cannon in Chatham, England, some ten years before, he had

made sure that there was no powder in the cannon before the fuse was lit. As a family man, Harry Houdini now took steps to provide for Bess. He took out a large insurance policy with the Union Central Insurance Company of Cincinnati. Before assuming the risk, the company satisfied themselves that Houdini used a double in his dangerous movie stunts. Their records also indicated that the water torture cell "was practically foolproof." To the insurance company and to Harry Houdini, there was no "hazard" in the occupation of being an escapologist. Although all of the adventure had been left, all of the danger had been extracted by careful planning. That was his *real* insurance!

The Grim Game was a moderate success, but *Terror Island* was not. It was an old-fashioned barn-burner that most critics, and even members of Houdini's immediate family, like his nephew Harry Houdini Hardeen, "didn't think much of." Between them, they grossed less than

the average first-run feature with a recognized star did. So Lasky and Famous Players, not having made the "small fortune" Houdini had predicted, allowed his contract to lapse.

The expiration of Houdini's contract late in 1920 came at a time when Hollywood was in the throes of convulsive reorganization. Mary Pickford, Charlie Chaplin, and Douglas Fairbanks had just established their own production company, United Artists. Observers joked that "the lunatics had just taken over the asylum." Other stars followed suit, and soon nearly every major star had his own company. Harry Langdon and Will Rogers did. So did Harry Houdini.

He moved his base of operations back to New York and formed the Houdini Pictures Corporation, where Harry Houdini would star in the title role, write the scripts, choose locales, supervise the camera work, edit the film, direct the other actors, write the titles, oversee the pub-

licity campaign, and generally provide artistic supervision for the two movies, *The Man from Beyond* and *Haldeen of the Secret Service.*

He also established the Film Development Corporation and called on his brother Dash to leave magic and join him in the new enterprise, an enterprise Hardeen wasn't to leave until his brother's death. The Film Development Corporation bought a plant near Union City, New Jersey, and produced not only the pictures turned out by the Houdini Picture Corporation but also newsreels and other feature films by means of a new process for which Houdini had purchased the patent rights. Unfortunately, the chemicals necessary for the new process were nearly impossible to acquire during the immediate postwar years, and the plant became a drain on Houdini's resources.

New Jersey had been the cradle of the movie industry. Edison had developed the motion picture camera in Menlo Park, and the first feature film, *The Great Train Robbery*, starring the Lackawanna Railroad, was filmed there in 1903. D. W. Griffith had made seventy-five of his pictures in the Garden State, and Theda Bara, forty of hers. From Pearl White's *Perils of Pauline* to Mary Pickford's *Rebecca of Sunnybrook Farm*, the dream factories of New Jersey had turned out thousands of films, but just as Houdini was coming east to film there, most moviemakers were going to California, where better weather and cheaper labor costs beckoned. It was a telling com-

mentary on Houdini the businessman.

Houdini's first production, *The Man from Beyond*, was based on a story he first saw in *The American Weekly* about the body of a Viking that had been found perfectly preserved after one thousand years in ice. This theme of a cryonically preserved man has been used many times since—recently by Woody Allen in *Sleeper*—but never with as much action and derring-do. In the picture, Houdini is revived after having been frozen for a hundred years in "Arctic" ice, found in Lake Placid. Then the story switches to tried-and-true melodrama. Houdini and his adversary clash on the sheer rock cliffs of the New Jersey Palisades, overlooking the George Washington Bridge. After dashing the villain to his doom, in a thundering climax, with a piano wire around his waist, Houdini catches the heroine in her wild flight before she goes over the edge of Niagara Falls. Throw in escaping from sheets and scaling the outside of a building and you have not only an old-fashioned potboiler but an expensive vehicle for the display of Houdini's skills.

Houdini the director and Houdini the actor both favored a style of exaggerated acting whose day was past. The film also suffered from one other major flaw. The love scenes, more in the style of Charlie Chaplin than Rudolph Valentino, were hilarious. Houdini's nervous reluctance to emote in love scenes gave his fellow actors some amusement and his directors, when he had them, great trouble. One frantic director, after trying all morn-

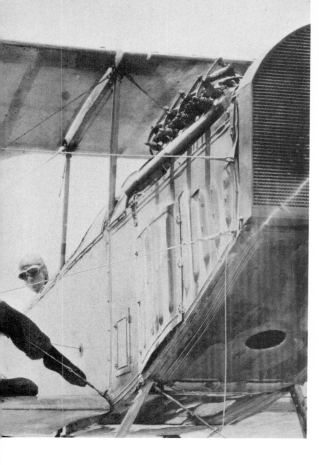

Publicity stills from **The Grim Game**.

*With Nita Naldi in **Haldeen of the Secret Service**.*

ing to persuade Houdini to embrace the heroine as if he meant it, finally asked Bess to leave the lot. "Whenever we get him to the point of kissing the girl," the director said to Bess, "he spoils the shot by glancing anxiously at you." Houdini himself admitted, "I am afraid I am not much of a lady's man. I am so old-fashioned that I have been in love with the same wife for twenty-five years!

Houdini toured the country publicizing *The Man from Beyond* and designed what he called "simple type promotions" (one of these was a two-page flier with the headline "How to Bring Up Children" on the front cover and on the second page, the answer: "Bring Them Up to See Houdini's Performance in *The Man from Beyond*"). The picture was a modest success. One scene, Houdini's battle with the majestic Niagara, saved it, and became as memorable to moviegoers as Lon Chaney's face in *Phantom of the Opera*. *Variety* said the scene on the rapids "has a kick that would carry any audience."

The Man from Beyond came close to recouping its high production costs, but Houdini's second picture, *Haldeen of the Secret Service*, released two years later and filmed completely indoors to conserve on costs, was a total disaster. One reviewer said, "The name Houdini is supposed to carry a strong box office draw, therefore it

may or may not be surprising that when reviewed there was a slim crowd at a house which usually is packed to the doors. Perhaps the renown of Houdini is fading or more probably the Broadway filmgoers were wise to how bad a film this one is. The pity of it all is that the film is reputed to have cost a great deal of money, but it is the company's own fault because added to the weak plot they have inefficient direction, poor acting and carelessness in detail." Another review of *Haldeen* was more succinct: "Way out in the sticks they may flock to see this because of the name Houdini, but they won't like it!" The reviewer was half right: they *didn't* like it, but they didn't flock to see it either. Houdini's noble experiment was at an end.

As Houdini's zeal for his work had gained in intensity, his feelings for his mother had also intensified. During the four years he spent making movies, he devoted every available extra moment to mastering the fourth dimension and communicating with her. But the results were as before—disappointing. He could never persuade himself that any of the messages that were purported to emanate from her were genuine, and the traces of outright fraud that he repeatedly encountered in the frustrating course of his quest so disgusted him that he now contemptuously turned against spiritualism and mediums.

Even the best of mediums could never guarantee the production of phenomena every time. They developed escape clauses of their own, telling those present that nothing would happen if conditions were not favorable—if there were not enough power, or if the presence of a particular person or of too many people hampered the spirits, or if they did not talk more or sing more, or if they did not sit upright and draw in their legs, or if they did not maintain contact around the séance table, or if the light had not been completely extinguished, or if . . . but Harry Houdini never failed.

For that reason, the spiritualists believed him to be a true medium. But because he disavowed or misued his psychic powers, these spiritual leaders said, Houdini could not receive any communication from his mother.

As he sat through séance after séance, he observed no phenomenon—from mind reading and spirit messages on slate boards by celestial hands to materializations of ectoplasm and table levitations—that he felt he couldn't reproduce by natural means.

Houdini always claimed that everything he did was "accomplished by natural means" and "by art and practice." Still, there were many who couldn't explain Houdini's white magic and who could only attribute his getting out of handcuffs as if his "hands were made of jelly," walking through walls, and continually escaping from what they felt was certain death, to mystical qualities.

One of these leaders, Hewat McKenzie, recounts in his book *Spirit Intercourse* his own impression of Houdini's escape from the milk can: "A small iron tank filled with water completely covering his body. . . . The body was then dematerialized within the tank in one and a half minutes, while the author stood immediately over it. Without disturbing any of the locks Houdini was transferred from the tank direct to the back of the stage in a dematerialized state. He was there materialized and returned to the stage front. . . . This startling manifestation of one of Nature's profoundest miracles was probably regarded by most of the audience as a very clever trick."

Houdini angrily replied: "Some spiritualistic leaders have insisted that I am a great medium, whether I realized it or not, simply because I perform such unbelievable tricks. That is foolish on the face of it. I am perfect in the art of trickery because I've made a life study of it."

At a Halloween party at the country home of Irene Sophie Loeb, he showed his art of trickery. One of the literary guests at the party suggested that Houdini provide some of the necessary spooky atmosphere by staging a séance. Getting into the spirit of the night, he agreed to be a medium and "went into a trance." According to Houdini, "Suddenly I announced to this literary group, huddled in the dimly lighted room, that I was communicating with Jack London, the novelist. I produced a slate and scribbled a message. The room was lighted brightly and I passed the slate to each guest. Miss Loeb, who knew Mr. London well, gasped in astonishment. The writing, she said was unquestionably Mr. London's and certain words used in the message were code, expressions known to only a few of the novelist's intimates. . . . 'If I didn't know you were faking, Mr. Houdini,' she said, 'I would swear you went to Mr. London's vault for that message.' But I didn't, of course. The performance was a trick. I readily admitted it."

He began to see that if he could succeed in fooling a circle of intellectual writers like those at Mrs. Loeb's estate, what chance would a grief-stricken human being eager to receive messages from a departed loved one have against him?

Houdini had painstakingly researched the background of spiritualism and mediumistic practices to the point where his library at 278 was now packed with voluminous files of data and books concerning the world of mysticism. His research had carried him to the little burg of Mayville, New York, where he had visited the remaining Davenport Brother just before he died in 1911. There he had learned the secret of the Davenport bolt (a gimmick bolt with an opposite thread), the famous Davenport rope-tie, and their specially made cabinet, techniques he later adapted to his own specialty.

The Davenport Brothers were still of great interest to spiritualists, particularly in England, where they had performed as onstage mediums in the 1860s and created quite a furor. *Punch* called their act of being tied up in a séance cabinet "Tie-Fuss Fever," and the Davenport Brothers themselves, "Ministers of the Interior."

One of those profoundly interested in the brothers was Sir Arthur Conan Doyle, creator of Sherlock Holmes and one of Great Britain's leading intellectuals and spiritualists. Houdini in 1920 was making his first visit to the British Isles in six years and playing to a whole new generation of theatergoers. The trip was noteworthy for Houdini's purchasing, in the course of it, shoes for all of Edinburgh's shoeless children. Doyle contacted him at the Empire Theatre in Sheffield, inquiring about the Davenports. Houdini, desiring to achieve the social and academic respectability of being associated with the famed author, responded at once. On March 17, 1920, he wrote telling Doyle "I trust you will not think I am egotistical by making this statement, that I know more about the Davenport Brothers than anyone living." Conan Doyle was elated by the correspondence, and an association that was to be what one book title called *A Strange Friendship* commenced, lasting until the publication of Houdini's book *A Magician Among the Spirits* in 1924.

The creator of Sherlock Holmes had suffered cruel bereavement in recent years. His first wife had died in 1906. His son, Kingsley Conan Doyle, a captain at Somme, was one of the 60,000 casualties on the first day of battle; he came back to England with two bullet wounds in his neck and later died from the effects of the wounds coupled with influenza. Doyle's brother-in-law had been killed in the war; and his beloved mother, "the Ma'am," had just died.

Doyle's critics pictured him as a good man gone wrong, for he studied spiritualism for over thirty years in a search for a faith to replace the Catholicism he had given up in medical school. He also belonged to a group known as the New Forest Group, whose members, including H. G. Wells, T. E. Shaw (Lawrence of Arabia), and Aldous Huxley, discussed spiritualism continually and rabidly. According to one of his biographers, during an "automatic" writing session in 1915, Doyle received a message from his recently killed brother-in-law which contained an intimate detail Doyle was convinced only he could know. That was the final evidentiary test he had been waiting for, and he became a convert to spiritualism. Thus, the man who was to write in *The Adventures of the Devil's Foot,* "I take it in the first place we must rule out the intrusion of mysterious forces," himself became a crusader for just such mysterious forces. Like

Houdini with Ira Davenport (left), and visiting the grave of William Davenport (above).

Houdini, he sought to communicate with his mother; unlike Houdini, he never felt his mother was dead.

The center for all his belief was the New Testament, with Christ and His teachings as its inspiration. Doyle believed there was no such thing as death. When a man died, in the accepted sense, it was not his material body which survived. What survived death was the etheric body; that is, the soul clothed in its bodily likeness at the best period of its earthly life. The etheric body—sometimes immediately, sometimes after a brief sleep—passed into another world, or another series of worlds.

It was inevitable that the two men should come together, although they were as dissimilar in their thoughts as in their physical appearance: Harry Houdini, now a graying and slightly balding little man just over five feet eight inches in his elevator shoes and Sir Arthur Conan Doyle, white-maned and moustachioed and standing over six foot seven. Doyle had taken up the cause of spiritualism because of his beliefs and study. Houdini had taken up the cause of antispiritualism and become, in the words of Doyle, "the greatest medium-baiter of all time" because of his frustration and bitterness at not being able to communicate with Mama and also because, quite frankly, it was good business.

In March 1922, Houdini was fifth on a nine-act bill in Brooklyn. For the third time in his long career, his star was sinking, and he was running out of acts and rabbits to save himself. Once he had resorted to the milk can to

rescue himself from the obscurity of being just another handcuff king. Another time he had come up with the water torture cell. Now, at forty-seven, the man who had made himself an American institution was challenged again—but this time by changing times and tastes. People were no longer interested in escapes that took over an hour to effect. Postwar America marched to a different beat—jazz, comedy, song. Houdini, always sensitive to the desire of the public, accepted the challenge and fought even harder to stay where he had been for 22 years—on top! His theatrical prescience, coupled with his commercial intuition, told him that spirit debunking would be just the vehicle to right his falling star.

The 1920s was an age of cynicism, a logical successor to the postwar disillusionment. It was smart to mock everything. Literature had its Babbitts, society had its prohibition, and religion had its spiritualism. All that was needed was a magnet to pull together all the disparate filings and elements of those who believed that spiritualism and mediums were frauds. That magnet was Houdini.

His appearance at a critical moment in the history of spiritualism—as Conan Doyle and others tried to spread the gospel of belief—gave Houdini a new kind of celebrity. He was news again. Before he came on the stage as a crusader against mediumistic fraud, it had been the custom to have spiritualistic phenomena authenticated by scientists of various sorts. But doctors, scientists, and physicians were no better qualified to check up on spiritual phenomena than lawyers, preachers, and poets. They were deceived just as readily as anyone else in the audience by magicians on the stage, or mediums. The problem was whether the medium was a real medium or merely a conjuror; something usually only a conjuror could tell. Houdini was therefore the first investigator of spiritualism who was competent for the task. *He* became the scientist.

Houdini began to include an exposé of mediumistic trickery in his act, complete with reproductions of some of the more elaborate phenomena. Houdini the crusader and Houdini the showman were one and the same. His opening comments were: "We laugh at the old story of witches astride broomsticks flying through space. But what could be more ridiculous than to believe that our beloved dead appear in the form of ectoplasm through the decayed teeth or any other part of a medium's body? Why, if our dear ones wish to communicate with us, do they resort to table flying, raps, etc., at so much per rap? Are our dead financiers?" It was thought-provoking and popular. He went on, "It is against all ethics to expose legitimate mysteries. But it is the duty of every citizen to expose cheats and frauds, and the most despicable cheats are the fraud mediums who use spiritualism as a cloak to prey on the gullible."

As once he had challenged the world to tie him up, now he challenged it to convince him of the supernatural. He declared that he had never been duped, never failed to see through a trick. But he also lived in continual terror of some day being outwitted by a medium. Then his denials would be made to look ridiculous. This gave him a certain edge, a certain nervous excitement, as of a man engaged in a critical fight, much as he had viewed his possible failure to escape from handcuffs during his youth as the ruination of his career.

With Sir Arthur Conan Doyle (far left), and visiting Anna Eva Fay, a reformed spirit medium (below).

Yet ironically the current that charged him to begin his challenge of mediums could also charge him alternately, so that he occasionally would still hope against hope that he could get through to his mother. One such occasion was on July 17, 1922, when Bess and Harry joined Sir Arthur and his wife, Lady Jane, in Atlantic City during vacation breaks from their respective arduous schedules. Because it was the day after Mama's birthday, Harry longed to be remembered to her. Doyle, knowing that his wife had a great gift for what he called inspired, or automatic, writing, suggested that Lady Jane might try to obtain a message from Houdini's mother.

They repaired to the Doyles' sitting room and closed the curtains. Lady Doyle was at one side of the table and Houdini at the other, when Lady Doyle felt the power come and started to write. She wrote with extraordinary speed, covering page after page, which she then tore off and passed across the table to Houdini, who paginated and initialed them. Houdini was asked by Sir Arthur if he wanted to ask a mental question (without speech). He did, and the medium's hand rapidly wrote what Houdini admitted to Doyle was an answer. The letter said, in essence: "Oh, my darling, my darling, thank God, at last I am through. I've tried, oh, so often. Now I am happy. Of course, I want to talk to my boy, my own beloved boy. . . . My only shadow has been that my beloved one has not known how often I have been with him all the while. . . . I want him only to know that—that—I have bridged the gulf—that is what I wanted—oh so much. Now I can rest in peace."

At the end of the writing, Houdini appeared much moved by what went on and picked up the pencil. Bending to the paper, he said, "I wonder if I could do anything at this." As he said it the pencil moved. There was one word on the paper, *Powell.* Doyle said the word proved that Houdini was really a medium; his friend Ellis Powell had just died in England, so the name had a clear meaning to him. Houdini muttered that he also knew a man named Powell (Frederick Eugene Powell, an American magician he was then corresponding with), picked up the seventeen sheets of paper, and hurried back to his room to show them to Bess.

Two days later, when Houdini next saw Conan Doyle in the presence of others in New York, he said, "I have been walking on air ever since." But the troubled Houdini continued to reflect on the message for many months to come, and he slowly made up his mind that it could not have come from his mother. In it he could find no "evidentiary" word. Much of it was in a style of expression that Doyle later admitted was his wife's; and also it was in English, a language alien to his mother (although Harry Houdini Hardeen later said that he had spoken with his grandmother, and since he knew no German or Yiddish, they must have been speaking recognizable English). Moreover, it was the day after her birthday, but it went unmentioned, and, finally, there was a

cross at the top of the paper, which was a normal mark for a medium to make, but not one the wife of a rabbi would be likely to communicate.

For Houdini, with his duality of passions, the letter had originally seemed the long-sought message from his mother in the afterworld. Then afterthoughts overcame his initial joy, and he vacillated between the fantasy he usually indulged in and the truth of reality. This time the truth won out, coupled with the pragmatic need of maintaining his current status as a medium-baiter and not a medium. He wouldn't be deceived by wishing it were so even if Sir Arthur was.

Houdini now incorporated his exposé of mediumistic trickery into his act, developing it from a straight lecture into an entire show. Crusader Houdini had by no means impaired the powers of Houdini the showman. More and more the lecturers turned into fascinating performances, in which Houdini managed to give the spectators all the thrills involved in "spooky" séances and at the same time to reveal to them how it was all done.

He would invite members of the audience up on the stage to take part in a séance; they would be hooded and seated hand in hand, forming the usual semicircle around a table, with Houdini's neighbors on either side of him holding his hands and pressing their feet upon his. Soon they would hear the "spirits" tapping sharply upon the table, which would then levitate, while tambourines and bells would sound and objects would appear to float around their heads. One of them, unhooded for a moment, would write a question on a slate board, hiding it so Houdini couldn't see it. When the slate was held under the table, the scraping of a pencil could be plainly heard, and when the slate was brought back up to the table again, they would find that a relevant reply had been written by the spirits.

To those seated at the table the phenomena seemed unexplainable. They would swear that Houdini's hands and feet were touching theirs and that he couldn't move, and the man who wrote on the slate was certain that it was never tampered with.

For years those who had visited Houdini during his few hours of repose had observed him whiling away his time by unobtrusively removing his shoe and stocking and tying and retying knots with his toes, never so much as glancing at his own remarkable manipulations and not missing any of the conversation. But his total capabilities weren't fully discovered until Dr. Ales Hrdlicka, the father of American physical anthropology, made a study of magicians and found that not only did Houdini possess a magnificent mind, but also that he had developed prehensile toes through constant practice. This finding confirmed what many Houdini fans had always believed—that his strange powers lay not in his hands, but in his feet.

And it was this unusual capability that aided him in this act, as it had in so many others during his career. For

Simulating spirit "manifestations" for a delegation of New York clergymen on the stage of the Hippodrome.

what really had happened while the committee sat on the stage, and what the audience seated in front could plainly see, was that Houdini had slipped his foot out of a trick shoe and sock and had left the shoe still firmly held by his unsuspecting neighbor. He then rang the bell and shook the tambourine with his toes and, by virtue of another subterfuge, freed one of his hands and with his foot and hand made the table shake. The audience also saw how he simulated the scratching of the spirit pencil with his fingernail and, finally, substituted the slate, handing it to a hidden confederate who wrote an answer to the submitted question.

It was all a great show, totally novel and uproariously successful, but it also served Houdini's purpose of striking a blow at the fraudulent spiritualists he had come to despise.

One reviewer who saw the show said, "It is difficult to understand how a credulous disposition towards mediums can long survive such public exposures. Here one can see Houdini reproduce the classic phenomena of the megaphone that floats, the bells that ring and the ghostly hands that brush one's face in full sight of the audience, who see how the tricks are done—but to the bewilderment of a blindfolded man who sits with him on an isolated platform. When one watches Houdini with his hands and feet both held by his vis-a-vis get hold of a megaphone by his teeth one does not find it surprising that so many should have been fooled by the same trick

performed in a dark room. And when we have heard him by means of devices, that he afterwards gives away, tell members of the audience whom he has never seen before, their names and their addresses and facts about their private affairs, we are prepared to accept any marvels of this kind that mediums with their elaborate intelligence service are reported to be able to accomplish."

For the next two and a half years, Houdini's crusade crisscrossed the country. He alternated his show now with lectures, complete with slides. As he went from town to town, he usually chose to speak at colleges and universities, a long-time desire for an association with learning in the man who had never gone beyond the third grade.

But if his lectures were semi-erudite and quasi-scholarly, his road show was a traveling circus. Before he hit a town, Houdini would send a dozen or more advance agents ahead of him to pose as clients of spiritualists and investigate the most conspicuous mediums. (One of his investigators even had the *chutzpah* to call himself Reverend F. Raud, a name the spiritualists never caught on to.) The agents would obtain scores of messages from dead children (who never existed), talk to their mothers (still very much alive), and then, surreptitiously leave small marks about the room with an indelible pencil.

By the time Houdini and all his attendant publicity swept into town, he was fully primed with information on the local spirit community. At his opening show, peo-

Making reproductions of the floating "ghostly hands" that brushed one's face during a séance.

pled with curious members of the medium market, Houdini would call out the local spiritualists by name, have the spotlight focused on them—their seat numbers having been ascertained by his advance agents, now acting as spotters—and confront them with some recent bogus séance: "Yesterday afternoon, for two dollars you gave my agent messages from the spirit of her deceased husband and child. My agent has never been married nor had a child." If the medium protested and denied the accusation, Houdini would have a second spot turned on his agent for identification. If the medium persisted in denying Houdini's allegation, he would then make mention of the mark left by the agent and would "gladly have a committee accompany the medium home to verify or disprove" the incident. Usually by this time, the medium was in full flight, to the guffaws and sneers of the appreciative audience.

Then Houdini would step forward and wager $10,000—holding aloft ten $1,000 New York City bonds—"against an equal amount" to "any medium in the world—male or female—who will produce any so-called psychical phenomena I cannot reproduce or explain as being accomplished by natural means." This challenge, like most of Houdini's, was conditioned by the small print in the program: "The medium must present the manifestation three times in the presence of Houdini and the selected committee." There were no takers!

His tour was successful, his name was in the news

again, and Houdini was back on top—this time as a spiritualist debunker. Even Sir Arthur Conan Doyle was forced to admit, "Houdini's campaign against mediums did temporary good so far as false mediums goes. . . . The unmasking of false mediums is our urgent duty." Then Doyle, having seen "price lists from some firm which manufactures fraudulent instruments for performing tricks," added sadly, "I admit that I underrated the corruption in the States."

The twin tours by Sir Arthur Conan Doyle and Houdini kept spiritualism in the headlines. While Houdini was careful to avoid any direct confrontation with his friend, the publishers of *Scientific American* were stimulated by Sir Arthur's tour to offer two prizes as publicity g．mmicks: $2,000 to anyone who could take a spirit photograph under test conditions, and $2,500 to any medium who could prove authentic communication with departed spirits while strictly controlled.

The magazine named a five-man committee to investigate all claims: Dr. William McDougall, formerly of Oxford and the British Society of Psychical Research and Harvard University; Hereward Carrington, psychic investigator; Dr. Walter Franklin Prince, research officer for the American Society for Psychical Research; Dr. Daniel Fisk Comstock, former professor at M.I.T.; and Harry Houdini. J. Malcolm Bird, associate editor of *Scientific American*, served as secretary of the investigating committee.

20ᵗʰ Annual Dinner

There are things O Silent One about Magic and Spiritualism you never knew

SOCIETY OF AMERICAN MAGICIANS

HOTEL McALPIN
NEW YORK
— Grant Wright — JUNE·6·1924

Throughout 1923 and into 1924 there was only one serious applicant for the $2,500 prize. This was Nino Pecoraro, an Italian medium who demonstrated that even when tied up he could cause a tambourine to fly through the air, bells to ring, and a toy piano to play. His former manager, Hereward Carrington, now a member of the *Scientific American* blue-ribbon committee, arranged for the committee to investigate him—inexplicably without Houdini. When Houdini heard that the committee planned to investigate Pecoraro without him and that they planned on using one long rope, he returned unannounced from his engagement in Little Rock, Arkansas, to see for himself. He exploded. Seizing the single piece of rope, he cut it into smaller pieces and tied up the Italian in knots. There were no manifestations and there was no prize winner.

There the matter rested until the summer of 1924. Most mediums preferred obscurity to a confrontation with Houdini. But in 1924 a certain medium's name was put into contention by her husband, and the spiritualist battle of the century ensued.

The challenger for the prize was no back-street charlatan. She was Mina Crandon, the twenty-seven-year-old blond socialite wife of Dr. LeRoi Goddard Crandon, a distinguished surgeon from one of Boston's first families

and a member of the Harvard faculty. Nicknamed Margery by *Scientific American* editor Malcolm Bird, she was also referred to in the press as "the blond witch of Boston," "a psychic lighthouse on the border of the world," and "the most brilliant star in the firmament of mediumship." It was generally agreed that her amateur séances on the fourth floor of her fashionable house at 10 Lime Street had brought her no commercial gain, so therefore there seemed to be no ulterior motive in her claiming supernatural powers. The Crandons let it be known that it was not the money, but proof of spirit communication certified by a committee of renowned scientists that they sought.

Various members of the committee had sat through almost fifty séances with her and had been completely captivated.by her clairvoyant visions, the extrusion of ectoplasmic pseudopods from her bodily orifices, the materialization of full forms and spirit gloves, and other psychic phenomena. They were on the verge of awarding her the prize. But for some strange reason, although he was a member of the committee, Houdini had never been informed of the challenge by Margery, let alone invited to one of her séances.

Thus, it was with some agitation that Houdini first read about the Boston challenger in the *New York Times*. He saw a headline proclaiming "Margery, the Boston Medium, Passes All Psychic Tests," and read the accompanying premature account of the successful investigations then being conducted in Boston without him. The next day he received a letter from Bird: "You will observe when you get your July *Scientific American,* we are engaged in the investigation of another case of mediumship."

Houdini rushed immediately to the offices of *Scientific American,* stormed into the office of the publisher, O. D. Munn, and demanded to know if the *Times* article and Bird's letter were correct. Were they prepared to give Margery the prize? If so, Houdini exclaimed, *Scientific American* would lose its prestige and become the laughingstock of the country when he exposed her, as he intended to do. Houdini backed up his threat with an offer of $1,000 in additional prize money if he could not detect trickery, believing that as a professional conjuror he was the only one qualified to judge whether or not a conjuror was using his or her skills to pass as a mystic. The publisher immediately agreed that no further séances would be held until Houdini was present and went directly to Boston with the medium-baiter.

Although other members of the committee had partaken of the Crandons' home for weeks at a time, Houdini believed that familiarity bred more than contempt and checked into a nearby hotel. Dr. Crandon, who was a year older than the fifty-year-old Houdini, offhandedly dismissed the master magician as a judge of his wife's talents, calling him one "whose knowledge of wriggling out of handcuffs and straitjackets was almost as great as his ignorance of psychics." This verbal challenge could hardly have endeared the doctor to the man who would tolerate no deprecation of his talents or his name—particularly when the suggestion was made that he was a mountebank.

On July 23, everyone gathered for dinner at the Crandons', including Houdini and Munn. In studying the procedure of the Crandon séance circle, Houdini had noted that Margery's controls were her husband, who held his wife's right hand, and Bird, to the doctor's right, who held both their hands with his right hand and kept his left hand free for "exploring purposes."

The room that was to be the scene for the séance that night was book-lined and chintz-curtained, with a brick fireplace, faded orientals on the floor, and one door leading to the hallway. Scattered about the room were Margery's props—her famous bell-box, a fourteen-inch wooden box with a flap that resembled a telegraph key, which rang a bell when suppressed by supposed spirit pressure; a megaphone; a phonograph; and a three-sided cabinet.

The principals took their places around the table. Dr. Crandon sat to the right of Margery, Dr. Bird to his right, and in the seat of honor to the left of the medium, Harry

Houdini with Mrs. Benninghofen, another reformed spirit medium, this time holding a horn used to listen to "spirit voices" during séances.

Houdini. The bell-box was placed between Houdini's feet. He also held the medium's left hand and pressed his right ankle against her left ankle—uncomfortable on a hot July night, but necessary for further control. For, unknown to anyone, Houdini had worn a tight rubber bandage around his right leg all day to make his calf extremely tender and hypersensitive even to the slightest touch.

The spirit "control" was Walter Stinson, Mina Crandon's older brother, who had been killed in a Canadian railroading accident nine years earlier. His voice was not the voice of usual "controls," given to lisping or Pidgin English, but a robust, rough voice, often speaking in slang, most of it profane—very different indeed from the soft-spoken, ladylike Margery. "Walter" would whistle, chant limericks, and make rude remarks, while admitting frequently that he didn't have all the answers—a refreshing departure from the ambiguous utterances of most spirit voices.

The room was darkened for the séance, and almost immediately the bell-box sounded. Then Walter contributed his deep-throated comments to the session, giving the impression of being a very real and live entity, separate and distinct from Margery, as he discussed poetry and the state of the world with the committee. As Houdini felt Margery moving her leg around so that she could get to the bell-box, her leg rubbing the inside of his, Walter announced it to the room, even specifying the place touched on Houdini's leg. Then, in answer to a request by Walter for a luminous board, Bird jumped up, leaving the Crandons' hands unattended. When Bird returned to his seat, after placing the board over the bell-box, Walter announced that the megaphone was flying through the air, and asked his bête noire, Houdini, where he should throw it. "Towards me," Houdini cried, and almost instantly the megaphone came tumbling down on the table in front of him. After an intermission, the luminous board and table both moved, the cabinet fell over, Walter said good night, and the séance was over.

Throughout all of these occurrences, Houdini remained silent. His only comment, as he left his host and hostess, was that it had been an interesting evening, and that he looked forward to their next meeting. But once he got back to the hotel, Houdini gave full vent to anger. He had felt the movement of Margery's hands and feet and had detected her using her head to create effects, including the throwing of the megaphone in his direction and the picking up of the table. Houdini then vehemently decried the use of her husband as her other control and told the committee members what to look for in the next séance.

But each séance during the first series was different. The looked-for effects in one didn't reappear in another. Even Walter's pithy comments were different. Houdini, silent throughout each session, told the committee members how each manifestation could have been done after-

ward, but never halted the proceeding, even though once he had felt Margery's stocking catch on his garter. He merely unfastened it.

At the behest of Dr. Prince and Dr. Comstock, Houdini built a box to "humanely control" the medium for the second series of séances. The box, called by Houdini the "Margie Box," had a sloping top and apertures for the head and both arms, with ample seating room inside. It was secured on the outside by eight padlocks. This was now to be Margery's base of operations.

The second set of séances began at the Charlesgate Hotel on August 25. But not before Malcolm Bird had been excluded from them. Bird had not only written several articles favorable to Margery in *Scientific American* and thus compromised the committee, but he was now making pronouncements to the press that would indicate that the medium had baffled and stumped the committee. As an ex officio member of the five-man committee, deputized to be secretary, his absence was missed only in the absence of accurate records, of which there are none.

While the second series proved to be unsatisfactory and inconclusive, it was not uneventful. After an investigation of the "Margie Box" by the Crandons, Mina acceded to the committee's request to get into the cabinet. Almost immediately the brass that held the cabinet's top in place broke open. Houdini claimed Margery did it. Margery claimed it was Walter. Nobody ever successfully explained why it happened, or why Houdini's contraption was so vulnerable (or, in the words of Sir Arthur Conan Doyle, "why it was worth while to bring it with so much pomp and circumstance)".

Then the bell-box wouldn't ring. Houdini claimed that there had been no manifestation because of the "Margie Box." Walter cried out, "You have put something to stop the bell ringing, Houdini, you bastard." Upon examination it was found that an eraser from the end of a pencil had been wedged under the flap of the bell-box.

Finally, just as everything was quieting down a third disruption took place, worse than the other two. After Margery was put back into the reconstructed box and her hands were taken by Houdini and Dr. Prince, the terrible voice of Walter thundered, "Houdini, you God damned blackguard! You have put a rule into the cabinet. You son-of-a-bitch! Remember, Houdini, you won't live forever. Some day you've got to die." The lights were turned on and, sure enough, a two-foot folding ruler was found in the cabinet. Houdini claimed that Margery had smuggled it into the "Margie Box" to produce manifestations by using it with her teeth. Dr. Crandon and Margery claimed that Houdini had put it there to discredit the medium. Walter claimed that Houdini's assistant, Jimmy Collins, had put it in the box before the séance started. Collins pledged his word of honor that he hadn't done it. (Years later, according to one biographer, Collins was quoted as saying, "I chucked it in the box

In the "Margie Box," shown here with ruler and bell box.

meself. The Boss told me to do it. 'E wanted to fix her good.")

The last séance disintegrated into a shouting match of recriminations. Walter claimed that Houdini's mental attitude disrupted the conditions necessary for psychical communication and that "if Houdini did not leave, he would go and not return." The séances were over, but the episode was not. Towards the end of the affair, Dr. Crandon blatantly said to Houdini that he would gladly contribute ten thousand dollars if Houdini would "see the light." Houdini never did see the light, and as a member of the Committee, cast his vote in the negative. Carrington claimed the medium had produced some genuine phenomena. Prince, McDougall, and Comstock asserted they had no proof of Margery's alleged supernatural powers. *Scientific American* saved $2,500, Dr. Crandon saved $10,000, and Harry Houdini not only saved his $1,000 but had a new gimmick to add to his traveling antispiritualism show.

For the first time in his "never-fail" life, Houdini had not succeeded. Although his program now included "the Margery Test Explained" and an exposé of the well-

known Boston medium, Houdini had failed to satisfy those who were looking for final proof, which was, of course, impossible to give because, logically, he couldn't prove a negative—that spiritualism does *not* exist and that the dead do *not* survive. Houdini could not prove that just because his manifestations were performed by trickery, *all* spirit manifestations must therefore be performed by trickery.

If Houdini thought he had heard the last of psychic believers, he was wrong. Not satisfied with telling the world that he was a drunkard and a drug addict, they now began to predict his impending doom. Arthur Conan Doyle told how by 1925 he "began to hear the message: 'Houdini is doomed, doomed, doomed!'" Others heard it, too, including Houdini. He began to allude to a premonition of death continually. One time he called Bess and said, "I am marked for death. I mean that they are predicting my death in spirit circles all over the country." But Houdini was too busy preparing for his life's desire—a full evening show on tour—to be too concerned. It was to be his last tour. Within a year and a half he would be dead.

ACT 7
THE CLOSING

For twenty-four years Harry Kellar had been the most famous American magician. Called "the unrivalled magician and presti-digitateur" by some and the "dean of American magicians" by others, to a whole generation of theatergoers his name meant magic.

After serving as business manager for the popular stage spiritualists the Davenport Brothers, Kellar had gone out on his own. He soon became the toast of four continents. Returning to his native country, he opened at Horticultural Hall in Boston in December 1887 with his own one-man show, known as Kellar's Wonders.

The three-part show consisted of "Psycho," "Kellar's Wonders" (feats of prestidigitation), and the "Cabinet Séance" (The Davenport Brothers' tests"). "Psycho" was by far the most sensational of all of Kellar's sensational acts. Described in the program as "A Mechanical Autom-aton, champion calculator, whist player, poker player," it was a little figure on a glass base which indicated an-swers to the audience's requests by selecting numbers or picking out cards. Reputed to have beaten Ben Franklin in chess, it was operated from backstage by compressed air forced through the glass shaft by hoses.

Through his artistic showmanship and illusory magic,

Kellar stayed center stage for the next thirty years as America's premier magician. Then, on the evening of May 16, 1908, at Ford's Theatre in Baltimore, Kellar an-nounced his retirement, bestowing the mantle of magic on his hand-picked successor, thirty-nine-year-old How-ard Thurston. Kellar claimed that in time Thurston would be the greatest magician the world had ever known.

Thus, in 1908 the two leading magicians in the United States were Howard Thurston and Harry Houdini. Sev-eral students of magic have pointed out that while Thur-ston proudly wore Kellar's mantle of magic, Harry Hou-dini had just as proudly adopted his first name. The two magicians now became more than just competitors for parts of Kellar's rich legacy; they became competitors for the whole of the magical stage.

Houdini and Thurston had more in common than merely being at the top of their profession in 1908— Houdini with the galvanized milk can and Thurston as Kellar's successor. In addition, they had both run away from home as children; they had both been strong-ly influenced by religion, Houdini through his Jewish fa-ther and Thurston by his early evangelical training; they had both had their vaudeville start playing at Tony Pas-

Best
wishes

Houdini

tor's; they had both gone to Europe to establish their credentials; they had both opened in London in 1900; and they had both used their younger brothers in hand-me-down road shows.

But for all their similarities, Houdini and Thurston were totally dissimilar in one important respect: their morals. Houdini, in order to keep in first-class physical condition, neither drank nor smoked, nor did he, in the vernacular of the day, "womanize." Thurston, however, despite his religious upbringing, was given to pursuing all three areas of intemperance. When his effects were auctioned off by the Federal Storage Company in Chicago twenty-five years after his death, three trunks were found full of interesting objects that bore mute testimony to his life-style. One trunk was filled with empty beer cans, collected from around the world; the second had nothing but empty matchboxes in it; and the third was filled with ladies' undergarments, all marked in crayon with the cryptic words *good* or *very good*.

But still it was Thurston, not Houdini, who wore Kellar's mantle and had been chosen to succeed him. The extremely egocentric Houdini was naturally envious.

Houdini, however, never allowed his envy of Thurston to get in the way of his admiration for Kellar, an admiration that Kellar, in later years, reciprocated. In 1917, at his farewell performance at New York's Hippodrome, Kellar gratefully thanked the audience for their enthusiastic reception and then turned to thank the man who had introduced him, Houdini. As he did so, he said, "Ladies and gentlemen, this is positively my last public appearance as an entertainer, I am both happy and sad. I am finished giving performances after this evening's entertainment. As I will have no further use for the cabinet and table, I publicly present it to my very dear friend, Houdini." In later years, Kellar was also to present Houdini with his most prized possession, "Psycho," the automaton. But in spite of this, Kellar had presented Thurston with his mantle, and for that alone, although he was too political to show it, Houdini never fully forgave Kellar. And he was never able to mask his petty jealousy of Thurston.

His envy was aggravated by the success of Thurston's one-man "Wonder Show of the Universe," a theatrical phenomenon that revamped the traditional full-evening magic show. Houdini determined on a similar show for himself. Twice before he had tried, in 1906 and 1914, and both times the shows had failed. Now, in 1925, Houdini laid plans for a full two-and-a-half-hour evening show. This time he would show Thurston!

Harry Houdini opened his "Three Shows in One—An Entire Evening's Entertainment" in Pittsburgh on September 14, 1925. He came out on the stage of the Shuber Theatre in full evening dress, and as the crowd applauded his entrance, took off his detachable sleeves and dramatically threw them backstage, declaring he wanted to show the audience "there was nothing up my sleeve."

More applause.

Houdini opened his act with the crystal casket trick, originally called "the Miser's Dream" by Robert-Houdin. Holding up a coin in his hand, visible to the audience in the glitter of spotlights, he tossed it up towards a closed plate-glass box rimmed in gold-plated metal hanging by rings on either side from shining wires. The audience heard an audible clink in the casket. The process was repeated time and again, as the audience assured itself that the coins had gone through the air into the closed box. The previously empty casket was then lowered, and as Houdini turned the box over and a rush of coins worthy of Midas poured out, he exclaimed, "Will wonders never cease?" (The trick was that Houdini had palmed the coin and the clinking sound in the box was made by an electromagnetic switch, which caused the gold-plated rim to strike against the heavy glass. The coins were inside a hinged flap in the middle bar which held the rings on either side of the box.)

After the crystal casket, Houdini performed ten more magic tricks, including a medley of silks, rabbits, and a substitution trunk, which, according to the program, "Startled and Pleased Your Grand and Great-Grand-parents." Then there was an intermission.

The second act was a combination of challenges, card tricks, the East Indian needle trick, and the water torture cell.

Before the show, Houdini's advance men had scoured the house to see if there were any handcuffs brought by members of the audience for challenges. And, as Houdini asked from the stage, "Hasn't anyone got any handcuffs?", his advance men would hustle those with handcuffs up onto the stage. Houdini would appraise the cuffs as they were handed to him and dismiss most with a chilling "Nonstandard," throwing them away until he got the pair he liked. If any of those who had brought "nonstandard" cuffs on the stage protested or became obstreperous, he would be "winked" offstage. (This stage seduction of the uncooperative customer took the form of having one of Houdini's assistants making faces and wagging his finger in a "come here" gesture from behind the curtains, and signaling the customer to come offstage into the wings, where, out of the sight of the audience, he would be grabbed and dragged away.) All the audience saw was one of their fellow members hopping mad one moment and walking off into the wings the next, never to be seen again.

On those evenings when no one would materialize from the audience, Houdini would merely shrug and announce, "Well, from my own private collection here is...."; and producing an ancient pair of cuffs, he would give its history and then announce, "Anyone can come up and examine them."

If handcuff or straitjacket challenges were "slow," Houdini would fill in the remainder of the allotted time with card tricks, spreading an entire pack the length of

Kellar, Houdini, and "Psycho," Kellar's automaton.

his arm and throwing them up and catching all of them in the same hand.

But the *pièce de résistance* and the high point of the show was the Chinese water torture cell. Never fearing investigation, even inviting it, Houdini had the top to the Chinese water cell exhibited in the lobby of the Shubert before the show. But the top in the lobby was not the top used in the act. It was four times the size of the stocks Houdini would have his feet trussed up in, and looked very much like the oversized stocks Tony Curtis used in the movie *Houdini*. Unlike Curtis—who perished in his very first attempt to get out of the "U.S.D."—Houdini would escape from the cell, just as he had hundreds of

times before. Second intermission.

The third and final act was dedicated to exposing fraudulent local mediums. He explained the Margery test, exposed fraudulent medium messages on slates, caused baby hands and fingers to materialize, rang bells and rattled tambourines, and wound up by making his standard $10,000 challenge to any spiritualists who could "produce any physical phenomena that I, Houdini, cannot reproduce or explain by natural means." Curtain.

Harry Houdini's one-man show was well received not only by audiences who flocked to see him in Syracuse, Columbus, Baltimore, Indianapolis, Dayton, New York, Boston, and every other city he played, but also by the

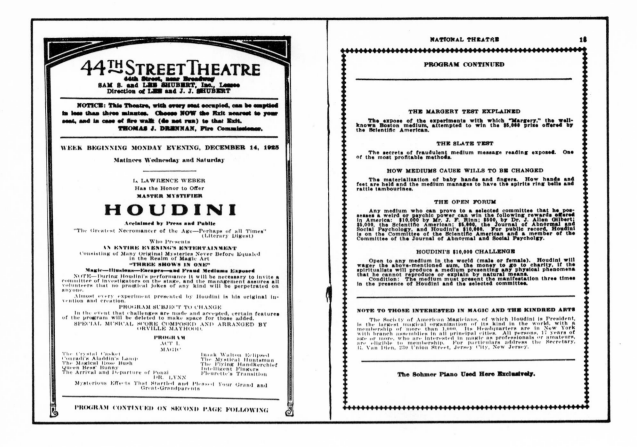

PROGRAM CONTINUED ON SECOND PAGE FOLLOWING

reviewers. One review, found in Houdini's own scrapbook, made the entire tour worthwhile: "Last season Thurston presented a remarkable entertainment. But Houdini captivated this reviewer in a much greater measure than his predecessor in magic."

As 1925 turned into 1926, Harry Houdini could look forward with anticipation to a good year and reflect back on his accomplishments during a good life. At the age of fifty-one, he had risen to the heights of his profession; he had received the adoration of the public and of the press, and the acceptance of his own peer group—having been elected president of both the Society of American Magicians and the Magicians Club of London. But most important of all, his home and his home life had given him the necessary ballast and base for accomplishing all of this.

If 278 was really a haven where he could tuck in during a storm, then Bess was now his heaven, where he could find succor and solace during those days when he needed comforting. Their relationship, which had started in an impetuous fashion with a week's courtship, and had had to be nurtured through times when Harry would prevail upon Bess to go hungry in order to satisfy his mother's need by sending home money, had now gained a golden glow of devotion.

His deeply affectionate nature, once devoted almost totally to Mama, was now directed to Bess. After his

mother's death, Houdini adopted the practice of writing a short endearing note to her every day, even though they were apart. These humorous little notes filled with a delicacy of feeling—such as "Hairbreath Harry has gone down to the coffee shop leaving Beautiful Belinda"—were usually left in the open, just as this one was left on the pillow for Bess to wake to. But more often, they were secreted in some hiding place, and for months after Houdini's death, Bess would find these little notes, showing up like long-forgotten Easter eggs, secretly meant for only one person.

Houdini was constantly concerned about Bess's frailty and bad health. The hysteria he had once had her employ successfully in places like Moscow to aid his escape now worried him. Another concern of the abstemious Harry was Bess's appreciation of fine champagne. Although he could usually limit her to two glasses, there were times when he could not control her. On one such night, backstage at the Hippodrome Theatre, the woman who had mortgaged her entire being to the show and the showman—only to be dropped ultimately from the act because of her ill health and his development of the act beyond the Metamorphosis—let some of Houdini's associates momentarily through the curtain of her feelings. As the master magician's voice thundered and ricocheted throughout the theater and backstage, Bess, in the dressing room celebrating his opening night with more than her allotted share, said, "'I'...'I'...'I'...That's all he ever says. That's his favorite word. 'I' ... 'I' ... 'I.'"

And Harry, knowing that sometimes she felt left out, would go out of his way either to include her in the act—as he did at the Hippodrome the previous spring in the substitution trunk act—or to develop a new act especially for her, such as "Queen Bess Bunny."

By 1926, the man who had taken so much from the world now dedicated himself to putting back as much as he could, especially into the area he had devoted his life to—magic. People were continually coming to him for help—former retainers, down-and-out magicians, actors, circus performers, friends who were on their "uppers"—and they seldom went away empty-handed. He was indulgently accessible to all.

He was far more the total man than he had ever been before. While still believing in himself and in his calling, he had mellowed to the point where he no longer stood alone in studied combat against his audiences, his competitors, and all the elements. No less a battler, he now believed there was room for others both on the stage and in his life.

But if Houdini had mellowed in some areas, one area he hadn't softened his stand on was spiritualism. The Copeland-Bloom Bill, a bill sponsored by Senator Royal S. Copeland and Representative Sol Bloom to prevent fortune-telling for fees in Washington, D.C., was under consideration by Congress. This was an opportunity for Houdini to go from the entertainment pages to the front pages, and also an opportunity to make larger headlines in Washington than Howard Thurston had a year before when he arrived with twenty-two assistants, a full orchestra and truckloads of props and equipment to perform for President Coolidge.

Houdini wouldn't need an orchestra, twenty-two assistants, and truckloads of equipment. He would appear before the joint congressional committees by himself! He went to Washington with an open letter to President Coolidge demanding that "the criminal practices of spirit mediums and other charlatans who rob and cheat grief-stricken people" be abolished. He prepared to appear before the Congress of the United States of America. It was an unheard-of honor for a magician, one that would serve as Houdini's capstone and monument in his long battle against spiritualism.

But it didn't turn out that way. On February 26, 1926, Harry Houdini appeared as the star witness at the Congressional Committee hearings to consider Bill H.R. 8989. As Houdini charged the spiritualists with being fakers and several psychic followers in the gallery answered with angry shouts, Capitol guards were summoned to the committee room to stand ready to prevent physical com-

Houdini and his assistants in his workshop, preparing for his last great New York show.

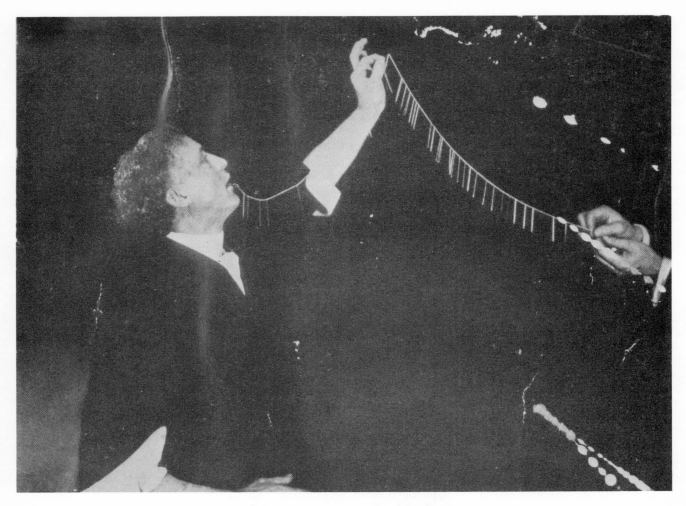

Performing the East Indian Needle Trick.

bat. Then, when one of the spiritualists took the stand, the hearings became even nastier. Houdini, who had never attacked spiritualism as a creed, now found himself attacked for his own. One psychic follower jumped up, pointed at Houdini and Congressman Bloom, and screamed out, "They crucified our Lord once and now they're doing it again, those damned—" He was gaveled down before he could spout out the rest of the religious pejorative, but everyone knew what he meant. Houdini was stunned. He muttered that he had never intended to criticize any religion, or bargained on having to distinguish the religion of spiritualism from spiritualistic frauds such as gypsy fortune-tellers to a group of sophisticated lawmakers. For the first time, Harry Houdini was totally out of his element. The man who had spent all his life as an outsider wanting to get in now suddenly found himself inside—and he wanted to get out.

Houdini tried to get the hearings back on a footing that was more familiar and comfortable to him. He showed the assembled congressmen how fraudulent mediums performed supernatural slate writings and other tricks that had long captivated his audiences. But this wasn't *any* audience; this was the Congress of the United States.

Finally, to impress them, Houdini offered $10,000 to anyone who could tell him what was in the telegram he tossed on the table in front of him. He had made such a challenge many times before from the stage, offering any medium in the audience $1,000 for each correct answer to five sealed questions. (The only time he ever had a taker was the previous year, when the Reverend Alice S. Dooley of Pittsburgh Church of Divine Healing had stepped forward and accepted his challenge. Her reply to the first question was "All is well. March 30, 1894." To another, "Is it possible?" The two questions had proved to be "Where did I meet the chief of police of Pittsburgh last summer?" and "What is the name of the man who taught me the East Indian Needle Trick?") But this time he was dealing not with spiritualists, but with congressmen, and one of them, Representative Reid of Illinois, ventured a guess. "Why, it says 'I can't be there today,'" said the Republican congressman without blinking. Houdini was caught by surprise. "That's a guess," he said to the congressman. "You're no clairvoyant."

"Oh, yes, I am," said the congressman, indicating that that—and the need for money—were the only two reasons telegrams were sent. He was correct, but Houdini insisted it was all an accident. But even if it was an accident, it was symbolic of Houdini's ineffectiveness. He was sadly out of his element. As further testimony developed that there were statutes already on the books to deal with fraudulent taking of money from unsuspecting people, the House dropped the hearings, never to report the bill out of the committee.

His next challenge was more to his liking and was something he understood. Relaxing after the strenuous 1925-26 season, he read about a supposed Egyptian yogi named Rahmen Bey, who professed supernatural power by which he could suspend animation in his own body. Under the management of Hereward Carrington, the fakir had astounded audiences at the Selwyn Theatre that June by going into a self-imposed cataleptic trance. After stopping his pulse, he would demonstrate the Oriental yogi's power of mind over matter by doing tricks that Houdini had seen years before at circuses and carnivals: pushing needles through his cheeks; lying on a bed of nails; exhibiting "eyeless vision"; having a lump of sandstone broken on his chest while he lay on two upraised scimitars; and, finally, being buried alive in a coffin onstage under a mound of sand.

Bey then took his act offstage, in much the same manner as Houdini had, to be buried alive twice—once for nineteen minutes in the Hudson River and once for an hour at the Dalton swimming pool in downtown New York City. Both times he emerged alive and bowing. His publicity and his claims of being an Egyptian miracle man infuriated Houdini, who recognized Bey's tricks as the gimmicks of a dime-museum sideshow performer, not those of a yogi.

When addressed in Egyptian, Turkish, or Indian, Bey professed no knowledge of the language. But if his ancestry was unknown, his feats were not, and Houdini rose to the challenge. He would prove that Bey's feats were not those of a yogi and that being buried alive needed no supernatural powers.

After three weeks of rigorous training, Houdini had lost twelve pounds and was down to 157-1/2 pounds. He then contacted the same casket company that had made Rahmen Bey's bronze casket, the Boyertown Casket Company, and had them make him a coffin designed by his assistant Jimmy Collins. He made two secret tests on their premises. The first test went smoothly; Houdini lay in the coffin for one hour and ten minutes without being submerged. His second test took place on August 4 in a coffin made to specifications. "It had a lining of galvanized iron and was strengthened and tested until it was air-tight." Houdini remained submerged for "one hour and thirteen minutes. This time I was comfortable . . . much more comfortable than at the first test as far as my body was concerned. Started to draw long breaths after

about fifty minutes." Satisfied with his experimentation, Houdini gave the signal to his assistants to pull him out "at seventy minutes." It took them three minutes to unscrew the thirty-two bolt and screws on the coffin.

Confident of his ability to outdo the fakir and to prove that "the copybook maxims are wrong when they say a man can live but three minutes without air," Houdini and his staff transferred operations to New York's Shelton Hotel swimming pool for the big moment. There on August 5 he was to conduct the public demonstration of his underwater burial.

The 22' x 22' x 6' 6" tin box that served as a metal coffin—complete with a telephone and emergency bell for constant communication with his assistants—was placed on the edge of the Shelton Pool. Houdini, in a one-piece black bathing suit, stepped into the coffin and lay down.

The top was closed and soldered into place. Two round plates were screwed over the air vents, one at Houdini's head and the other at his feet. Weights were attached to the sides of the casket, and the tin box was lowered into the shallow pool.

Because the box floated, even with the weights, two teams of sturdy-looking men, working in relays, had to keep the coffin down under the water. Occasionally they rocked the casket to give Houdini the "air action" he wanted. In continual contact with Jimmy Collins by telephone, Houdini noted that he was breathing heavily after about fifty minutes and "was not sure of staying an hour." The temperature in the box was 99.2, and Houdini tried moving to the foot of the coffin to get air.

As the first team of four holding down the coffin turned it over to the second, one of those holding it slipped and the coffin popped to the surface. According to Houdini, "When the box jumped in the air, I felt water under my shoulders and reaching over found the handkerchief I brought into the coffin was wet." But Collins reassured him, telling him the reason why the box had jumped in the air, minimizing the leaking.

Now the time was announced—as it had been every five minutes—as one hour. Rahmen Bey's record was equaled. Excitement ran through the gallery of onlookers and those at pool-side. Houdini had proven himself, and more. For with each passing minute—the time now being announced at one-minute intervals—Houdini was breaking Bey's mark and setting his own. After an hour and a quarter the time was called every thirty seconds.

Every time Houdini spoke to Collins, he would gasp for air. He was angry that Collins made him raise his hand to ring the bell.

Houdini had told Collins at the one-hour mark that he was drawing "rather long breaths" and that his respirations were at seventeen a minute. But he continued to talk to Collins in steady communication and held on. At the hour-and-twenty-eight-minute point, Houdini told Collins that he had commenced to see yellow lights" and had to "watch myself not to go to sleep." Houdini kept

Houdini in Glasgow, Scotland
(above), accepting a challenge to be
enclosed in an antique gibbet that
encased his form in riveted steel,
with a steel tube around his head
keeping it away from his body;
Bessie in the Glass Box (left), and
one of Harry's Christmas cards
(right).

his eyes wide open and lay on his back. Then he rolled over and lay on his right side, "left buttock against the coffin so that I could keep the telephone receiver to my ear without holding it." At this point he told Collins, "Get me up at an hour and a half," believing that even if he went to sleep, they could still get him up safely.

The box was brought to the surface, and the air-vent cap at the bottom was unscrewed. Houdini said "the rush of air" lifted him "practically off my back" and he "wondered why they didn't take off the second plate." They did, and then opened the soldered top with tin snips, and the man who had been buried alive for one hour and thirty-one minutes stepped out of the coffin to the cheers of the throng of well-wishers.

Some followers of Bey tried to imply that the batteries in Houdini's alarm bell contained oxygen-liberating chemicals and even soda lime to absorb the carbon dioxide, but the Bureau of Standards found that Houdini was "sincere and honest in every detail," and used his test as an important part of their findings that "any individual could do it...when they were not alarmed."

Like so many others who had gotten out of tight spots, Houdini himself was now said by the newspapers to have "pulled a 'Houdini.'" In fact, his fame was so widespread that the word *houdinize* was included in *Funk and Wagnalls Standard Dictionary* as a transitive verb. (But ironically the verb, pronounced hou'di-nize, honored not Houdini, but his namesake Robert-Houdin in its pronounciation and stem.)

As he planned his 1926-27 tour, the fifty-two-year-old Houdini sought a new *shtick*. By his own estimate, he had "escaped from drowning on 2,000 occasions. I have extricated myself from approximately 12,500 straitjackets, and picked, roughly, 8,300 locks." But it wasn't the fact that he had tired of "getting out of all sorts of things human ingenuity has devised to confine a human being" that motivated him to look for something new. It was the fact that he was aging. "See these gray hairs? They mean something. I'm not as young as I was. I've had to work hard to keep up with my profession. I'll still be entertaining for many years to come. But I intend to do it along lines not quite so spectacular. As an escapist extraordinary, I feel I am about through!"

But age was only one part of the reason; the other was the changing character of show business. Where once people had been content to wait patiently for over an hour, watching closed curtains in anticipation of the self-liberator freeing himself from his bonds, audiences in the twenties were substantially different. They had neither the time nor the patience for such entertainment, but marched and danced instead to the frenzied beat of jazz.

Houdini saw the dual challenges of age and changing interests as demanding something new. His antispiritualism crusade was running out of steam. The postwar fad of spiritualism and communication with the dead had given way to a full enjoyment of life. The congressional hearing served as spiritualism's watershed, both in terms of its own popularity and of Houdini's

antispiritualism.

Anticipating with his theatrical prescience that there were no more headlines to be made in exposing spiritualism as a fraud, Houdini turned to the newest con on the block—fraudulent gambling. The likes of Arnold Rothstein and Nicky Arnstein were making the headlines along with the Charles Ponzis who were conning people out of money by fixing card games, baseball games, and investments. This was to be the next challenge for Houdini. The man who wrote *The Right Way to Do Wrong* in 1906 and who had once been the "King of Cards" and "Cardo" would collaborate with a fellow conjuror named Sam Horowitz—renamed Mohammed Bey—to expose fraudulent gambling and con men. This new *shtick,* which Houdini felt would be his new draw and headline-maker and which he hoped would prevent him once again from being a has-been, was to become part of his full evening show in 1927.

The 1926-27 tour started with high promise. Houdini opened in Worcester, Massachusetts, exhibiting a glass and bronze casket. The new casket, ordered from Boyertown Casket Company at a cost of $2,500, replaced the tin box which had been hacked opened and was to lie beside the Shelton Hotel pool for the next twenty years, advertised as the "casket Houdini was buried alive in."

From Worcester he went to the Providence, Rhode Island, Opera House, where he opened on October 4. Three days later Bess was stricken with ptomaine poisoning. The frail Bess was a source of constant concern to Harry. Never weighing over ninety pounds, she had always been susceptible to every kind of sickness imaginable. Already weighted down with the problems of the tour, Houdini now had another problem. He sat up all night with her, and assigned relays of nurses to care for her. Then Houdini supervised the crating up of the show and sent all of the props to Albany, together with Bess, who was kept under the care of nurses.

Before entraining to Albany, the extremely exhausted Houdini, still very much upset over Bess's illness, went back to New York to visit his attorney and pick up some things at 278.

There, on the night of October 10, he called his friend Joseph Dunninger to ask for a ride to the station with his props and material. According to Dunninger, who had just sold Houdini an illusion known as "Cutting a Girl in Eighths," which Houdini had redesigned so that the girl's head and feet could be seen to heighten the illusion, Houdini for the first time showed a clear sense of impending doom during their drive to the station. He cried to Dunninger, "Go back to the house, Joe!" And after getting out to look at the house, he climbed back in for his ride to the station, saying, "I've seen that house for the last time. . . . I'll never see my house again!"

Taking a late night train, Houdini returned in the very early morning hours to Albany. Still suffering from extreme fatigue and exhaustion, he went ahead with the

show that night—a show that would be the prelude to worse disaster.

The show started with the usual magic tricks. Houdini only walked through them, showing signs of wilted health. The second section of the show that night was to be the Chinese water torture cell. When his ankles were clamped into the wooden and metal stocks and he was being lifted up off the stage to be put head down into the water cell, he felt a crack. The frame had loosened and wrenched his left foot, injuring the bone. He was brought back to the stage and released, where his foot was massaged. A call for a doctor in the house brought Dr. Elwyn Hannock up onto the stage. He immediately diagnosed the injury as a bad bruise and a broken bone in the ankle. Houdini, though in great pain, went ahead with the remainder of the performance, substituting his East Indian needle trick for the U.S.D., and finished even the third part of the program, the spiritualist debunking. He showed what the Albany *Journal* called "grit." That night he went to Memorial Hospital and had a splint put on his injured left foot. The pain kept him awake all night, but it gave him an opportunity to devise a special brace for his ankle so that, against the best medical advice, he could finish the rest of his engagement in Albany.

Paradoxically, it was Harry Houdini's iron determination that was to cause his untimely death. For over thirty years, the man who had been straining his physical powers to their utmost limit had believed himself to be superhuman in body as well as in spirit. He exuded machismo and believed he was as immune from injury as he had been made of india rubber. And, indeed, in the past it had really seemed as if he had the resiliency of india rubber, performing in pain and distress despite broken blood vessels, broken fingers, broken wrists, and many other injuries that would have debilitated a less hearty or a less stubborn man. His reaction to illness and injury was a strange combination of ego and a high threshold of pain. Houdini would never admit to the outside world that he was anything but superhuman, and when forced to—and only then—he retired from public view to convalesce and lick his wounds in private. But those times were few and far between. Until now.

After Albany the tour went to nearby Schenectady, where it opened at the Van Curler Theatre on Thursday, October 4.

While he was starring at the Van Curler Theatre, he lectured at a local college. During the past three years, Houdini had taken great pride in addressing college groups either when booked by the affiliated Lyceum and Chautauqua Association or on his own. So when Professor Harold A. Larabee of Union College approached him on Thursday to address his philosophy class on the subject of logic and ethics the following day, the frustrated intellectual who yearned to be thought of as one, accepted immediately. He was like a little kid showing off. Af-

AN OPEN LETTER TO
HIS EXCELLENCY CALVIN COOLIDGE
PRESIDENT OF THE UNITED STATES

Whereas, a Spiritualistic newspaper, known as "The Progressive Thinker," has prepared a petition, and is now soliciting signatures with the intention of persuading your Excellency to use your high office, and personal influence, to bring about the repeal of certain just laws that deal with the criminal practices of alleged "spirit-mediums," and

Whereas, practically every one of these so-called "mediums" who have been accessible to competent investigators, have been shown to be either self-deluded, or wilfully fraudulent, and

Whereas, the investigations of competent persons have invariably shown that nearly all of the outright professional "mediums" are mercenary mountebanks and charlatans, even though they might be accepted as genuine by a few distinguished, but hopelessly credulous gentlemen, and

Whereas, the attempt is being made in the petition which the Spiritualists are preparing for you, to make it appear that the alleged "mediums" are "persecuted" on account of their "religion," and are victims of unjust discrimination, and

Whereas, the Spiritualists are constantly boasting that their claims can be scientifically demonstrated, yet they, in their petition to your Excellency, carefully avoid any invitation to you to witness any such demonstration; and, what is still worse, they actually have the effrontery to ask you to believe in the genuineness of present day hocus-pocus, on the ground that Saul, King of Israel, talked with the deceased prophet, Samuel, through the "Witch of Endor," or words to that effect, etc. (In other words, the "phenomena" offered to us today by men and women of very questionable reputation, many of whom have been caught in fraud, must be genuine because records dating back several thousand years bear evidence of miracles), and

Whereas, any class of criminals or law-breakers, could, with equal right, add a pseudo-religious service to their unlawful practices, and, when run down by the authorities, claim that they too were being "persecuted" because of their religion,

NOW, THEREFORE, in view of the facts herein set forth, it is the height of presumption, for the Spiritualists, in the petition to your Excellency, to remind you that under the Constitution of the United States, "Congress shall make no law respecting an establishment of Religion."

As an argument and justifiable reason for writing this open letter to your Excellency, I beg to call your attention to the fact that I have devoted more than thirty years of my life to a most searching, and painstaking investigation of this matter; that I am the author of "A Magician Among the Spirits," "Margery," and various other books, magazine and newspaper articles on illusions, delusions and occultism; that I am a professional mystifier myself of many years training; that I have visited and I am now visiting every accessible "medium" in every town and city, in my constant trips from coast to coast; that I am the President of the Society of American Magicians; a member of the Scientific American's Committee for the Investigation of alleged "Spirit" manifestations; that I have repeatedly offered cash rewards of from $5,000 to $40,000 for bona fide demonstrations. In all of my researches and investigations I have found only delusion and fraud.

The Spiritualists themselves base their belief in the genuineness of alleged "Spirit-phenomena" solely and exclusively upon the fact that they cannot discover fraud. They do not discover anything, either against or in favor of their proclaimed theory. They ask us to believe, that their "Scientific" ignorance of the real nature of the "phenomena" is proof of genuine spiritism, and that to deny it, is to impeach the Holy Bible, and the ancient literature of India, Egypt, China and Japan.

In conclusion, I trust most earnestly that your Excellency, if, perchance, you have not had the opportunity to make a personal study of this complicated, and difficult subject, will not be influenced by the Spiritualistic petitioners; and that you will not suppose that there is any "religious persecution," or any reason for modifying the entirely just laws which make it a crime for charlatans to rob and cheat grief-stricken people with alleged messages from the dead. I am not actuated by prejudice or ill-feeling in making this appeal. I do not consider it a victory to have found only error where I had hoped to find truth. My experience has been a keen disappointment.

Very respectfully.

Houdini

We, the undersigned, being in sympathy with the views as expressed by Houdini in the above open letter to your Excellency, Mr. President, hereby affix our signatures, with the hope that you will not be swayed to act in causing the repeal or modification of laws which now protect us from the unlawful practices of unscrupulous persons;

Signed;

---

ter entertaining the class with coin and handkerchief tricks, "puncturing" his cheek with a needle as Rahmen Bey did, and telling them how he was able to hold his breath, Houdini discussed the importance of coincidence and luck. The example that stuck most in the mind of student Harry Markson, later to become head of Madison Square Garden Boxing, was Houdini's story about having lunch in the captain's quarters aboard ship with Theodore Roosevelt. According to the story Houdini told that day, Roosevelt and Houdini sat at opposite ends of a table with a pencil and a piece of paper. Then they wrote simultaneously and the phrase that was on both pieces of paper when they finished was "River of Doubt," the river TR had just explored the previous Christmas. Houdini told the class that because the River of Doubt was a household phrase, he figured his chances of duplicating Roosevelt's note were seven out of ten. (Perhaps this is really the way his meeting aboard the *Imperator* with TR took place, and the slate writing incident was merely a fabrication of Houdini's fertile imagination!)

The following week, on October 18, Houdini opened at the Princess Theatre in Montreal. On the nineteenth he once again addressed a group of students, this time at McGill University, on spiritualism and the powers of the supernatural. One of the students, Samuel J. Smilovitz, whose hobby was "studying figures," stood at the back of the class and drew a sketch of the lecturer. Afterwards, Smilovitz showed the sketch to Houdini. Houdini was pleased with the likeness and invited the student to join him backstage at the Princess on Friday to make some additional sketches for his scrapbook.

That Friday, October 22, Smilovitz, together with two friends—one of whom was Joselyn Gordon Whitehead, a former McGill student from British Columbia—visited Houdini backstage in his small, cramped dressing room at the Princess before the matinee.

Houdini usually sent and received between sixty and seventy letters a day. But that day the incoming mail seemed abnormally heavy. Maybe it was just catching up to him after a week split between Albany and Schenectady or maybe it was some of the responses to the many letters he had been sending out daily to friends and magicians. Whatever the reason, Houdini settled down on the couch to read and answer the mail as Smilovitz sketched. One person Houdini sent a letter to that morning was Frank Durcrot, owner of the famed Martinka Magic Shop—once owned by Houdini and the founding and meeting place of S.A.M.—informing him that he was in the market for "a number of tricks and mathematical things. Could you give me a few on a number tricks. Just with figures or objects."

As Houdini read and answered his stack of mail, Whitehead asked if what Houdini had said during his lecture was correct—that he could withstand heavy blows in the midsection without any pain. Houdini, paying slight attention to the colloquy, murmured his assent, adding that he could do so if he braced himself before the blow. Whitehead, mistaking his absentminded assent for a responsive answer, asked if he could test the master magician. Houdini, again engrossed in his mail, mumbled something back to the boy, which Whitehead mistook for an acceptance of his challenge to test Houdini's powers of endurance. The next instant, the relaxed Houdini, with his injured left foot stretched out on the couch, was startled to find Whitehead atop him, hitting him in the stomach. Houdini, with the aid of Smilovitz, finally prevailed upon Whitehead to stop, but not before he had been struck three heavy blows to the left side of his abdomen.

The incident, which was over in seconds, was not thought important by Houdini, who went back to reading his mail, leaving Smilovitz to finish his illustrations. The students finally departed and Houdini concluded his mail. Later that afternoon, Houdini felt some pain and thought it was purely muscular. He rubbed it and dismissed it from his mind. But by that evening it had become unbearable, and he couldn't sleep. He finally got Bess up to massage his aching abdomen with alcohol, still believing it to be nothing more than a torn muscle. Bess's nurse suggested he see a doctor, but Harry predictably refused.

On Saturday morning, the exhausted Houdini, who had gone once more without any sleep, fitfully dozed on a cot in the dressing room when he could and suffered spasmodic chills. He complained bitterly of acute stomach cramps and broke out in a cold sweat at the close of the evening show.

The show closed Saturday, October 23, in Montreal. The following day it was scheduled to open at Detroit's Garrick Theatre. Houdini, ever the *Ubermensch*, helped pack the props aboard the overnight train to Detroit, all the while sweating profusely with a temperature of 102. By now he was so weak that Collins had to help him get into his street clothes.

On the train, his pain was so acute he couldn't mask it anymore. Collins wired ahead for a doctor to meet the train when it got into Detroit. But even the doctor—or more precisely, the committee of doctors—could not prevail upon Houdini to go to the hospital. Their diagnosis: appendicitis. His reaction: he would lie in bed until the pain went away. He lay on the bed for twenty-five minutes, wracked with chills. Then he got up and made his way uneasily and unsteadily to the theater.

Houdini was informed the house was sold out. That did it. Whatever else he may have been thinking of, no matter how bad he felt, he would perform. His temperature, now 104, and his pain were sublimated to the task at hand. In the best show business tradition, the show had to go on.

His performance for that opening night crowd was a strange one. To the audience, he was the dynamic and electrifying performer they had paid to see. To those in the wings, he was a member of the walking wounded, performing only through stubbornness and courage, almost as if by rote, every move obviously torturous. Smiling and outwardly suave, Houdini stripped the sleeves off his tuxedo jacket "to show that nothing is up my sleeves." Offstage, he was held up.

One of his opening numbers was an innocuous little trick in which four girls disappear from a cabinet. He made as if to run through the cabinet to show that it was empty. But as he poised with his right foot in the air to take that first step, the combination of his broken ankle, exhaustion, and the internal pain and chills that were sweeping over him was too much. He froze, then started to crumple. Houdini did not have time to signal for help, but the ever-alert Collins ran through the cabinet and onto the stage to assist. Next, Houdini tried to perform the simple silks-from-bowl effect, but floundered again. Collins once more raced out onto the stage, and half carrying, half dragging his master, got him offstage into the wings, where he collapsed—a martyr to his own desire to please thousands of admirers who made his fame possible.

There were no protestations now. His assistants and the house doctors immediately took him out on a stretcher to Grace Hospital.

Houdini's condition was diagnosed as a gangrenous appendix and an advanced case of peritonitis. The surgeons prepared to operate instantly. The weakened magician was proud enough to demand that he be allowed to walk into the operating room. Even now, he still had to prove something.

Houdini regained consciousness with drains in his abdomen. The prognosis: his condition was so acute that he couldn't survive a disease from which recovery is rare for more than twelve hours.

But hospital records hadn't taken into account that one intangible—courage. And they didn't reckon on Houdini's. The twelve hours came and went. And if anything, Houdini's condition stabilized and even improved as he grimly fought his last challenge—death. Bess, still recu-

Emerging from a sealed iron box after being submerged in the pool of the Hotel Shelton in New York.

perating from ptomaine poisoning and weak from medication, suffered a relapse. She was given the room next to his, and wheeled in every day to be with her husband.

For the remainder of the week Houdini hung on, determinedly, even desperately. He underwent a second operation, for streptococcus peritonitis, and false hope abounded that he would escape from this challenge, too. Twice a day the hospital posted bulletins on his condition.

Occasionally Houdini would look up from his deathbed and communicate with those around him. One time he saw the figure of Dr. Charles S. Kennedy, head surgeon of Grace Hospital, hovering over him. Slowly Houdini said, "Doctor, you know I always wanted to be a surgeon, but I never could. I have always regretted it." The astonished doctor looked down at the wasted figure

of a man who even in his final illness longed to be an accepted professional member of the community, and said "Why, Mr. Houdini, that's one of the most amazing statements I've ever heard. Here you are the greatest magician and the greatest entertainer of your age. You make countless thousands of people happy. You have an unlimited income and you are admired and respected by everybody. While I am just an ordinary 'dub' of a surgeon." And Dr. Kennedy smiled in his best professional manner. The patient smiled back and replied, "Perhaps those things are true, doctor, but the difference between me and you is that you actually do things for people and I am in most every respect a fake." As the day of judgment neared, the man who had more than touched greatness, even nudging it, was unmoved by his own contributions. Again, the outsider wanted to come inside and be accepted.

149

On Friday the twenty-ninth, he called Bess close and gave her the secret words by which she would know him if and when he could break through. It was his fourteenth pact to pierce the veil. He had made compacts with his associates and other magician-friends, like Lafayette, and still the picklock to break through the barrier eluded him. But if he could get through as a spiritual guide to anyone, it was his wife.

Then on Saturday he told his assembled family, including Bess and his brother Dash, "I'm licking them." Later he told the doctors, "I'll get out of this, like I get out of other things." With the end nearing, the superman believed he could somehow escape the fate of lesser men. He refused to yield to death just as he refused to yield in life. But his was a death by inches, and the end was drawing closer.

On Sunday, October 31, seven days after entering Grace Hospital, Houdini must have sensed there was to be no escape from this, his final challenge. He called his brother over to him and said, "I'm tired of fighting, Dash. I guess this thing is going to get me."

He lay quietly for a while, and when he reopened his eyes, he saw Bess standing over him, crying. He couldn't bring himself to speak, but looked at her longingly for a moment before his head fell back on the pillow.

Just before ten-thirty in the evening, the semiconscious Houdini was heard by a nurse to say "Robert Ingersoll"—the great agnostic of the nineteenth century—in what might well have been Houdini's last and most classic misdirection. At ten-thirty he laid his head on the pillow for the last time. The Great Liberator had

failed to escape from life's final trick. He had died on Halloween.

All of the properties that had accompanied Houdini on his final tour were sent back to New York the day he went into the hospital. All, that is, except the bronze casket he had exhibited throughout the tour as the coffin which he intended to use in the Buried Alive stunt. Inexplicably, it was the one crate not shipped back. The hermetically sealed casket was to be his funeral bier.

His body was brought back to New York aboard a special Pullman car attached to the *Detroiter*. After lying in state on the stage of the New York Hippodrome, services were held at the Elks Club in New York City. There Rabbi Bernard Drachman delivered the eulogy: "Houdini possessed a wondrous power that he never revealed to anyone in life. He was one of the truly great men of our age." And members of the Society of American Magicians, which Houdini had served as president from 1917 until his death, broke a wand in half over his coffin and chanted: "The curtain has at last been rung down. The wand is broken."

From the Elks Club, the cortege wound its sorrowful way to Machpelah Cemetery in Cyprus Hills, to bury another patriarch—this time a patriarch of magic. There, under a bust that Houdini had himself designed, as his final act of ego—the only graven image in the cemetery, or for that matter, known to be in any Jewish cemetery by the American Jewish Archives—Houdini was laid to rest by his friends and associates.

Under his head was a pillow made up of a packet of letters sent to Ehrich by his mother.

Believing that Houdini had defied death in life, many believed he would also be able to defy life in death. For although his stage voice was stilled, Houdini's echo still lived.

Sholem Aleichem, the Yiddish writer and idol of the East European Jewish masses, requested in his last will that his stories be read on the anniversary of his death each year to his friends and followers; similarly, Harry Houdini's friends and followers gathered each year on the anniversary of his death to attempt to pierce the veil and contact him in the world beyond the stage.

During his lifetime, Houdini had made many pacts with "dearly beloved friends and relatives, wherein we each have taken an oath that the first to pass away would return and be the spiritual guide for the other....We agreed upon a secret sign and word, which I have never divulged to any living human being."

The thought of posthumous communication possessed those who were close to Houdini, especially his widow, Bess, the last to make a compact with the master magician. She believed that, like all of Houdini's tricks, his death was a mere illusion.

Bess was now a lonely woman. Her life's helpmate was gone after thirty-two years, and there was nothing to fill up that yawning void, no one to fuss over, no little notes in the morning to look forward to. All she had was the hope that she could continue to communicate with him—and become almost a professional widow and keep his memory alive.

Bess's emptiness was not monetary. Although Houdini's escapades in making and processing his own movies, together with his neurotic acquisition of eclectic ephemera to add to his many collections, had drained almost everything they had saved in their lifetime, his death brought her money. Houdini had two policies on his life, one with Union Central Life Insurance of Cincinnati and a smaller one with New York Life, and both had a double indemnity clause calling for payment in case of accidental death.

The cause of Houdini's death has always inspired much controversy—especially with the two insurance companies, who sent various representatives to Dr. Kennedy to try to convince him that the injury sustained in Montreal had nothing to do with Houdini's death. Dr. Kennedy's report showed that Houdini "had been struck on the left side of the abdomen. There can be no doubt his symptoms started immediately following the blow. He had no symptoms prior to that injury. And from the

One of many séances held attempting to summon Houdini's spirit. This one took place at the Houdini Museum in Niagara Falls, Canada.

beginning of the injury events progressed steadily to his death." It was the only case of traumatic appendicitis that the doctor had ever seen, but he had no other recourse than to verify to the insurance company representatives that he believed that Houdini had indeed died from it.

Many people, including Sir Arthur Conan Doyle, thought the story about Houdini's "suffering a blow from a student...apocryphal." Others thought that it was part truth and part publicity release, for the student who was reputed to have hit him was supposed to have been a member of the boxing team (he wasn't), and from a publicity standpoint, the only person who could hurt the superman Houdini must also have been a superman. Some thought that the story was a cover-up, owing to the rumor then going around in Montreal that Houdini "had had a fight with a newspaper man." But this turned out to be Houdini's normal arm wrestling, which he practiced with any and all visiting newsmen to prove his superiority—nothing more, but nothing less, than little boy showing-offmanship. The only clue in any of the papers at the time was found in the *Montreal Star* after Houdini's death. Unlike the other obituaries, it simply stated that Houdini had "suffered a blow in the stomach." And that was what the insurance companies found in their investigation.

The estate, other than the $150,000 paid by the insurance companies, consisted, according to one source, of cash ($2,871.95); personal effects and books ($34,356); stocks and bonds ($29,609); and notes and mortgages ($3,118). Charged against this were $30,000 for funeral expenses and expenses for the administration of the estate; $46,367 in debts; and a commission of $694 payable to the executrix, Mrs. Houdini, who also claimed she had lent her husband over $5,500 to pay his insurance premiums. The net worth of the estate—excluding the house, which was in Mrs. Houdini's name—was minus $12,900, hardly the king's ransom one would have expected the king of magicians to leave for all his majestic efforts!

The effects were then disposed of. Houdini's will had provided that his books and memorabilia were to go to the Library of Congress. But an unimaginative librarian, who came and assessed the mammoth and monumental collection, selectively chose just 4,000 volumes—mostly on magic and white magic and spiritualism—and left the remainder at 278. Bess sold the remainder of the collection, amounting to some 5,000 volumes plus all of his playbills and theatrical posters and memorabilia, to Messmore Kendall, publishing executive and theater owners, for $35,000. Kendall immediately put an evaluation of $500,000 on the collection, which he ultimately donated to the University of Texas, where it is today part of the Hobitzelle Theatre Arts Library. Other important pieces of Houdini's collection were given to former friends who claimed that Houdini had promised them this or that during his lifetime. And so, very shortly after Houdini's death, his material legacy had been scattered to the winds.

The first order of business in keeping his memory alive was to perpetuate his show. Once before, Hardeen had taken over his brother's act. Now, under the fourth provision in Houdini's will, Hardeen was to receive "all my theatrical effects, new mysteries and illusions and accompanying paraphernalia, to be burnt and destroyed upon his death." So the man who had once been introduced by Houdini to Conan Doyle as "the brother of the Great Houdini" and who had quit the field of magic to assist his brother in handling the Film Processing Company five years before, now reentered it, taking over the show and all of Houdini's assistants and finishing the tour.

Meanwhile Bess, bereft of her constant anchor and companion, was completely despondent. She wanted somehow and somewhere to communicate with the man she had shared so much with before and now shared a compact with to pierce the darkness that surrounded her. The sixteen-word cipher that Houdini had left behind—both at Grace Hospital and in his safe deposit box at the Manufacturers Trust Company in New York—and which would be a test of his return, had still never been uttered.

That is, it had never been uttered in the form of a message purported to come from the great beyond by Houdini. Other magicians knew it, but they had never communicated it to Mrs. Houdini as a sign. Nobody had, until January 1929, when the Reverend Arthur Ford, minister of the First Spiritualist Church at Carnegie Hall in New York, claimed he had the code words. The words, he said, began "Rosabelle, believe," referring to the song Wilhelmina Beatrice Rahner was singing as a member of the Floral Girls when Houdini first saw her. Mrs. Houdini, upon hearing the words, took off her wedding band. There, engraved on the inside, were the words to the song "Rosabelle." Mrs. Houdini, ill with nervous excitement, went to bed in her apartment at 67 Payson Avenue in the Bronx and lapsed into unconsciousness. These were the words that Houdini had given her two days before his death; they were the arranged communication.

It was claimed that a former confidante of Mrs. Houdini's was now a confidante of Reverend Ford and that she had told the minister of the secret cipher. But Mrs. Houdini refused at first to accept this explanation. No one but her husband and herself could possibly have known the details of the code, and it could not have been gleaned either overtly or covertly. But it *had* been gleaned from the confidante. Bess recanted her belief that this *was* the message, and the Reverend—who was to enter the head-

lines again some thirty years later when he claimed that he had heard from Reverend James Pike—was disgraced. Dismissed from his pulpit, he turned to drink as his only source of comfort.

But the messages did not end there. A Milwaukee woman claimed voices drove her to a vision revealing the magician's message. A Boston medium claimed he had received a spirit message signed "Weiss." So did a Houston medium, who claimed that "Houdini realized before his death that all his power was psychic, and that his scoffer's pose about spiritualism was merely for box office purposes." They continued to come to Bess and Hardeen by the thousands. Many a medium, once Houdini's adversary in life, now became his champion in death, believing that his objections to spiritualism were not very deep and that he had found the true way back only through them.

Bess tried every year on the anniversary of his death, Halloween, to contact her husband. She kept a shrine on a table in the living room of her apartment in the shape of a huge keyhole with two burning candles on top. As soon as the candles burned down, they were replaced. For nine years they cast a flickering glow over the shrine and the photograph of Houdini it contained. And every year the result of the one-hour séance was the same, as Bess knelt before the shrine, alternately staring at the likeness of her late husband and closing her eyes in reverential prayer: nothing. "I held these trysts alone with the shrine and photograph, pleading and praying for Harry to come to me," she said.

By 1936, a full decade after Houdini's death, Bess had become resigned to never hearing from him. After years of keeping an open mind, she too had become a skeptic of pyschic phenomena. But she determined to give it one last try.

For by 1936 a new motivating force had entered Bess's life—Dr. Edward Saint. Saint was Charles David Meyers, a former carney and memory expert, who had performed under the name of Sesrad. Some people thought he was just a hanger-on, a "go-fer" (as in go-fer coffee, go-fer the morning paper, etc.). Others described him as her constant companion, her prince consort. Some, including Dr. Morris Young, the noted Houdiniana collector whose massive collection now forms the basis of the Library of Congress's magic collection, said he was her husband. According to Bess, Saint had "given me the only peace and happiness I've known since Houdini left me." She was also concerned about the "gossip regarding this fine man. He is keeping the name alive in every way and the good Lord knows I need the money."

In the intervening ten years since the death of her husband, things had not gone well with Bess. She had opened up a tea room, but was prey to every down-and-outer in show business, a profession known for having more than its share. She had prepared to appear in a one-woman show as "the greatest lady magician" and had

had the equipment constructed for such feats as an escape from a block of ice—something Houdini was to have introduced in his 1927 show—but the show never got off the ground. She was also easily misled. She began selling Houdiniana or giving it away to friends, including such priceless art objects as the ancient Mary Magdalene lock, which was hundreds of years old. She was also continually leaking to papers evidentiary manifestations of Houdini attempting to contact her, which she would later deny as untruths.

The Society of American Magicians formed an unofficial committee designed to keep her in line. But that was before Saint came on the scene and served as a committee of one. With Bess's help, he made Halloween, the eve of Houdini's death, National Magic Day. He also spent sixteen months with Bess trying to sell an original story based on Houdini's life. However, as Bess found out, "One can starve gracefully in Hollywood and the

high moguls of movieland keep you waiting. And that's what we are doing, waiting." The frustration of trying to sell the script got to her, and she wrote her brother-in-law Dash, "We were told repeatedly that they or any studio could take anything pertaining to Houdini and call the picture The Great Bordini, Fordini or any-dini. And when we asked for real money, they answered they could make a picture of Houdini for nothing."

The waiting had made Bess, in her own words, "a nervous wreck." Never in good health, she suffered a heart attack in 1934, but said, "as the insurance money is all I have to live on, I cannot afford being ill."

If Bess was faring poorly, her brother-in-law Hardeen was doing no better. Even though he had swallowed his pride and had posters printed up reading "Hardeen, Brother of Houdini and Successor to Houdini," his show was a dismal flop. No one had wanted to see an imitation of the one and only Houdini. He had appeared in Olson

*Two pictures of Bess Houdini
in her later years.*

and Johnson's *Hellzapoppin'*, a bright revue that was the forerunner to such zaniness as Ken Murray's *Blackouts* and *Laugh-In*. Hardeen's act was to purposely bungle over half of his straight tricks—which had also been Houdini's tricks. But this was fool's gold; it brought laughs and little more; the name of Houdini was tarnished and the future of Hardeen was equally tarnished. By 1936 he had been reduced to appearing at stores like Gimbel's in New York, where he was hired to do old coin tricks to advertise jackets with "magic pockets"; tricks he could barely do because of his advanced case of rheumatism. Hardeen also made extra money by selling authentic, signed Houdini handcuffs—at least that is how he advertised them.

But for one last moment—on Halloween, 1936—Bess, Hardeen, and Houdini made news together again. It was the tenth anniversary of Harry Houdini's death, and the last time Bess would try to contact him. After this, she

was to stop searching.

The occasion was celebrated on the roof high atop the Knickerbocker Hotel in Hollywood, California, in front of noted celebrities and three hundred fans seated on bleachers. The inner circle of the séance was made up of Saint, Bess, Hardeen, a California Supreme Court judge, two newspapermen, two magicians, and a member of the American Institute of Psychic Research.

On a table in front of Mrs. Houdini and Dr. Saint was a small altar Bess had had in her apartment with a picture of Houdini on it. Over the table was a tiny candle which had burned for ten years. On a low stand in the center of the inner circle were a set of props: a mocked-up pair of silver handcuffs which hadn't been unlocked since Houdini's death, a plate, a slate board and a piece of chalk, a writing tablet and pencil, a large bell, a trumpet, a pistol loaded with blank cartridges, and a tambourine. The spirit of Harry Houdini was asked by Dr.

Saint to manifest himself to Bess through the secret code and also to shoot the gun, unlock the cuffs, talk through the trumpet, and, in the words of an onlooker, "so on, through the list of objects."

At exactly eight o'clock, to the regal music of "Pomp and Circumstance," the last music Houdini had used at the Garrick Theatre ten years and one week before, the séance started. Dr. Edward Saint's strange, almost Satanic stage voice intoned: "All is in readiness. Please now, the time is at hand. Make yourself known to us. Any of you, please. Manifest yourself in any way possible. Houdini, we wish to contact you. Houdini, are you here? Are you here, Houdini?...We have waited, Houdini, oh so long. Never have you been able to present the evidence you promised....Bessie is here. Your Bessie, who is part of you for thirty-three [sic] years. She's here, Harry, pleading in her heart for a prearranged sign from you. It means so much to her. To all of us. To the world, Harry." But the only answer was silence. Again Saint entreated: "Levitate the table, move it. Lift the table, move it, rap on it....Spell out a code, Harry, please. Ring the bell. Let its tinkle be heard around the world. I ask that you come through with the evidence. By the love of a little silver haired widow....Hardeen, your brother, has joined us in the circle. He is from New York City, three thousand miles away. He has joined us to seek the truth. Do it, Harry, please. Please, Harry. We are waiting." But again, only silence.

Saint turned to Bess and said, "Mrs. Houdini, the zero hour has passed. The ten years are up. Have you reached a decision?"

"Yes," replied Bess. "I do not believe that Houdini can come back to me or to anyone. After faithfully following through for ten years the compact, using every type of medium and séance, it is now my personal and positive belief that spirit communication in any form is impossible. This light has burned for ten years. I now regretfully turn out the light. This is the end. Good night, Harry!"

As Bess, Hardeen, and Saint left the rooftop of the Knickerbocker, the clear skies suddenly clouded over, the low rumble of thunder was heard, and it began to pour—just long enough to drench everyone on the Knickerbocker roof. Then it stopped, not to rain again for the rest of the evening.

One magician in attendance said, "Houdini was too big a man to come back and shake insignificant little bells, to write his name on a piece of slate or to toot horns. Harry Houdini was a dynamic personality. Harry Houdini was a man of great ego. Harry Houdini was a man of great force. Harry Houdini, if he *could* return, would not have returned as a horn tooter, but perhaps as something dynamic. As something great and forceful. Perhaps as a drop of rain from heaven."

Convinced that "he never will be able to come through," Bess extinguished "the lights on his shrine. My last hope is gone."

Bess lived out the remaining years of her life without hope, without money, and soon without Edward Saint, who, like Houdini, died at the age of fifty-two, leaving Bess with "files and files of junk." According to Bess, Saint "took every picture that Harry ever had taken and had hundreds of copies made, hundreds of busts, even photostats of his letters. Who the devil wants all that?...[He] spent every cent he could get to have something made from Houdini, even sent to Washington Harry Houdini copyrighted games....Although I never got angry with Ed while he lived, I'm sore at him for leaving me this mess."

Believing that she would only "meet Harry in heaven," Bess died aboard a train taking her from Los Angeles to New York, on May 11, 1943, two years before Hardeen died. Ironically, she died at a little stopover in California named Needles, the only town in the United States with the same name as one of her husband's famous tricks.

Because Bess was Catholic, she was not buried in the Jewish Machpelah Cemetery next to the husband she had tried so hard to get together with after his death. She was denied this even in *her* death. She was interred in the Gate of Heaven Cemetery in Hawthorne, New York, in a single grave, and she has since had someone buried on top of her. The inscription on her gravestone reads simply: "HOUDINI/Wilhelmina Beatrice/1876-1943." She was many miles apart from her husband, both in distance and in the style of the gravestone.

Houdini's attorney, Bernard M. L. Ernst, once said, "There was only one Houdini and he is gone!" But if Houdini is gone, his legacy and name continue on, the performer who pitted himself against the world, challenging anything that stood in his way—locks, manacles, supposedly insuperable bonds, anything. He was a profoundly individual person, the romantic master of a romantic trade.

It was widely rumored that his secrets were kept in a safe deposit vault in a bank in the East under some name other than Houdini, and that this vault also housed secret papers, jewels, medals, and a diamond question mark pin with a rare pearl drop that was a gift from Harry Kellar to Houdini. Many Houdini scholars have been determined that a code exists to locate this treasure trove of Houdiniana. Another legend also became widespread, that a box containing his secrets would surface on the occasion of the hundredth anniversary of his birth. No such box was ever found. Author Milbourne Christopher has wryly suggested, "A hundred years after his birth the great magician is still delighting and deceiving the public."

PART II

A PEEK
BEHIND
THE
CURTAIN

HOUDINI THE SHOWMAN

There have been numerous accounts of the life and times of Harry Houdini, some of them excellent, some of them severely lacking in one respect or another. Any attempt at biography must depend upon written records, recollection of acquaintances, and word-of-mouth information, all or none of which may be dependable. In discussing the art of the man called Harry Houdini, I find it necessary to depend upon the verbal accounts that I have been given over the years from those who had personal encounters with the great escape artist, previous material already fashioned about his life, and parallels that might have occurred between his career and my own. In this last respect, I feel that I am offering a different approach than has been hitherto available.

It will be necessary from time to time for me to refer to actual events that have occurred to me, simply because they frequently bear a striking resemblance to events in Houdini's life. And, before we begin, I must make it very clear that aside from a few early years of my somewhat unwise youth, there has not been a time when I have sought to borrow on the strength of Houdini's name. You will believe me, I am sure, when I tell you that the press and the other media have taken the somewhat trite ap-

proach of almost always attempting to compare me favorably or unfavorably with the great Houdini. It has seldom been to my advantage, even when a headline such as "Houdini Outdone" has appeared. There is simply no point in attempting to equal or surpass a legend, particularly a legend of the scope outlined in this book.

Of course, much of what I now write is pure surmise. But I feel that my analysis of the personality behind the name Houdini is quite possibly more accurate than other interpretations by psychiatrists, historians, and magicians, who have not been as deeply involved as I have been in the business of escape. I cannot help but believe that the thoughts that have passed through my mind in moments of stress and great challenge also passed through the mind of Harry Houdini. I think I may be forgiven for that presumption.

As you will have seen from Mr. Sugar's account, Houdini was born with anything but a silver spoon in his mouth; perhaps a lockpick replaced the spoon. We are accustomed, in biographies of this sort, to hear the Horatio Alger story told all over again, a rags-to-riches tale with a predictable ending. But there was little about Harry Houdini that was predictable. His early childhood gave little indication of the greatness that lay ahead of

him, and even into his early twenties, fame seems to have been throwing him only a bone or two and withholding the real prize.

To read of the accounts dealing with his early life, when he was knocking about on the road as a literal two-bit entertainer on one of the countless circuits that abounded in America at that time, makes the reader wish most vehemently for him to have an eventual success. If it were not known in advance that the story was written about a man destined to become a household name around the world, it would fail miserably. It is a highly improbable tale about a highly improbable gentleman.

One thing is very evident—his love, admiration, and devotion for little Beatrice Rahner, who made a momentous decision that was to both thrill and grieve her over the years: she married young Ehrich Weiss. As Houdini himself was to declare many times during their years together, nothing better ever happened to him in his life. That was probably quite true.

I have always felt that the story of Bess Houdini very much needs telling. Marrying an almost penniless actor with no visible future and devoting herself single-mindedly to his eventual success by slaving day and night both to assist him in the act and to keep a clean collar about his neck, this tiny lady deserves a very special monument in the annals of show business. Though the early life they shared together was probably quite difficult and beset with many frustrations and crises of one kind or another, I hardly think those days compared with the later days of their great success from Bess's point of view. For during this period, she was often away from Harry, and even when she was with him she would find him intensely preoccupied with the matter that most imminently concerned him: the next show.

For the Houdinis, there was never a period when resting on his laurels was considered appropriate. Show business was and always has been highly competitive, and there was always an imitator ready to step in and fill a vacated position on the huge but overburdened ladder of success. There were few times in his history when Houdini can be said to have relaxed his constant vigil against such usurpers.

And along the way, there was a particularly difficult burden that Houdini had to bear. Before Bess entered the picture, Harry had shared the limelight with his brother Theodore, familiarly known to them as Dash. When Harry attained success in Europe and theaters were trying to buy his contract away from other theaters in Germany, he cabled to Dash to join them and reap the benefits of Houdini's vacated dates. Thus was born a "competitor" to Houdini (he took the name Hardeen) who at the same time created a rather unique problem for him. Houdini's basic character could allow of no serious competition that might take work away from him or steal an inch of newspaper space that he might obtain. Since Dash had once shared the act with him, he was ob-

viously as knowledgeable about the escape business and magic in general as Harry Houdini ever was. What neither of them realized at the beginning was that brother Dash was no competition at all to Harry when it came to personality or flair. And, after all, that's what show business is all about. The escape artist Hardeen was to plod along, not exactly in his brother's footsteps, but certainly in his shadow. Even after Houdini's death in 1926, his shadow still fell far enough to compel Hardeen to advertise himself as "the brother of Houdini." To be born into near fame is a dreadful fate indeed.

If I may be forgiven a parallel here, I should like to say that many times during my thirty years of learning the escape art, I've been tempted to write a book on the subject. In this oft-considered manuscript, I have contemplated telling of all the nuances of deception that I have accumulated, as well as the mechanics of how I have learned to defeat locks and other restraints. But I simply cannot bring myself to sit down before a typewriter and begin this job, because I cannot tell into whose hands it might fall. I find it a wiser and more satisfying plan to allow myself to be sought out by those youngsters who, like myself, want desperately to mount that rickety and somewhat illusionary ladder that all magicians see shimmering before them. And in the past few decades, I have found only three such. For one of them, at least, I have great hopes. But as he leaves his apprenticeship with me, I must hasten to fill the void once more with a deserving acolyte. They are few and far between.

Houdini, too, found it necessary to bring people into his inner circle, who not only knew all of the secrets, but were prepared to deal with any emergency that might arise. Collins, Vickery, and Kukol were only three of these trusted assistants. But there was never a ghost of a chance that any of them would aspire to displace the master or even go off on his own as an actor. These men were born assistants who had no greater aspirations than to serve their master long and well. In that, they were very successful.

Could Houdini have had an apprentice? I very much doubt it, knowing the character of the man. His ego would have automatically assumed that no other person would be capable of his accomplishments, and he would not have dared to try passing these secrets on to another for fear of creating a Frankenstein's monster he might not be able to control. His brother Hardeen was his only serious adversary, and not too dangerous a one at that. They had a brotherly understanding which allowed them both to operate, though Hardeen would never have dreamt of encroaching on Houdini's territory. For I believe that he fully realized what the consequences of such an act would be. I believe Houdini would have effectively opposed and demolished him, though not without a great deal of regret.

Houdini was very much a family man. He was forever changing his will every time someone in the family displeased him or stepped beyond his puritanical standards. That he could have enjoyed romances with other women is unthinkable, in my view. Yet, as with all great personalities, stories abound about his amorous escapades, to the delight of third-rate journalists. Perhaps Harry would have been amused to learn of the turns of events.

I've singled out Bess and Hardeen because I believe them to be very much the victims of his bright star. They were both burned by it. Bess signed on for the job; Hardeen was catapulated into *his* situation as Harry's comet took off. For almost half a century, the comet was to blaze across the horizons of show business, attracting admirers in every station of life, from his peers in the magic profession to the crowned heads of the world.

It was not difficult to like the engaging little man that no restraint could hold. Onstage, certainly, he could charm them out of their seats. And to hear Bess's sister, Marie Hinson, tell of the humorous byplay that went on between Bess and Harry, it is obvious that his home life, what there was of it, was a circus. Rose Bonanno, who lives in one of Houdini's former homes in New York City, recalls that as a girl she once stood with a crowd of admirers across the street while Harry Houdini clambered up the face of his three-story house to the sun porch, where he presented the startled Bess with a bouquet of roses on their anniversary. That's about as charming as a man can get!

There was also a dark side to Houdini's character which has never been satisfactorily explained, in spite of several efforts to do so. He seemed to be preoccupied with death. All through his life, whether in the United States or abroad, he visited the graves of long-dead magicians and other entertainers, laying wreaths or otherwise beautifying the graves whenever he could. This in itself may not seem morbid, since it is indeed a noble gesture to honor those of your profession who have paved the way for your success. But it is also a fact that, upon buying a family plot at Machpelah Cemetery in New York, Harry had the remains of his father and his half-brother Herman exhumed and brought to the site to be reinterred, and that he actually had the coffins opened and examined the contents with great interest. He later wrote, "Brother Herman's teeth in a remarkable state of preservation." I do not know if I, or any of my readers, could look into the mouths of long-dead relatives and find interest in their teeth.

This fascination with death is further reflected in his diary, in which he frequently mentioned the exact number of days since the death of a friend or a member of the family, and almost always carefully noted the death-day anniversary of any prominent family member. His moth-

er's death changed his whole life and brought about his deep interest in the possibilities of survival after death. Later in his career, this was to give rise to his dogged pursuit of the so-called "spiritual mediums" who purported to be able to bring back the shades of the dear departed.

It has been said that this morbid interest of Houdini was part and parcel of his death-defying career. I cannot agree. Since I am a special consultant to the Houdini Museum in Niagara Falls, Canada, I am in a position to examine thoroughly the equipment used by Houdini during his long career. Every time I discover something new about this man by means of such an examination, I discover as well that he took no chances, as far as his equipment was concerned. He was determined to live to a ripe old age, and if the equipment had not been properly designed so that the chance of failure was absolutely minimal, he might also have failed to fulfill his promise to the audience. In some ways, that might have been much worse than severe injury to Houdini. He might have preferred even death!

There are, in my experience, three kinds of conjurors: there are the fumblers, without which the profession and the rest of the world could well manage; there are the accomplished professionals who turn out a very satisfactory and exciting performance day after day; and there are those who are *born* magicians. Houdini certainly belonged to this last class. The distinction I make between the second and third classes is simply this: performers can learn their art, either from the published literature or by apprenticeship; whereas those born to the art, though they may learn the bread-and-butter matters of the profession in the same way, are *naturally* equipped to be able to invent, improvise, and salvage any intention entered upon while performing.

Certainly, no one had ever envisioned the escape act before Houdini. True, there had been contortionists and physical culture exponents who struggled or wriggled out of difficult situations for the edification of the public, but no man before Houdini had so convinced the audience that he had a "secret" that no other man was privy to. Ironically, Houdini was destined later in his life to *deny* again and again that there was any Secret, for the spiritualists and other varieties of disturbed persons that he worked to disabuse of their silly notions decided in their incomplete wisdom that he really *had* supernatural powers.

Now let us deal with the events in Houdini's life related to his show-business career and examine them in the light of what we know about the man. It is, I believe, an exciting investigation that we undertake here, and the astute reader will find between the lines much more than appears to be there on first examination.

Handcuffs must not be thought of as some sort of padlock built to hold a prisoner. Whether we consider Houdini's time or today, the design of a satisfactory manacle to hold a prisoner involves much more than merely a locking mechanism. It is essential that the manacle be humane, secure, and at the same time easily managed by the person applying the device both as regards facility of application and ease of subsequent removal with the proper tool, that is, the key.

In the author's personal collection, 168 pairs of handcuffs show the great diversity of inventive skill that has gone into designing manacles. Some of these items never achieved wide circulation or popularity with law-enforcement officials. Others were manufactured by the tens of thousands and distributed across the globe. The escape artist was therefore much more likely to find himself facing one of the latter. But here arises a most peculiar problem for the escape artist.

Mastering the most common makes of handcuffs and leg irons was not the escape artist's greatest problem; rather, it was the "bastard" manacle that would occasionally pop up in the hands of a spectator who wished to test the real skill of the artist, or it might well be one of a rare make of handcuffs. And in this last-mentioned cate-

gory, the most feared of all challenges was the poorly working lock mechanism that might have made that make of manacle unpopular and caused its very limited use among law officials.

In Houdini's day, by far the most common type of handcuffs in use, at least during the early part of his career, were the "Darbies." These cuffs, pictured here, are shaped like a *D*. The locking mechanism consists simply of a hollow tube (the straight part of the *D*) with a slot in the side of one end. Into this slot the curved end of the cuff would slip, and be engaged by a simple rod located in the straight section. This rod was surrounded by a coiled spring, which pressed it in the direction of the inserted end. Since the arc of the handcuff was hinged at the other end, the rod effectively held the cuff closed. Access to this rod was by means of a hole in the end of the tube, and the key consisted, in most cases, of a hollow tube which reached into the larger tube of the cuff and grasped the rod, pulling it back against the spring and thus releasing the cuff.

The defects of a simple cuff like this are obvious. Any kind of a tool that would reach into the tube and grasp the rod would open the cuff. This rod was usually threaded, and engaged the key, which had a "female" thread

162

and was screwed into the cuff, then pulled to effect the unlocking process. Though the spring was usually quite a formidable one, it was still possible to design various tools to do the job. It is of interest to note that in England today, the Darbies are still in common use. In America, on the other hand, the "swing-thru" kind of handcuff is in almost universal use. We will discuss this type of handcuff shortly.

One of Houdini's books describes the process whereby handcuffs may be opened by "rapping" them. I have always considered that this was one of Houdini's private jokes with the escape artists. Though he had recommended that a large lump of sheet-lead be fastened to the leg above the knee, underneath the trousers, to rap

the cuffs upon, I am pretty sure that the great artist never used this method himself. And I can imagine the number of would-be imitators who found themselves with bruised wrists and torn trousers as a result of this not-so-clever system. Fundamentally, however, there are some merits to the system of "rapping" handcuffs to open them.

Indeed, the Darbies can be opened in many cases if the cuff is very sharply rapped on the hinge so that the spring-loaded rod inside is caused to pop down momentarily, thus releasing its hold on the arc of the cuff. But sometimes the blow required for this process is enough to discourage the most ardent self-releaser.

Houdini's jail-breaking and handcuff-escaping career

hardly consisted of rapping Darbies open day after day. As can be seen from many of his photographs, he frequently was presented with all sorts of much more fearsome devices from which he had to release himself. One such handcuff, here pictured, is the "Dortmunder" handcuff, named by Houdini himself, since he first discovered it in the town of Dortmund, Germany. These cuffs could be placed upon the wrists with both hands pointing in the same direction (considered to be the usual position for application of handcuffs) or with the hands pointing in opposite directions, even behind the back. Handcuffs applied in the latter position present a far different problem from that of merely opening a lock. The contortions necessary to escape from them may seem to the uninitiated almost insurmountable. Naturally, any escape artist who knows what he's doing is going to try to avoid having the handcuffs applied in this way. But the choice was not always Houdini's, and he had to be versatile enough to handle such a situation when it occurred.

According to Houdini, and he is probably right in this claim, the great dread of the escape artist had to be Bean Giants. These handcuffs had a huge lock case, on each end of which was a locking arc. The key, a tiny one, had to be inserted in the center of this lock case and turned one whole rotation to open the cuffs. But while both hands were locked into the Bean Giants, especially if the keyhole was located away from the fingertips, it seemed literally impossible, even if one had the original key, to insert that key and release oneself. For this situation, Harry Houdini of course had to have a solution. And his solution for this was typical of most of his solutions, because it was so basically simple.

For such "problem" handcuffs, he built an extender, about ten inches long and equipped with hinges. This enabled him to fasten a key or a pick into the end of the extender and, by using his teeth, effectively work at the keyhole. Luckily for the escape artist, 95 percent of all handcuffs are designed with flexible swivels or hinges between the two hands, and this makes it unnecessary to use such an extender. But it was not the general case with which Houdini was concerned; he was mostly concerned with the exceptional situation that might arise and cause him to fail at a challenge.

Let us deal for a moment with a perfect example of a "problem" handcuff. I refer to a manacle that Houdini often faced in his career, and that I myself have had to deal with on three separate occasions, in widely separated parts of the world. The handcuff under discussion is known as the "Plug-8," and it gets its name from the fact that it is shaped like a figure eight (see illustration). There is a small screw-in plug that is tightened into position after the cuff has been locked, to prevent tampering with the keyhole. Though it is similar in some ways in design to the old-fashioned Darbies, it is really quite a step up from the simplicity of those cuffs. There is absolutely

no flexibility between the cuffs, and as we have already seen, this creates a severe difficulty. On several occasions I have presented a pair of these in my collection to an unknowing neophyte and challenged him to open them, not even fastened upon his wrists, using the original key. In most cases, total failure is the result.

I have always referred to the key for the plug-8 handcuff as a "Christmas tree." One end of it has two small studs that are used to screw the plug referred to in and out. The other end, however, is a formidable set of spikes arranged in a spiral. After the plug is removed and set aside, the working end of the key is screwed into the tubular lock case and turned clockwise. It goes straight in for an inch or so, then reverses to be turned an additional two rotations counterclockwise. At this point, the cuff is opened. But, as might be imagined, even with the original key to the device, the escape artist can flounder around for an hour trying to figure out exactly how the designer intended the handcuff to work!

About the year 1910, the "swing-thru" handcuff, previously referred to, came into common use. This handcuff has the advantage of being always unlocked while not fastened upon the wrist, so that it is not necessary to use the key to unlock it before applying it to a prisoner. Half of the arc of this manacle consists of two parallel pieces of steel through which the other half can freely rotate in a "forward" direction when being locked, and in a "backward" direction when the key has been inserted and turned. As the cuff tightens up fractionally, owing to the ratchet construction, it approaches the "breaking" point where, if there is no impediment such as a wrist inside the circle, the solid part of the arc will pass between the two parallel paths of the other section, and the cuff will swing around again full circle and begin entering the "locked" condition. (see illustration). There is also a position on the cuffs called "double-locking," which simply means that by further application of the key after the cuff is fastened in place, the arc is prevented from further advancing or retreating, so that the comfort and safety of the prisoner are assured. Otherwise, of course, any jar or blow on the handcuff might tend to tighten it up painfully on the prisoner.

Think, for a moment, what the problem was that Harry Houdini faced as an escape artist. With literally hundreds of makes of handcuffs and hundreds of possible variations, he had to be prepared at all times for a "strange" or "problem" cuff to be brought up on the stage. True, to a large extent, these cuffs could be weeded out by his assistants as they saw them being brought out onstage. That is not to say that they could not be used in the demonstration, but they would merely be placed in such a position (such as between two other commoner pairs of handcuffs) that they would not be of critical importance in the release process. Since Houdini usually insisted that the handcuffs be locked and unlocked in his presence with the original key, it was also of

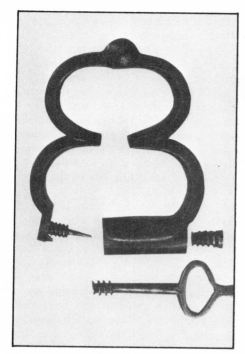

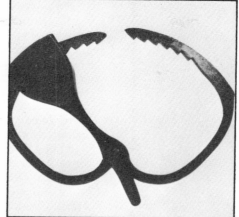

English Plug-8 cuffs (left), "Dortmunder" cuffs (middle), and modern swing-through handcuffs.

course possible for him to study the way in which the cuffs operated at this time. Though the probabilities are that he would be already well aware of the process being shown him, there was already a slight advantage to be had in observing the process actually being performed.

Another way of handling problem handcuffs was frequently used by Houdini when as many as five or six pairs would be fastened on his wrists. He would make sure that the easier cuffs were fastened on lower down on the actual wrists and the troublesome handcuffs were placed above them on the larger part of his forearm. In this way, after he had released himself from the first manacles, the others were adjusted to such a size that they could be more easily slipped off his hands. This simple rule seems never to have occurred to his audiences.

As we have seen, Houdini's greatest fame came to him during his visit to England. There he really established himself as a top-notch performer, and not the least stunt that he used to establish this reputation was the one that has come down to us in history as the Challenge of the Mirror Handcuffs. The *London Illustrated Mirror* was a newspaper of considerable importance in the early nineteen hundreds. When the Elusive American arrived in the British Isles, the editors of the *Mirror* saw a perfect opportunity to make some very fancy headlines. They set up a challenge which they felt, for once and for all, would prove whether or not Harry Houdini could really do what he said he could.

A Nottingham blacksmith was engaged by the newspaper to manufacture a pair of "escape-proof" manacles.

The device, when finished, resembled a large *B* (see photo). There was the usual tubular body, and a hinged section fastened to one end of it made up the two loops of the *B*. There was one key and one key only to open this formidable pair of handcuffs.

At this point I should digress to tell you that there has been a great deal of speculation concerning the performance of this great Houdini stunt. From newspaper accounts of the day, we know that he struggled for several hours in the grip of the cuffs, emerging from the small curtained-off booth still tightly manacled. While Bess waited tearfully offstage, Harry struggled, finally removing his topcoat by cutting it into two pieces with a borrowed penknife held in his teeth. It was a dramatic moment and a showy gesture that was not lost upon his audience.

Finally, hours after he had been placed in the handcuffs, he emerged from the booth free of the restraint and received such a tumultuous welcome as he was seldom, if ever, to experience again. London went literally wild over the Yankee daredevil who had proven their very best effort of no avail against his superior skill.

Now for some of the fiction. It has been said that Houdini despaired of escaping from the handcuffs, and so asked Bess for a glass of water, giving her an affectionate kiss as if for encouragement. The myth goes on to tell us that during this tender kiss onstage, Bess slipped him the key, from her mouth to his. If so, I must say that Bess Houdini had a mouth that would make Martha Raye's look small. For people who have seen the original handcuffs have told me that the key is at least six inches long,

165

(Top to botom) Bean prison cuffs, Towers double-
locking handcuffs, Palmer and Baldwin leg irons,
Bean-Cumming cuffs, Marlin "bottle" cuffs, rare
American cuffs, and English Plug-8 handcuffs.

and of a very complex nature indeed.

How he did achieve his escape from the *Mirror* handcuffs is not known. Obviously, the newspapers would
have had the handcuffs constructed to very exacting
specifications, and would have been well assured that
Houdini could not easily effect his escape, if at all. I can
personally think of many subterfuges that Harry could
have employed to escape, and I'm sure that some of these
have already occurred to my readers. I must add that the
handcuffs were in perfect working order when Houdini
had freed himself from them. There were no marks or
signs of their having been forced in any way by the master escape artist.

This escape, of course, differed greatly from those
Harry Houdini usually had to accomplish for his audiences. He was relatively new in England at that time, so
he needed some spectacular publicity stunt to bring him
to the attention of the press. Whether he coerced the
London Illustrated Mirror into challenging him with a
pair of handcuffs, we may never know. Suffice it to say,
that it was a fortunate audience who attended the theater
that night in London, England, and who waited through
the long hours while Houdini struggled onstage with this
great challenge. If ever Houdini deserved the title of the
World's Greatest Escape Artist, he deserved it then, and
had proven his claim to that throne once and for all.

The handcuff escape as an item of his regular show
served Harry Houdini faithfully throughout his lifetime.
Audiences never tired of watching him pit his skill
against these curious devices, and the expertise that he
must have accumulated after almost forty years of experience with handcuffs might well have filled several books.
One such book does exist, entitled *My Handcuff Secrets,*
but the information contained in it is really of very little
use to the escape artist. It is more likely that Houdini carried these secrets with him to the grave.

In the Houdini Museum, Niagara Falls, Canada, there
are sets of hundreds of keys that can be identified as fitting handcuffs of various makes. Obviously, one of the
problems of the escape artist is not only how to carry
these keys during the performance, but also how to
choose the correct one as needed. Just as obviously, any
such process is strictly impractical and could not have
been employed unless Houdini were content to walk as
though severely ruptured!

When it came to other kinds of locks, such as padlocks
and jail-cell locks, the situation was entirely different.
You must understand that in Houdini's day, the Yale pin-
tumbler lock was not a very commonly used device. An
older style of lock, known as a lever lock, was much more
common. Though methods of course exist for "picking"
all of these locks, the process is never easy and often *very*
difficult. Among Houdini's effects were found many ingenious devices for opening locks of both sorts, with a
great deal of stress upon the large and often precision-
made jail locks with which he had to deal so often.

Typical jail lock (above).

Here is an illustration of a typical jail lock. I will not attempt complicated explanations of how the lock works or how it is opened. I believe the reason is quite obvious. If the reader will compare the size of the key used for the jail lock with the size of an ordinary latch-key shown in the same photograph, he will realize upon what scale we are now speaking. My personal experience has been that carrying tools to open such a lock, if one is to be searched by jail wardens, is almost literally impossible. Other means must be found, and on several occasions I have resorted to laboriously straightening out the small coiled springs that are attached to many prison cell cots, thus making a very usable "lock pick" for opening such locks as this.

But I fear I am growing too technical for my readers. It would probably be best to leave the subject of jail locks at this time, and I imagine that law-enforcement officials will be grateful to me for this change of subject.

It is not known exactly how many jailbreaks Houdini performed in his lifetime. It was probably less than fifty, though some of them stand out more than others. Those

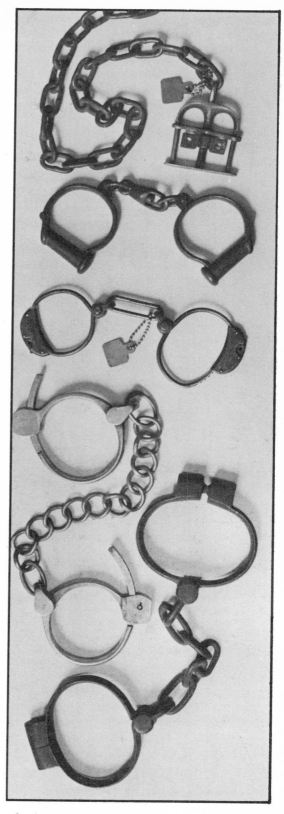

(Right, bottom to top) "Bastille" thumb cuffs, Darbies, Boston lady cuffs, leg irons, Towers lightweight detective leg irons, "flexible" Lilly irons.

The legend lives on: Dunninger, one of Houdini's later disciples, points out handcuffs to the young Tony Curtis, who is preparing for his film portrayal of Houdini.

in which he switched the prisoners around from cell to cell after effecting his escape were, of course, bound to get him more publicity, and he almost always had some sort of a twist that he could put on the performance to make it more exciting. Wardens, chiefs of police, and turnkeys were always astonished when the little man in the briefs managed not only to free himself from the manacles, but also succeeded in vanishing from the jail cell as well!

One of the most difficult problems in performing a jailbreak is to avoid stepping on the finer sensibilities of the officials involved. After all, jails were meant to hold prisoners, and were not designed as vehicles for sensational stunts! It seems that Harry Houdini was able to avoid this problem by using his flashing smile and his

quick wit when reconstructing events for reporters. The police officials ended up more his friends at the finish than they were at the start, no mean feat in itself. On two occasions, police chiefs have tried to slip me the key to the cell in which I have been incarcerated, feeling that I would be terribly embarrassed if I failed to free myself. Wisely, I feel, I refused their offers and discovered that they are truly astonished that the escape can still be done without "special" help. Harry Houdini, of course, made that discovery more than half a century ago.

Perhaps other "dressed-up" stunts that Houdini performed onstage stayed with his audiences longer. But the handcuff escape and the jail escape were the bread and butter of his act. They never lost their popularity or their utility for the great escape artist.

Several years ago when I was working in Cologne, Germany, I had the opportunity to visit a local library where newspaper files were kept. I examined a copy of the *Rheinische Zeitung* for February 1902, and found in it something quite revelatory about Harry Houdini. I had for a long time suspected that his story about an encounter there with the German police might be less than strictly factual. I was right. Thus, I was able for the first time to isolate a perfect example of how Harry Houdini's half-truths enabled him to add to his own legend.

Let us, first of all, understand one thing: all of us, at one time or another, are guilty of half-truths. They are probably one of those things that make the world go round. And in the hands of a versatile artist like Harry Houdini, a half-truth or a slight variation from the actual facts can make a miracle out of what is otherwise only a very clever performance. This was perfectly illustrated by the affair in Cologne.

A police official named Werner Graff had made what Houdini considered to be a slanderous statement about the great escape artist. Graff said Houdini had claimed he could get out of "anything," and he declared that this was, of course, impossible and that it was an obvious mis-

representation. His accusation was published in the popular press. Houdini, in typical fashion, could not let this accusation go unopposed, and he soon appeared to bring a case against Graff for slander. It was to be one of his major victories.

As the case developed in court, it became obvious that the only way to settle it was to put Houdini to the test. There was nothing that he would have liked better. At last he had the opportunity to appear in a court of law and demonstrate his claim to the escape-artist throne once and for all.

At that time in Germany, as well as in other European countries, it was not uncommon to fasten a prisoner in a simple piece of chain secured by a padlock. Such a device was known as a transport chain. Devices like this had been Houdini's meat for a long time back in America, second only in effectiveness to the handcuff escape itself. So when he faced such a simple device in a German courtroom, he must have been highly amused. Indeed, his demonstration in the courtroom won him instant approval from the magistrate, as the padlock-plus-chain combination merely slipped from his wrists.

When Graff was ordered to publicly apologize to Houdini by means of a statement in the press, the embarrassed police official decided instead to take the matter to a higher court. This time, they were equipped with a lock which, once closed, could not be opened. This, of course, was not by strict definition an actual "lock." It was as final as a rivet, since the definition of a lock would naturally include the fact that a lock may be opened repeatedly by a properly designed key. Thus, as we shall see, Houdini was not only ready to accept this challenge but knew well that he would make very good press by doing so.

I quote now from a rather elaborate poster that Houdini had printed up to advertise his success in convincing the German courts of his fantastic ability. "The police...were unable to fetter or chain Houdini in an unescapable manner. He was even successful in opening a special lock that they had constructed which after it had once been locked could not be opened!" It would seem that Houdini had gone as far as any escape artist could hope to. In this performance, he seemed to have done the impossible.

To get down to the mechanics of the matter, it must be realized by my readers that it would have been quite possible for Houdini to have equipped himself with a small drill or other tool by means of which he could have violated the lock case in a minor fashion so as to slide back the locking bolt inside and thus release the lock. One of the stipulations of his escape to the court was that he could go into another room and enjoy the privacy he needed for the performance. It has been surmised in print that this process was precisely what he used on this occasion in Germany.

The newspaper account from the *Rheinische Zeitung* that I had the opportunity to examine was translated to me by a German friend, who gave me a somewhat different version of the affair. Referring to the quotation taken from Houdini's own poster, we note that he claimed he had *opened* the special lock. I fear this was not so. We read in the *Zeitung* that Houdini—in the same way that he had handled the first transport chain—returned to the courtroom with the chain and the unopenable padlock "removed from his wrists." Thus we observe a slight semantic twist in Houdini's account, whereas the newspaper's account of the same event provides us with the truth.

I have engaged in this nit-picking in order to illustrate a very important fact about Houdini's methods of operation. I, of course, do not fault him for this procedure, since I confess to having been guilty of it many times myself. I draw attention to it more in admiration than in censure.

Regardless of what really occurred in that courtroom, the magistrates were sufficiently impressed that once again Houdini was declared the winner. Though Werner Graff tried a third time to salvage his damaged honor by taking the case to an even higher court, he lost there as well and had to pay a sizable fine. Meanwhile Harry Houdini was allowed, at Graff's expense, to publish in the newspapers a brief account of the court cases and the eventual verdict.

In the Germany of the day, where the police were anything but popular and every citizen was in fear of falling into their clutches, Houdini became not only a popular hero, as he had been even before his "victory," but the shining ideal of every young lad who could scrape up the few marks necessary to see one of his standing-room-only performances in that country.

The court case in Cologne proved conclusively to everyone that Houdini would fight back in courts if any attempt were made to slander him. And from then on, no one dared try.

"TO RESTRAIN THE MURDEROUSLY INSANE"

One of Houdini's most obviously "physical" escapes, certainly the most strenuous one, was the escape from a straitjacket. Early in 1896, while Houdini was traveling with a magician called Marco in Canada, he had the opportunity for the first time to see a legitimate straitjacket. He was totally fascinated, as he recounted later, with the fact that the jacket appeared to hold the victim in an absolutely inescapable condition. Now, of course, nothing would do for Houdini except an attempt to escape from such a device. He probably little expected at that time that the straitjacket would become one of his most popular performance items. By 1900, Houdini had performed the straitjacket escape successfully countless times. But as yet, the most important fact about this kind of performance had not yet occurred to him. It was to occur strictly by accident.

His brother, Hardeen, had also been featuring the straitjacket as a part of his act. When, at one of his performances, the audience accused him of having an assistant concealed behind the curtained-off cabinet to free him from the straitjacket, Hardeen responded by promising to do it in full sight. Up until then, neither he nor his brother had thought that the audience would want to see

the actual escape, and they had always performed out of sight.

In its new form, done in full sight, the straitjacket escape was a sensation. Not only was it very exciting for the audience to see onstage, but it served as one of the most spectacular of outdoor attractions. Both Houdini and brother Hardeen took to dangling from high buildings or flagpoles wrapped in straitjackets and suspended by strong ropes tied about their ankles. It never failed to gain them considerable newspaper space.

What makes the straitjacket escape so formidable? First of all, there is tremendous variety in the design of straitjackets. Generally speaking, they are made of heavy canvas, or in some cases of leather, heavily reinforced to prevent their being torn. The primary purpose of the straitjacket is to restrain criminally insane persons from harming themselves or other people. It is usually equipped with very long arms, perhaps twice as long as seem necessary, and sealed at the ends. The jacket is often put on the body so that it may be laced or strapped up the back, and the arms are wrapped around the body after being crossed in front. Straps or ropes fastened to the ends of the extra-long arms are tied together or to the other parts of the jacket to keep the arms from being em-

171

THE WORLD FAMOUS
HOUDINI

THE FIRST
HUMAN BEING
TO SUCCESSFULLY
ESCAPE FROM
A REGULATION
STRAIT JACKET
AS USED ON THE
MURDEROUS INSANE

ployed in any way.

It goes without saying that the average patient legitimately placed in a straitjacket by hospital attendants would not be put into the jacket with the same dedication or perseverance that volunteers from the audience will use on the escape artist! Personally, I have had spectators fasten me so tightly in the jacket that I was unable to take a full breath and had to hurry along with the actual escape so as to prevent a blackout. A straitjacket is no fun at all!

There are some performers today who claim to be escape artists who not only use their own straitjackets, carefully tailored to fit their requirements, but insist upon being fastened into them by their own assistants! Such a performance is nothing more than a demonstration. It is hardly a challenge such as Houdini would have envisioned. His audiences were always assured that the straitjacket being used was quite legitimate, and those who wished to examine it were quite free to do so.

The straitjacket escape is, frankly, a combination of two basic elements. One, the performer must attempt to make use of any slack that it is possible to gather while the jacket is being applied. Two, he must learn to go through some pretty dreadful twisting of the body. I, myself, have frequently looked down to find my elbow in a position where Nature did not intend it to be at all! I have also developed some pretty strange sprains in obscure parts of my body which would puzzle any doctor, were he asked for a diagnosis and possible causes for these various afflictions. As for Houdini, at one point he strained himself so badly that he suffered for many years from kidney trouble as a direct result of a particularly strenuous straitjacket release.

I must at this point destroy another myth. I have heard it said many times that it is obviously easier to release oneself from a jacket while hanging upside down. Apparently the basis for this wild theory is that the jacket tends to "fall off" more easily. I can attest quite authoritatively that this is not so. There is one small advantage, however. I have discovered that the body tends to lengthen somewhat when suspended from the ankles, and although I have never gone through the process of measuring various cross sections of the rib cage, I think it quite possible that the chest section of the jacket is probably less tightly fastened to the body while the performer is upside down. Nevertheless, the strain of hanging by one's ankles far outweighs any advantage that the upside-down position might give. I recall that on one occasion, when the tackle hoisting me into the air ceased to function properly, I had to hang there for a *very* long seventeen minutes. I do not relish repeating *that* experience!

Houdini had several special straitjackets designed and manufactured for particularly dramatic purposes. Two of them are now on display at the Houdini Museum. One is

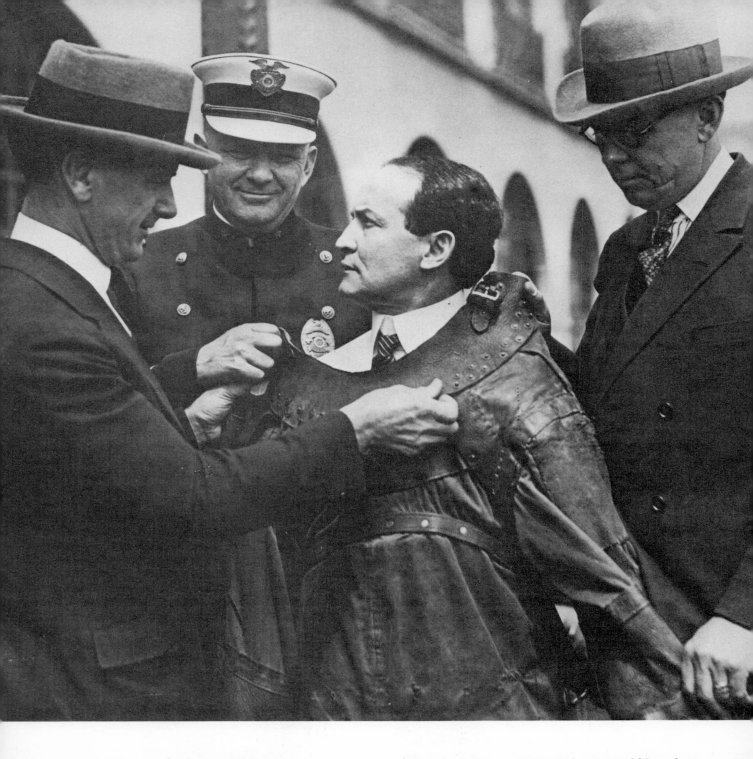

made of solid leather; it reaches down almost to the knees and has an intricate network of straps that holds the arms, not around the body, but tightly against the sides of the body, pointing down. There is also a large flared collar all the way around the neck which juts up in such a way that the victim cannot even see straight ahead of him, thus doing away with one very valuable method of determining the best way to effect one's release. Whether Harry Houdini used this straitjacket to any ex-

tent is not known, but if he did so, it would have been only on special occasions and to achieve the dramatic effect it was designed for.

Audiences who saw Houdini strapped in a canvas and leather straitjacket, leaping and twisting about on the stage to release himself, were not likely to forget the sight. I have spoken to many people who saw Houdini in his time, and the one demonstration most of them remember more than anything else is this one.

"FAILURE MEANS A DROWNING DEATH"

Early in 1908, Harry Houdini took another of the giant steps in his career that heralded a brand-new approach to the escape act. From now on, he would be hard put to surpass himself in a field that was eating up new material every season as fast as it could be originated. This new approach began with what has been touted as perhaps the most thrilling and puzzling of his feats—the Milk Can Escape.

I write now for a generation that has probably not seen a genuine milk can except for those that are used as decorative planters or catchalls in suburban homes. The exception, of course, will be those readers who find such an implement part of their everyday rural lives, still serving to contain milk on its way to the processing centers. Such a milk can bears an incomplete resemblance to the one Houdini made so famous as a fearsome death trap with which to thrill audiences.

The real thing is a straight-sided cylinder, usually of stainless steel nowadays, capacity about ten gallons, with a sloping shoulder which gives way to a straight neck, capped with a slightly "domed" lid which seals in the product. The Houdini prop milk can was of necessity much larger, with a neck wide enough so that he could enter and place his entire body inside. But there was also

a major structural difference: Houdini's can sloped inwards from the "shoulder" to the floor. This served two important functions. First, weight of the filled can was an important factor. Stages are made to support only so much weight, and the greater the taper of the can, the less the final weight. As Houdini was to discover when he developed the much heavier water torture cell in later years, it was sometimes required that adjustable jacks be installed under the stage just below the spot where the prop was to be placed. Second, if someone worked out a solution for the trick that said the outer and visible body of the can was only a "sleeve" that slid up so that an escape could be effected, the slope made that very obviously impossible.

The presentation was exceedingly dramatic. While assistants dressed in rain slickers and rubber boots were filling the can with water carried from offstage in buckets, the committee from the audience was onstage to examine and thump the can all they wanted. They found that the hasps were solidly soldered to the sides, that the thick galvanized steel was indeed impenetrable, and that the lid was clearly unfaked and formidable. Houdini, having changed into a bathing suit offstage, entered the can, quickly sliding in as the large clock onstage began ticking

175

off the seconds. The lid was not yet placed on, and the audience had been invited to take a deep breath at the moment the magician submerged below the surface. Within thirty seconds, members of the audience were letting out their breath explosively, and the thought occurred to each of them that if he were in the position Houdini was in, drowning would have claimed a victim!

Hardly did Houdini emerge from below the surface of the water than he plunged right back again, after a quick convulsive gasp for air. Quickly, additional water was poured onto the surface to replace the water that had of course slopped over in the preceding demonstration. Instantly, assistants slammed the lid on, snapping all six padlocks in place, and as they stepped back, a curtained enclosure dropped over the milk can. The orchestra burst into the sonorous strains of "Asleep in the Deep." And the miracle began.

The audience watched the clock as it now began ticking off the seconds that elapsed as Houdini tried to escape from the watery prison. Picture the audience as the clock indicated the spot at which *they* had found it necessary finally to take a breath! And imagine their dismay when the time passed at which Houdini himself had previously found it necessary to emerge! Some thirty seconds *past* that time, the curtains stirred once, then were still. Then they stirred once more, as Harry Houdini lurched from behind the enclosure, which then lifted away to show the milk can standing just as it had been, locks in place, except that it had somehow released its prisoner!

To say that the audience went wild would be to totally understate the case. Fred Keating, to whom I owe the description I have outlined here, said that the assistants would rush to the sides of the stage to restrain the more adventurous members of the audience who were so taken with the performance that they felt compelled to throw themselves at Houdini in their excitement. His victory was complete. Once more, the little man had faced and thwarted death.

Think of the wonder he had accomplished. A thoroughly examined steel can had been filled with water; he had immersed himself into its embrace without even a full breath of air—for to hold a full breath was impossible in the fetal position he had to assume in order to fully enter the device; the lid had been secured in place with six borrowed padlocks; and he had been left in a curtained cabinet to extricate himself as best he could. It was a scenario that no witness would ever forget, or would want to forget. It is no wonder that we hear of strong men weeping with relief when Harry Houdini stepped from behind that curtain to the cheers of his audience.

Today we are familiar with the frenzy that a younger generation can work up over a sequined rock star whose only claim to recognition may be his costume or some fantasy designed carefully by a highly paid press agent. But years before cacophony became the standard for modern music, a little man with steely eyes and an engaging smile was performing such miracles as this and thrilling audiences whose tastes were surfeited by the wonder of the impossible milk can escape. Houdini's accomplishment was the result of long years of work, courage, and absolute faith in himself, not just the result of puffery. He was the real thing, an enduring hero. And he proved it every night.

When Houdini finally unveiled his milk can escape routine to audiences, it was obviously the result of long and careful planning, both mechanically and psychologically. As with any of Houdini's presentations, the mechanics were only the means to the actual accomplishment; the rest was showmanship and "surround," which made a mere clever idea into a major miracle.

The basic appeal of the milk can was the apparent danger that accompanied each and every attempt. It seems not to have occurred to the audience that a man would hardly be attempting a really death-defying feat two or three times a day, week after week. That is not to say that the trick was without its genuine possibilities as the last that the magician would ever perform. Far from it. For only one small slip or piece of bad timing, a sudden cough or some small carelessness on the part of the assistants, and Houdini would have been in serious and deadly trouble.

The effect was grandly dramatic as it was presented to the audience. As the curtains parted, the spectators saw a grim-looking metal can which closely resembled the illustration that had fascinated them on numerous posters seen around town before the arrival of the magician in their midst. The poster, indeed, was probably responsible for a good deal of the excitement that was evinced from the crowd when they saw the device that had been pictured along with the chilling phrase "Failure Means a Drowning Death."

By the time the can was visible to the audience, there had of course been a goodly amount of conjecture as to what the presentation would consist of. The advertising had made it plain that the can was to be filled with water, and doubtless there were all kinds of theories passed about concerning the possible ways that the danger of drowning could be bypassed by the magician once he was inside the device. For there were two main problems presented: first, to escape from the can, and second, to do so within the very short period of time that was available while submerged under water. The lid of the can was to be fastened in place with six regular padlocks obtained locally from a merchant, the keys of which were held by him. And there were other major obstacles as well.

The lid of the can fitted on snugly from the top, and though the presence of the water seemed to offer only the problem of survival to the magician, it really was more trouble to him than that, because any attempt to open the can at any other point than where he entered it

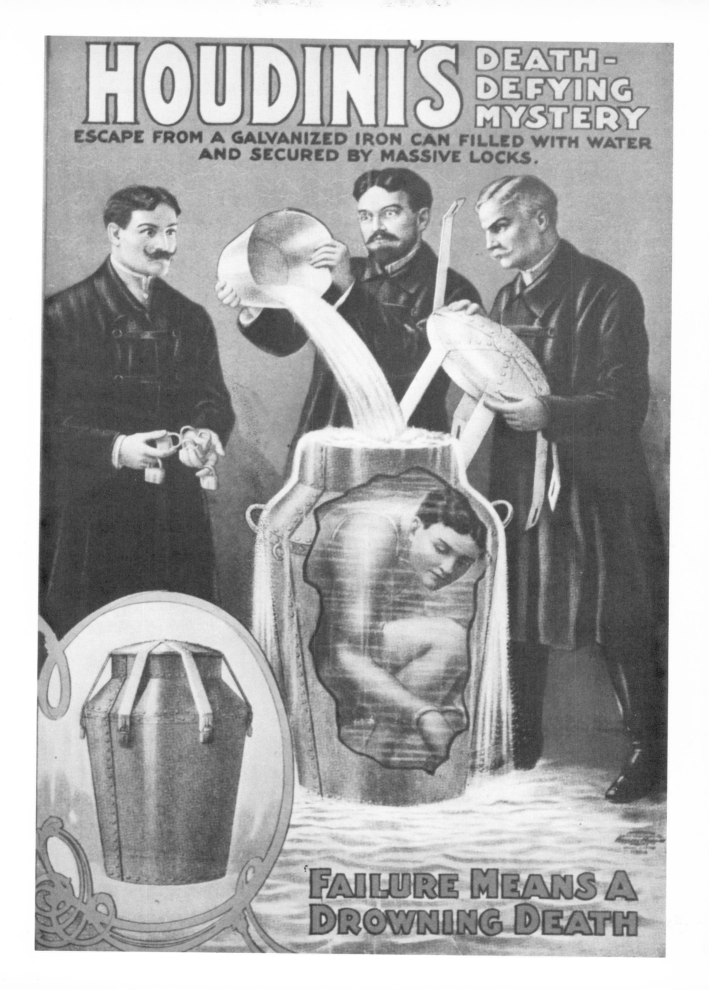

would result in water cascading out of the can and becoming very evident as it flooded over the stage from behind the curtain.

Mind you, there were several different models of the milk can. Two of them are on exhibit in the Houdini Magical Hall of Fame in Niagara Falls, Canada, both of them owned and loaned by Mr. Sidney Radner of Holyoke, Massachusetts. One can simply has six hasps as fasteners; it is the fundamental model. The other has, in addition to hasps, two sturdy locks built into the collar of the can, each of which is sufficient to lock the lid on, since each inserts a steel bolt into a receiving groove in the lid.

I should add that I, myself, have performed the Houdini Milk Can Escape, using the same can (the first mentioned above) that Houdini himself used. It was kindly furnished by Sid Radner. I have seen several explanations of how the milk can works, and some need not even be denied, since their very conception is ridiculous. One such clever explanation has the can coming apart at the shoulder and the top lifting off, and an illustration is even supplied. Luckily, the water level is not shown or the reader would be aware that a dozen gallons of water

would flood out into the orchestra pit the instant the can "broke"!

I cannot fully describe the feeling that is experienced at the instant that the last breath is taken and assistants slam that steel lid in place. Doubled over, arms around folded legs, head facing down to the bottom, I felt like some sort of colossal fool for having dared the feat, and as the really terrifying din of the locks being snapped in place sounded in my ears, I felt the slight twinge of panic that must always accompany any thinking man at a moment like that. I waiting, lungs bursting, until the first strains of music reached me. It was the signal that I could begin my efforts to escape, and that made it the sweetest music I'd ever heard.

Eventually, I emerged from behind the curtain as Houdini had done so many, many times. And I felt fully the impact of the man's genius, both in designing the device and in anticipating the effect it would have on an audience. It was one of the most moving moments of my life. The secret of the milk can, like the secret of all of Houdini's tricks, lies in the total presentation, and only very slightly in the mechanics of the effect.

THE CHINESE WATER TORTURE CELL

The trick that Harry Houdini called the Chinese Water Torture Cell was probably an outcome of the great success enjoyed by the milk can escape. A rather inferior Hollywood motion picture would have us believe that Houdini developed the presentation of the water torture cell, or the U.S.D. as he preferred to call it (the abbreviation stands for "upside down"), very late in his career; in fact, this film tried to tell us that he died while trying it for the first time. Nothing could be farther from the truth, for it was a very important part of Houdini's act for fifteen years.

Though it was not until late in 1913 that it really began to be featured in his act, he had tried it out for presentation purposes while in Germany the year before. It was probably during this early performance of the U.S.D. that the idea was boldly pirated by a lady calling herself Miss Undina, who performed a very close imitation of the trick. A lawsuit by Houdini soon put a stop to that, however. Miss Undina did her own spectacular magic trick by disappearing from the scene completely, and was never heard of again.

The water torture cell had all of the drama involved in the milk can presentation plus the added advantage that the performer was clearly visible to the audience. The milk can trick concealed him from sight even before the curtain was pulled in place to conceal the device while the escape was being made. In the water torture cell, there was no doubt in anyone's mind that Houdini was actually immersed in the water.

I will attempt a description of at least one of the models of the water torture cell that Houdini built. This one is owned by Mr. Sidney Radner and is on permanent exhibit at the Houdini Museum. It is apparently the model most frequently represented in photographs of Houdini performing the trick. The cell is constructed of heavy slabs of mahogany, arranged to fit together in a frame with strips of rubber between the pieces. This meant that the large telephone-booth-like apparatus could be broken down into much smaller sections, with the exception of the plate-glass front. The top of the torture cell was open, and the audience could see through the chrome-plated frame of the front panel, which was of solid glass. More than a ton of water was required to fill this cell, so the glass was exceptionally thick, and the assembly of the cell must have taken a considerable amount of time. The lid to the cell was constructed like a large pair of "stocks," which opened like a pair of scissors when the lid was placed on edge on the stage. Houdini, dressed in bathing trunks, would place himself prone on the stage on a specially constructed padded recliner. The stocks of the lid would open and close about his ankles, which were received in two cut-outs, after which the stocks were locked together with a large padlock. One model of the cell did away with this padlock and used instead a self-contained "cabinet lock." Heavy chains attached to the four corners of the lid would now be gathered together and stagehands offstage would start lifting the lid, with Houdini attached. He dangled, supported only by his ankles imprisoned in the closed lid, above the U.S.D., which was filled almost to the top with water. Upon his signal, he would be lowered headfirst into the cell, while the water displaced by his body poured in torrents down the sides.

The audience, of course, realized that from the moment his head entered the water he was in danger of drowning. Swiftly, he was lowered so that his head almost touched the bottom of the water-filled cell. As the lid approached the top of the cell, assistants on either side quickly placed ladders against the apparatus and began fastening the lid to the cell itself. This was accomplished by means of four heavy brass hasps, which were hinged to the body of the cell itself and received in sockets on the massive lid. Keys, already in place in each of four locks, were quickly turned to secure the hasps in place and then removed by the assistants, who scrambled down the ladders and stood to one side.

Instantly a large curtain enclosure was dropped from the flies to envelope the entire U.S.D. The last glimpse that the audience had of Houdini showed him in the water, upside down, moving his arms about as if vainly searching for an exit from the cell. From now on, the presentation was pretty much the same as it had been with the milk can escape; the performer and the equipment were out of sight, and the audience was left to imagine what might be going on behind the curtain.

The final revelation came when, just as the audience's excitement was reaching its maximum intensity, a dripping-wet magician would suddenly appear from behind the curtain, gasping and choking as if he had very nearly drowned. The curtain was quickly hauled away to reveal the water torture cell still intact, the water in it sloshing about as if Houdini's body had only left it instants before.

Though Houdini was known as a daredevil, he actually never took any chances with his safety, at least as far as the equipment was concerned. Careful examination of the U.S.D. at the Houdini Museum reveals that there are two large plugs about four inches in diameter located on each side of the cell at the very bottom. These plugs have handles both inside and outside the cell, so from inside Houdini could release them by giving the handles a half turn. The pressure of the water inside would force them out like corks from a popgun, and the water would quickly drain. By the same means, an assistant fearing for Houdini's life could do the same with the handles located on the outside of the cell. I leave my readers to imagine

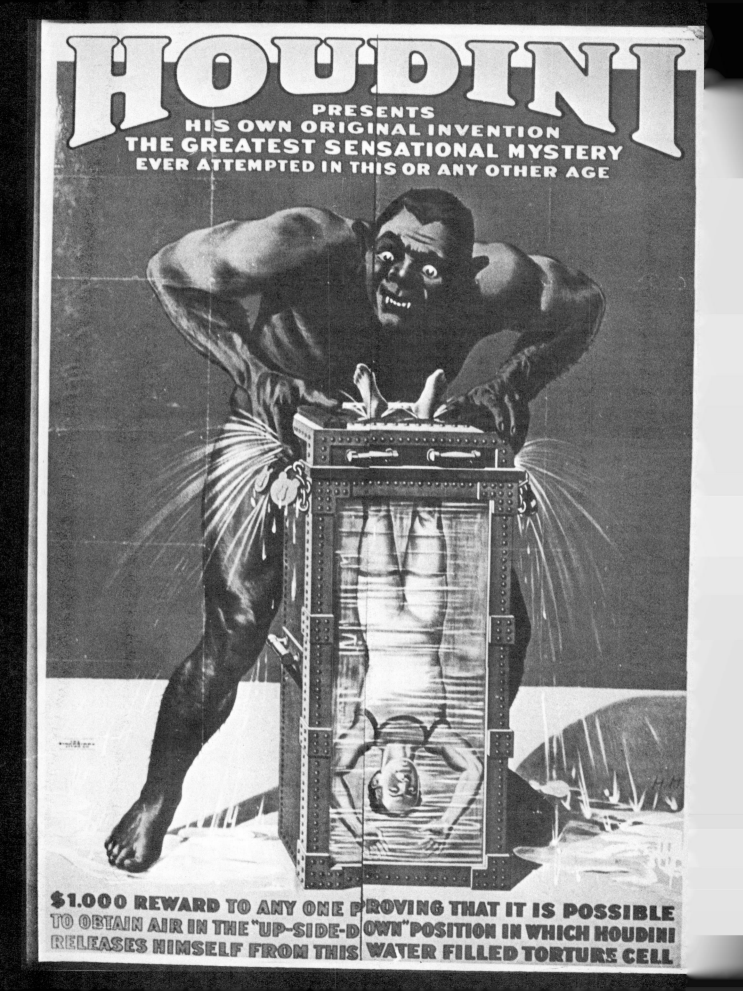

the mess that would have resulted if it had ever been necessary (there is no record that it ever was) to drain the water from the U.S.D. by this means! Theater managers would not be too happy to have more than a ton of water filling their orchestra pits.

Houdini offered a vast sum of money to anyone who could prove that it was possible for him, while performing the U.S.D., to obtain air in the upside-down position. This was a perfectly safe offer, since he had no need to do so. It reminds me very much of the late Joseph Dunninger's offer of $10,000 to anyone who could prove that he used stooges in the audience to accomplish his apparent miracles of mind reading. Joe's money was never safer, because, unlike other performers in the same field, he *never* used a confederate in the audience during his long career. I have many times heard this latter offer misquoted as an offer to give $10,000 to anyone who could prove that the act was not genuine mind reading! There is a distinct difference.

No doubt a large part of the charm and fascination of the water torture cell trick was in the instinctive fear that the average person has of being shut up in a closed container, particularly if that container is filled with water. People in the audience were known to have had most uncomfortable moments as they viewed Houdini performing the U.S.D. And no doubt Houdini chortled over every agonizing moment of it. Certainly, for a champion swimmer such as he was, there was very little discomfort in the performance of the water torture cell.

The stage instructions for the U.S.D. required that additional supports be placed underneath the stage directly beneath the cell so that the entire apparatus would not vanish into the basement suddenly. Also, the large caldrons of water situated backstage over charcoal fires were part of the equipment with which the Houdini troupe traveled, in order that the master magician would not have to immerse his body in ice-cold water every night! Houdini may have been a rugged individual, but he certainly was not about to make life any more uncomfortable than it had to be.

There has been a great deal of discussion in recent years about whether or not Houdini might possibly have obtained the idea for the water torture cell from a man who performed under the name of Zamora, the Man in the Bottle. Zamora was a dwarf who advertised himself as being multi-jointed. He was apparently able to get into the very small neck of a very large bottle made for him by a brewery. I have heard it said that Houdini denied ever having heard of Zamora, and if that statement attributed to him is true, then I fear I must chide the shade of the great escape artist for this prevarication. For the Houdini scrapbook reveals to us a program from the year 1894 which features in very large letters the said Zamora, and in much smaller letters lower down on the program "Houdini, Prince of Cards." If Houdini indeed never even heard of Zamora, then he was not reading the mar-

quee outside the theater or the advertisements for the show in which he played.

But I hardly feel it is necessary to dwell on this matter, for Houdini did not need Zamora in order to originate the idea of the water torture cell. It was a natural evolution of his other spectacular escapes, notably the milk can trick. But in comparing these two illusions, the U.S.D. and the milk can, I really find that I favor the latter for effectiveness of presentation. To my mind, there is something much more dramatic about a small, cramped steel can into which the escape artist can barely place his body and in which he is held by a solid lid clamped directly over his head. Though from my position as a performer I may not view these matters exactly as a layman would, I feel very strongly about my preference for the milk can over the water torture cell.

There have been imitations of Houdini's Chinese water torture cell presentation, at least seven that I know of. I had always hoped that magicians would let Houdini go to the grave with at least one of his tricks unimitated. But it seems to be the burden of The Great among us that they are carefully imitated and that every effort is made to top their performances after they have passed from the scene. That this should happen to Houdini was unavoidable, of course. Probably the most effective representation of the U.S.D. was performed by Doug Henning on a television special that was presented live on NBC recently. Given the changes in audiences' attitudes and sophistication, given the very nature of the media by means of which these things are exhibited, and in view of the wonders of science with which magicians now compete, one wonders whether or not such representations can compare at all with the original presentation as created and performed by Harry Houdini. It is a question to which we may never have an answer.

Think of the difficulty of setting up such a ponderous piece of equipment as the Chinese water torture cell. Houdini required that a small trapdoor about eight inches square be cut into the stage immediately beneath the torture cell, which was always installed over a large waterproof tarpaulin device equipped with a drain six inches in diameter in the center. This drain hole in the tarpaulin was located directly over the small trapdoor, so that at the close of the performance the 250 gallons of water that the U.S.D. contained would be easily and quickly drained. Obviously, the cell could not be moved with more than a ton of water in it.

The waterproof tarpaulin was then "flown" on a batten at the back of the stage so that it would drain and dry in time for the next performance. There may very well have been many stage situations where the water torture cell proved impracticable because of the great weight of the device.

Just how did Houdini manage to free himself from this watery tomb after the curtain had dropped in place to conceal it from the sight of the audience? As might be imagined, this has been a subject of discussion with magicians ever since Houdini designed the effect. Now that the original equipment is on display in the Houdini Museum, it is possible to examine the affair from only a few feet away. But even this advantage does not allow the inexperienced eye to solve the mystery, and so many "nut" theories have arisen concerning the secret of the water torture cell that it might be well to discuss a few of them here.

One of the most popular theories holds that Houdini was not really immersed in water at all! The genius who came up with this one has stated that the cell was built with a double-glass panel in front which held a six-inch-wide column of water. Thus, the magician was being lowered into a tank full of air with a watery panel between him and the audience. We are asked to believe that the water that flowed over onto the stage was supplied by a pump from underneath. This theory is easily demolished when one realizes that the committee who came up on the stage to authenticate the presentation were allowed to mount the ladder placed against the side of the tank and ascertain that the tank was indeed legitimately filled with water. Another fancy theory I have heard is that assistants were able to come up through trapdoors in the floor and extricate Houdini from his prison. This was impossible, however, because of the tarpaulin which covered the floor. There are also, of course, several other objections to this theory.

I recall that on one occasion when I was asked about the secret of the U.S.D. by a newspaper reporter, he actually began to write down my explanation when I asserted that Houdini went out through a trapdoor at the back of the cell! I swear, I believe that it almost got into print. Certainly it would compare favorably with many other ridiculous explanations that have been offered for Houdini's stunts.

I know of chess buffs who can walk by a game in progress, glance at the board, and announce with great authority that "white can mate in three moves." This capability is certainly beyond me, for I only know the basic moves of chess and I am a complete duffer when involved in the actual game. But just as the expert's acquaintance with this subject allows him such a pronouncement, so I may presume to assert that the secret of the water torture cell is one of the cleverest I have ever come upon in the magical galaxy of inventions. To the mechanically inclined, a careful examination of the cell itself, without any actual experimentation whatsoever, will reveal the secret. But again, I must stress that Houdini's audiences did not go to see the equipment or to see the trick; they went to the theater to see Houdini himself. The secret, the real secret that is, lay in the personality of the man involved rather than in the equipment used.

Whether Houdini or his very trusted assistant, Collins, was responsible for designing the *modus operandi* of the

U.S.D., we are not sure. Doubtless, both men contributed to the thinking and the creation of the illusion. Collins died without having said a word to betray his master's secrets, as did all of the other assistants. Those few who loudly claimed to be privy to the master's secrets were usually those least able to reveal anything of any importance. Houdini had chosen his staff very carefully and very well.

Imagine yourself suspended upside down, held firmly by the ankles in a heavy mahogany clamp, totally immersed in water except for your feet. What kinds of thoughts pass through your mind? There are only two possibilities. If you don't know what you are doing, and are not prepared for the experience, you will panic—and drown. If, like Houdini, you are well prepared and in complete control emotionally, you simply reach out and—ah, I almost revealed to you a cherished secret of the late great Houdini. And that I may not do.

I invite you, though, from a different vantage point, of course, to stand back in admiration with me and share the delight and sense of wonder that must accompany any consideration of the feats of Harry Houdini. For though my viewpoint must be radically different from yours, equipped as I am with the secrets of the trade and the advantage of thirty years of study, we may all delight in the fact that for more than a half a century a giant of the entertainment industry walked among us and thoroughly charmed and astounded us. I was born two years after Houdini departed this world, but I feel very much as if we have shared it together. I trust that this book has enabled you, too, to live through a small portion of the glorious career of Houdini.

You need not know the secrets of the master escape artist in order to fully appreciate his ingenuity, his daring, and his originality. He was a man among men and certainly the paramount magician of his time—if not of all time. Few people of his profession have dared to compare themselves with him or to belittle his accomplishments. To do that is to throw sand at the ankles of giants.

If there is indeed an immortality to which we are destined, Harry Houdini has certainly attained his. The unimaginative among us will believe that his remains, which lie in Machpelah Cemetery in New York, represent the man Houdini. Not so. For so long as a child's eye can widen in astonishment at some well-performed feat of magic, so long as an audience will draw in its breath in astonishment as a young lady is suspended in midair, and so long as a newspaper reporter will write the words *impossible* and *astonishing* in describing the feats of a conjuror, then the name of Harry Houdini will be spoken with reverence and awe.

For me, Harry Houdini is very much alive. And I am sure that if you could ask him if that is so, he would agree heartily and give you a huge wink.

And in that wink is everything.

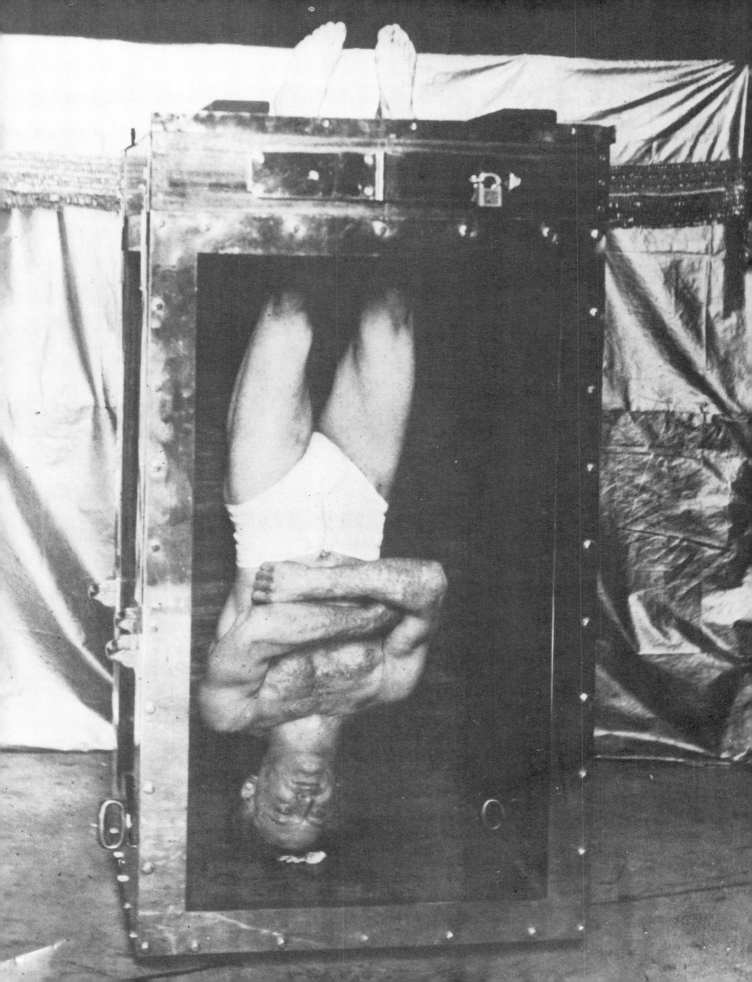

ACKNOWLEDGMENTS

The life of Houdini often resembles a crazy jigsaw puzzle put together by a drunken carpenter. The Publisher and the authors wish to thank the following people for the invaluable assistance in putting together this book: Leonard Beck of the Library of Congress, Curator of the MacManus-Young Collection of Houdiniana there; Dr. Morris Young, donor of that collection and a leading authority on Houdini and magic; Dave Haggerty and Henry Mueller of the Houdini Magical Hall of Fame in Niagara Falls, Ontario, repository of the largest and most exciting collection of Houdiniana available for public viewing; Louis Rachow, Curator of the Walter Hampden-Edwin Booth Theater Collection and Library at the Players Club, in New York; Jay Marshall of the "Magic Shop" in Chicago; Larry Weeks, magic aficionado and collector of Houdini's films; Milbourne Christopher, magician par excellence and leading authority on Houdini; Walter Gibson, outstanding Houdini author; Charles Chesnut of *Reader's Digest*; George Cobb, editor of the *McGill Daily*; Dr. Jacob Marcus of the American Jewish Archives; Dr. Donald H. Henzel, former Director of the Observatory at Harvard College; the Wisconsin Historical Society; Harry Houdini Hardeen, for sharing some personal family moments with us; Mrs. Marie Hinson and Rose Bonanno; the other friends, relatives and fans of Houdini who have given of their time and love to help maintain the flame; and, of course, Harry Houdini, whose like will never be seen again, in fact or in fiction.

PHOTO CREDITS

The publishers wish to thank the following for permission to use their material in this book: *The Bettmann Archive, Inc.*, p. 70, p. 102, p. 129 (top); *Brown Brothers*, p. 61, p. 86 (bottom), p. 87 (bottom), p. 106, p. 121 (top), p. 141; *Culver Pictures, Inc.*, p. 86 (top, left); *The Houdini Magical Hall of Fame in Niagara Falls, Canada*, p.12, p. 23, p. 57, p. 66 (left), pp. 66-67 (top, far right), p. 78 (top), pp. 74-75, p. 80, p. 84, p. 85, p. 87 (top), p. 90, p. 91, p. 99, p. 101, p. 103 (top), p. 104, p. 105, p. 107, p. 113, pp. 114-115, p.120 (top, left), p. 125, p. 127, p.130, p. 133, p. 135, p.137, p. 139, p. 144 (top, bottom), p. 152, p. 154, p. 155, p. 163, p. 168, p. 172, p. 173, p. 174, p. 178, p. 181, p. 182, p. 185; *The McManus-Young Collection at the Library of Congress*, p. 1, p. 4, p. 20, p. 21, p. 22, p. 24, p. 29, pp. 30-31, p. 39, p. 40, pp. 46-47, p. 50, p. 53, p. 54, p. 58, p. 79, p. 82, p. 89, p. 92, p. 98, p. 104 (bottom), p. 108, p. 109, p. 111, p. 117, p. 118 (top, left), p. 119 (top, bottom), pp. 120 (top right, bottom), p. 121 (bottom), p. 122, p. 124, p. 130, p. 131 (top left, right), p. 132, p. 140, p. 142, p. 147; *Mr. James Randi*, p. 34, p. 35, p. 42, p. 62, p. 165, p. 166, p. 167; *The Walter Hampden-Edwin Booth Theatre Collection and Library at the Players Club in New York*, p. 8, p. 13, p. 17, p. 26, p. 33, p. 41, p. 45, p. 46, p. 65, p. 67 (bottom), p. 68, P. 71, p. 73 (bottom), p. 77, p. 78, p. 81, p. 95, p. 112, p. 128, p. 145, p. 159, p. 178, p. 180; *Wide World Photos, Inc.*, p. 86 (top, right), p. 149.

INDEX

Hogan Envelope Company
EMPLOYEES
CHALLENGE TO THE
FAMOUS HOUDINI

Manager,
Majestic Theatre, Chicago.

Dear Sir:

We believe a giant Envelope can be made by us which will enclose Houdini and successfully prevent his escape therefrom under the following conditions.

His hands and feet to be securely tied with strong rope, after which he is to be placed in the Envelope, tieing the top of Envelope with rope and sealing same.

The Envelope will be the largest ever made, being constructed of the toughest heaviest rope manila paper obtainable. It will be open on the end with an 18 inch flap. 150 inches high by 54 inches wide and will contain 16,000 square inches of stock. The sides will be securely sealed also being riveted with our Tension fasteners, the bottom being of the Satchel variety. Weight 15 pounds. Kindly let us know if the great Houdini will accept our challenge.

Employees,
HOGAN ENVELOPE COMPANY.

EMPLOYEES,
Hogan Envelope Comp
86-96 E. Ohio

Challenge!
Jailer Lannon
CHALLENGES
HOUDINI

Erie County Jail
Buffalo. N. Y.
October 11th, 1916

Houdini,
Shea's Theatre,
City.

Dear Sir:—

Following a controversy among my guards, a committee selected from among the most experienced wish TO CHALLENGE YOU to escape from a full length Punishment Suit, used ONLY ON THE DANGEROUS INSANE which holds the criminal from the neck down to and including the feet.

When properly secured in same with the broad belting straps encircling your body you will be perfectly helpless to release yourself.

The only condition under which I will allow my guards to come on the stage and put you through this test, you must agree to make the attempt to escape in FULL VIEW OF THE AUDIENCE.

Signed,

JAMES J. LANNON,
Jailer.

HOUDINI HAS ACCEPTED THE ABOVE CHALLENGE TEST TO TAKE PLACE ON FRIDAY NIGHT, OCTOBER 13th, 1916, AT SHEA'S THEATRE, THE ONLY CONDITION HOUDINI HAS ___ IS THAT ANY STRAPS PLACED ___ MUST NOT BE

Shipwrights' Chall___
TO
HOUDIN__

January ___

Dear Sir,

We, the undersigned, Shipwrights emp___ yard of Vickers Limited, having heard of your ability to ___ apparently impossible and peculiar places, challenge yo___ us to construct a large and strong Packing Ca___ timber, secured by 3" French wire nails, into ___ will rope and nail you, and believe you will n___ to escape therefrom.

If you accept this challenge it must be clearl___ you are not to demolish the case in your attempt to escap___

We will send Box for examination, but rese___ to re-nail each and every board, to prevent any prepar___ part.

CLEMENT E. DENNIS, JOSEP___
JAMES FLETT, THOMAS C. ___
Shipwrights,

Employees of VICKERS L___

HOUDINI ACCEPTS THE ABOVE CHALLENGE for the Second House, Wednesday, January 14th, 1914, on the Stage of the Tivoli Theatre, Barrow-in-Furness, under the condition that the Box is not air-tight.

"Guardian" Printing Works, Barrow.

To-Night.   To-Night.
CHALLENGE!

Mr. E. F. NEWTON,
Principal Warder of the Wakefield Jail,
for 22 years, and

CHIEF WARDER of the NEWCASTLE PRISON

for 10 years,

HAS CHALLENGED HOUDINI to allow himself to be strapped up in a

STRAIT JACKET

such as is used on the Murderous Insane.

HOUDINI
HAS ACCEPTED THE CHALLENGE!
FOR THE
Second House To-Night, Dec. 2nd,

At the PAVILION, Westgate Road.

CASEY & BENT, NEWCASTLE-ON-TYNE.

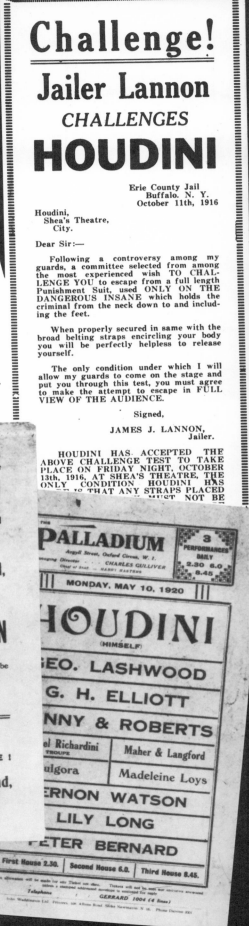

THE PALLADIUM
Argyll Street, Oxford Circus, W.1.

Managing Director — CHARLES GULLIVER
Chief of Staff — HARRY MASTERS

3 PERFORMANCES DAILY
2.30 6.0
8.45

MONDAY, MAY 10, 1920

HOUDINI
(HIMSELF)

GEO. LASHWOOD
G. H. ELLIOTT
___NNY & ROBERTS

| ___el Richardini TROUPE | Maher & Langford |
| ___ulgora | Madeleine Loys |

___ERNON WATSON
LILY LONG
___ETER BERNARD

| First House 2.30. | Second House 6.0. | Third House 8.45. |

Telephone ___   GERRARD 1004 (4 lines)